SEEN AND HEARD

LEXINGTON STUDIES IN POLITICAL COMMUNICATION

Series Editor: Robert E. Denton Jr., Virginia Tech

This series encourages focused work examining the role and function of communication in the realm of politics including campaigns and elections, media, and political institutions.

TITLES IN SERIES:

Governing Codes: Gender, Metaphor, and Political Identity, By Karrin Vasby Anderson and Kristina Horn Sheeler

Paving the Way for Madam President, By Nichola D. Gutgold

Maryland Politics and Political Communication, 1950-2005, By Theodore F. Sheckels

Images, Issues, and Attacks: Television Advertising by Incumbents and Challengers in Presidential Elections, By E. D. Dover

Democracy as Discussion: Civic Education and the American Forum Movement, By William Keith

Nuclear Legacies: Communication, Controversy, and the U. S. Nuclear Weapons Complex, Edited by Bryan C. Taylor, William J. Kinsella, Stephen P. Depoe, Maribeth S. Metzler

Picturing China in the American Press: The Visual Portrayal of Sino-American Relations in Time *Magazine, 1949–1973,* By David D. Perlmutter

Post-9/11 American Presidential Rhetoric: A Study of Protofascist Discourse, By Colleen Elizabeth Kelley

Making a Difference: A Comparative View of the Role of the Internet in Election Politics, Edited by Stephen Ward, Diana Owen, Richard Davis, and David Taras

Seen and Heard: The Women of Television News, By Nichola D. Gutgold

SEEN AND HEARD

The Women of Television News

Nichola D. Gutgold

LEXINGTON BOOKS

A division of

ROWMAN & LITTLEFIELD PUBLISHERS, INC.

Lanham • Boulder • New York • Toronto • Plymouth, UK

LEXINGTON BOOKS

A division of Rowman & Littlefield Publishers, Inc.
A wholly owned subsidiary of The Rowman & Littlefield Publishing Group, Inc.
4501 Forbes Boulevard, Suite 200
Lanham, MD 20706

Estover Road
Plymouth PL6 7PY
United Kingdom

British Library Cataloguing in Publication Information Available

Library of Congress Cataloging-in-Publication Data

Gutgold, Nichola D.
　　Seen and heard : the women of television news / Nichola D. Gutgold.
　　　　p. cm. — (Lexington studies in political communication)
　　Includes bibliographical references and index.
　　ISBN-13: 978-0-7391-2017-0 (cloth : alk. paper)
　　ISBN-10: 0-7391-2017-4 (cloth : alk. paper)
　　ISBN-13: 978-0-7391-2018-7 (pbk. : alk. paper)
　　ISBN-10: 0-7391-2018-2 (pbk. : alk. paper)
　　1. Women television journalists—United States—Biography. I. Title.
　PN4872.G88 2008
　　070.92'2—dc22
　　[B]　　　　　　　　　　　　　　　　　　　　　　　　2007048361

Printed in the United States of America

♾™ The paper used in this publication meets the minimum requirements of
American National Standard for Information Sciences—Permanence of Paper
for Printed Library Materials, ANSI/NISO Z39.48-1992.

This book is dedicated to my cherished sisters,
Julianne Flaim and Theresa DelBalso.
As the women of this book have enjoyed a sisterly camaraderie, my life
has been enhanced by the love and kindness of my two sisters.

CONTENTS

Acknowledgments   ix

Foreword by Helen Thomas   xi

1   Introduction: Anchors in America   1

2   From Persistent to Powerful: Barbara Walters   31

3   Anchors Away: Connie Chung and Elizabeth Vargas   63

4   The Worldly Wonder: Christiane Amanpour   91

5   Politically Speaking: Dana Bash, Candy Crowley, Andrea Mitchell, and Judy Woodruff   113

6   Veteran and Varied: Diane Sawyer, Lesley Stahl, and Paula Zahn   145

7   From Morning to Evening: Katie Couric   167

8   Turning Up the Volume: The Future of Women in Television Broadcasting   195

Bibliography   205

Index   219

About the Author   225

ACKNOWLEDGMENTS

Growing up in a home that kept the television blaring through the local and national news broadcasts each evening, I was convinced that becoming a broadcaster would be the ultimate career choice for me or any other woman. Though my career path altered from that initial idea, I still believe that the many women who have appeared on television as broadcasters, far too many to all be included in this study, have influenced the lives of countless young women watching and wondering what they will do with the rest of their lives. Even more profoundly, by being both seen and heard, these women helped to inch forward equality for women in all walks of life and in every profession. It was fun and interesting to tell their stories through the prisms of their distinct communication styles.

I'm grateful to several people who were as enthusiastic as I was about the project, including Barbara Berger, who carefully read and edited early chapter drafts, my husband Geoff, who sent many timely news articles to my e-mail "in-box," Dr. Roger Egolf, generously drove me to New York and arranged my interview with news veteran Marian Glick, and friend and wordsmith Alan Janesch, who directs the Penn State Grassroots Network, who shaped my thinking about many possible book titles. Special thanks to editor Joseph Parry who has tremendous insight and talent. Warm thanks also to Christine Craft, Candy Crowley, and Dana Bash, who were responsive to my interview requests, and the inimitable Helen Thomas, who very graciously wrote the foreword for the book. She is a trailblazing woman in journalism to be admired.

As always I remain indebted to my very supportive campus—Penn State Lehigh Valley where I was granted a semester sabbatical that allowed me to focus more intently on the completion of this project.

Thank you all very much!

Nichola D. Gutgold

FOREWORD

Helen Thomas, Hearst Newspaper Columnist

These women of television news toughed it out and fortunately were driven enough to insist on equity. It wasn't easy. They not only had to be devoted to the high ethical standards of journalism, they had to articulate and alas be pretty or at least good looking. The same criteria could be applied to men, but they could age and grow bald and last a little longer, but not too much longer. I've seen the best in the business sidelined in the networks' avid accent on youth over experience and gravitas.

I have met and admire all the women in television who are in this book, but know better those who covered the tough White House beat in different eras and went up the ladder. Among them are Andrea Mitchell, Judy Woodruff, and Connie Chung. I have seen Barbara Walters from time to time and I think she is great. She hit the boards during the Carter era when the principals involved in the Camp David peace negotiations only wanted to talk to her. It was a terrific coup. She reigns supreme in the field. I remember when she hosted a program years ago called "Not For Women Only" and lined up several women reporters to participate on one show. We were all seated on high stools and Walters turned to me with the first question: "Do the men at the White House think you are aggressive?" she asked. "I hope so," I replied. Walters nearly fell off of her chair and I realized why—because she obviously had colleagues who sneered at "aggressive" women when she started her career. As the cliché goes, it was always okay for a man to be aggressive. I have also realized a little late in the game that

I was wrong when I urged young women to go into journalism because it was an education every day. "You never stop learning," I said. "What more could you ask?" In that profession, I maintained, you don't go into it to be loved and popular. Just to get the news and do it well. I was wrong as far as television is concerned. You do have to be popular and liked if those attributes equate with the almighty "ratings" in the broadcast business. But to look on the bright side, women have more than arrived in television. At the White House, many women in television are beginning to dominate the field. At one point, ABC had four women on its presidential coverage and no men. History was made for women by Barbara Walters who began making $1 million as an evening coanchor with Harry Reasoner as the antagonist. As big money came into play some of the women on television began to be compared for the salaries and commissions they were making. Of course, the big coup in putting women front and center was when Katie Couric made history with her appointment as solo anchor for CBS. All of the women cited in this book are "pros." They can rise to any occasion when the big story comes along and they have. They have had to prove themselves over and over again in a tough, demanding, and sometimes merciless profession. I take my hat off to them.

Helen Thomas

1

INTRODUCTION

Anchors in America

Anchor. The word itself brings to mind a clear picture of the heft and weightiness needed to secure a vessel. An anchor is a source of security; support with enough power to make a force still. In television news, an anchorperson must make the audience pay attention—ideally stopping all other activity to focus on the narrator—who is the messenger of the news. "Anchors are our journalistic rocks; the news washes over them and recedes."[1] Americans have come to think of news anchors as the voice of authority, a television equivalent of the voice of God, even, for some news devotees, who get so used to tuning in to their favorite anchor that they think of them as family. Anchors project a friendly, yet powerful presence with the elegance and wisdom to tell the events of the world perched on their "electronic hearth" of sorts, in a way that anyone—from the barely educated to the most learned—could understand. Former *ABC News* anchor Frank Reynolds modestly described the role of the news anchor as someone "to help people understand what's going on,"[2] but anyone with even a passing knowledge of the history of television news in America knows that the anchor wields considerable power. Walter Cronkite, perhaps the most famed anchor of all, was considered "the most trusted man in America" in 1966, when the first survey was taken—and in 1996 over ten years after he stepped down from the anchor chair at CBS—he was named "the most trusted man in television news."[3] Some viewers simply called him "Uncle

Walter" and in a 2006 PBS documentary, *Witness to History*, Andy Rooney describes Cronkite by stating, "He typifies all the best of what television news should be and no longer is."[4]

Today, women have a strong presence in television news in America. Despite their slow start, as with politics and other mostly male-dominated industries, women have slowly but surely gained a presence on television news programs. The visibility and voice that women have gained in broadcasting have been important to the impact that women have made in other areas of business, industry, and politics. SheSource.org, an organization that supports the mission of getting women's voices in print and on television and radio, recognizes that for women to gain power in the United States, they have to be seen and heard. For this reason, the rise of women in broadcasting is significant, since it signals a greater acceptance of women's visibility *and* their voices. SheSource.org even holds training groups to give women the tools to write editorial articles and to serve as experts on radio and television.[5] This type of training will help to close the gap that exists in the visibility and voice of women in the media. According to communications scholar Maurine H. Beasley, "on the three main U.S. broadcast networks, 87 percent of the sound bites from experts are provided by men, while women represent only 23 percent of the news directors at television stations."[6] In 1971, Spiro Agnew, vice president of the United States, drew much media attention when he asserted that network news was run by "a small group of men, numbering perhaps no more than a dozen anchormen, commentators, and executive producers" who reserved the right to determine what their audience of tens of millions would learn about the "great issues of our nation."[7] Authors Mark Halpern and John F. Harris note that indeed, Agnew was right that "not that long ago there really was a 'small group of men'—and at the time they were all men—who served as gatekeepers for what the public learned about national politics."[8] This book will show the trajectory of a dozen important women who paved the way for many more women in broadcasting while describing some of the shifts that have occurred in television news. Most of the women in this book have experienced the most dramatic shift, from the three-network, male-dominated network news broadcast to the 24-hour news channels and the growth of the Internet and news. To their credit, most of the women who began in the old world of media are still working and thriving in today's multimedia extravaganza which has become the world of broadcasting.

SEVERAL TYPES OF ANCHORS IN BROADCASTING

There are morning anchors who create a cheerful "hello" atmosphere to viewers who are just starting their day. In the morning news programs, a male and female anchor team has been the most common combination. The anchors, often referred to as "hosts," cover both hard news, such as interviewing heads of state or reporting on the war, as well as lighter segments which may involve interviewing celebrities or participating in a cooking segment with a well-known chef. The early morning shows gave women in broadcasting their first opportunity to appear as anchors on television networks. Usually working alongside a male, they represented the typical American couple. Though a high-profile position, these morning anchor positions for women are viewed very differently than that of an evening news anchor, perhaps because so often the news they present is sprinkled heavily with entertainment features. There are also reporters or correspondents, who are "on the scene" covering stories. These journalists must be adept at doing "stand ups" or impromptu speaking on a topic while at the scene of the story. Frequently these jobs also include people involved in the news story and again, like the impromptu speaking required to report the story, the interviews are unscripted. In addition, the reporters are often asked a few questions by the anchor and again they need to be quick thinkers and able to adlib the answers to the anchors' questions in thoughtful and understandable precision. Other on-camera personnel are weather forecasters and sports anchors. Finally, there are news anchors who preside over the evening news and deliver the stories to the viewers. Since the anchor position is the pinnacle of success within a news organization, the focus of this study is on how well women have positioned themselves for anchor assignments. As Judith Marlane notes in her groundbreaking book, *Women in Television News Revisited*, the power, prestige, and symbolism of the network evening news anchor makes this on-air job the most coveted and important in television broadcasting. So while women may have cracked through some of the biggest barriers in the broadcasting business, it is crucial to evaluate the progress women have made toward gaining access to this most powerful position.[9]

It is important to examine the impact of women as news broadcasters, because the rhetoric of news is rhetoric of authority, as Roderick P. Hart has asserted.[10] The level of authority given to women in broadcasting has increased over the years, and to assess the roles of women today gives insight into their increased authority. However, because so few women have been anchors, the profiles in this book include prominent correspondents as well, but do not include morning television news anchors, with the exception of Katie Couric, who has transitioned to an evening anchor position, and Diane Sawyer, who works both on the ABC *Good Morning America* program as well as the evening ABC news program, *Prime Time Live*.

THE RISE OF WOMEN IN TELEVISION BROADCASTING

The inclusion of women in broadcasting has been on the rise since World War II when women joined the workforce in record numbers. During the late 1940s and through the 1950s and 1960s some women pioneered their way into working in television news. Pauline Frederick broke into television news at ABC during the 1948 political conventions and then became the first woman to work full time on the staff of an American television network.[11] In 1953, Frederick joined NBC as its chief United Nations correspondent and remained with that network until her mandatory retirement in 1975. She learned of her retirement from *The New York Times*.[12] After her retirement, Frederick served as an international affairs analyst and program host for National Public Radio and in 1976 she became the first woman to moderate a presidential debate.[13] In 1955 Marlene Sanders began her career in television news, and in the 1960s she joined ABC as a correspondent. Sanders is the first newswoman to achieve the rank of vice president when ABC appointed her vice president and director of television documentaries.[14] During this time Nancy Dickerson became a well-known *NBC News* correspondent. Dickerson was the first woman to cover the White House for television on a regular basis.[15] She tenaciously studied speech at Catholic University while she was a producer at CBS with the hope that she could become a correspondent, though the idea of that was outrageous at the time.[16] In 1965 Liz Trotta was television's first woman assigned full-time as a foreign correspondent. She stayed with NBC for thirteen years, covering major stories in Europe, Asia, Africa, and the Middle East.[17] In 1962 Barbara Walters became a reporter for NBC's *Today Show*. Lesley Stahl joined CBS as a correspondent in 1972 as the numbers of women increased in television news across the board. By 1974, the three networks had added about a dozen women reporters, and all were actively trying to recruit more.[18] Lesley Stahl was CBS's first woman to coanchor the coverage on election night. In *Reporting Live* Stahl remembers visiting the set before the broadcast with CBS News President Richard Salant and noticing that each chair had a name card. There was "Cronkite, Rather, Mudd, and Wallace." And then there was the card for her chair, which read simply, "Female."[19] This often-told story illustrates the tokenism toward women in television news at this time. These type of overt efforts to include women came after 1971 when the Federal Communications Commission ordered all businesses that made more than $50,000 and had 50 employees or more to mirror the gender balances of their communities.[20] This followed a landmark 1964 amendment to Title VII of the Civil Rights Act, which for the first time added gender to the discrimination taboos of race, color, creed, and national origin.[21] By the end of 1972, 50 percent of all television newsrooms employed at least one woman full time.[22] A study in *Journalism Quarterly*, however, contends that while affirmative action programs stimulated the growth of women in American broadcasting in the 1970s, deregulatory policies in the Reagan administration and increased local competition from local broadcasting companies brought this to a halt.[23] Although women were gaining employment in television news, they faced difficulties because their presence was "not welcomed into the world of television news as much as they were tolerated, indulged."[24] Barbara Matusow notes, "women had been unwelcome in the newsroom, partly because they spoiled the clubhouse atmosphere and partly because of paternalism."[25] The most important barrier [against women in broadcasting] comes from the attitudes of male colleagues and decision makers. Janice Castro reports the story of a woman applying for a vacancy at a television station who was told that there were no openings, "but we could possibly arrange something," and then was propositioned sexually.[26] Janet Vasil, a former local television news anchor and reporter in the Allentown, Pennsylvania, market, at WFMZ-TV, commented, "I gained experience through several internships in radio and television before landing my first on-air job. For one radio internship, I was hired by the program director to lend a hand in various departments around the station. After an interview and orientation tour, he told me to go introduce myself to the various department heads. The news director was a very famous voice in the market. When I entered the newsroom, he motioned for me to come into the sound booth while he was between on-air segments. I walked inside, introduced myself and he said "I don't talk to women with their clothes on." I was shocked but stayed calm enough to say "I guess we have nothing to talk about," turned on my heels, and left the newsroom. He later insisted it was a joke and apologized. I wrote it off as one individual's poor attempt at making a first impression.

Still, in talking to women colleagues over the years, I've found most put up with similar comments and in some cases, much worse actions.[27] Martha M. Lauzen and David M. Dozier analyzed prime-time programs from the 2002–2003 season and found that although Americans age 60 and older constituted 18 percent of the population, such individuals comprised only 4 percent of major characters in prime-time television. Overall, up to age 60, leadership and occupational power increased with age. However, middle-aged males were more likely to play leadership roles and wield occupational power than their female counterparts.[28]

Judy Woodruff notes, "Guys like Cronkite and Brokaw seem to gain wisdom with every gray hair. For women, it's the opposite. It's getting better, but it's still an uphill fight."[29] More succinctly Woodruff noted in her autobiography: "You don't see a lot of balding fat women on television."[30]

In Andrew Tyndall's 2005 study of the most frequent news correspondents on television (excluding anchors), Lisa Myers of NBC was ranked 6th with 214 minutes of airtime. There were seven women in the top twenty.[31] The number of women in news as well as the types of roles that they fill are important because getting significant air time means that women are performing the top jobs in news organizations. One need only to flip on the television to see women reporting the news.

A closer examination of the number of women and their assignments reveals that their roles are not on par with men, and that the model of three white males as anchors on the three major networks, while slowly changing, still remains the norm. The three original anchors at the major networks—Douglas Edwards, John Daly, and John Cameron Swayze—are now Brian Williams, Charlie Gibson, and in September, 2006, the very first woman sole anchor, Katie Couric, took over for Dan Rather as the anchor of the *CBS Evening News.*

In 1983 *TV Guide* asked, "Why Are There Still No Female Dan Rathers?"[32] And it took almost a quarter of a century—2006—for the question to be moot. With a five-year contract, a multimillion-dollar salary, and the title of managing editor, Katie Couric is in a strong position to reshape *CBS Evening News.* CBS President Les Moonves said he wasn't looking for a "voice of God" anchor when Couric was appointed. The CBS newscast has been dead last in the ratings for more than ten years, but it's shown some life under interim anchor Bob Schieffer. CBS executives are hoping that Katie Couric will build a bigger audience that includes more women and younger viewers.[33] That women are on the news isn't enough. They need to gain a strong presence in the areas of leadership, which in news means anchoring.

John Dickerson, editor of Slate.com, and son of former pioneering correspondent Nancy Dickerson, said that it has taken women over thirty years to get to the anchoring position because "men have always run the networks and it takes time to convince men that women can handle the task. But it's also the audience. Networks are risk averse and putting a woman in the anchor chair is a change for viewers and advertisers who fund that crucial hour of television. People took time to get used to a female face in the position of authority."[34]

CONTRIBUTING TO THE GROWING LITERATURE

Several books and articles examine television news history and specifically the progress of women in television news; themes that emerge in this book. *Women Come to the Front* is a book that spotlights women who covered World War II as journalists, photographers, and broadcasters. Jeff Allen and James Lane chronicle the history of network news in the comprehensive book, *Anchoring America: The Changing Face of Television News* (Bonus Books, 2003). Barbara Matusow offers an in-depth look at news anchors in her book *The Evening Stars: The Making of the Network News Anchor* (Houghton Mifflin, 1983). Marlene Sanders and Marcia Rock get to the issue of gender inequality in *Waiting for Prime Time: The Women of Television News* (University of Illinois Press, 1994). *Featuring Females* include feminist analyses of media edited by Ellen Cole and Jessica Henderson Daniel. An encyclopedia-type book, *Making Waves: The 50 Greatest Women in Radio and Television* (McMeel Publishing, 2001) offers profiles of women in media from Gracie Allen to Oprah Winfrey. Professor Judith Marlane offers *Women in Television News* and her updated *Women in Television News Revisited* which includes many interviews and draws from her experiences as a television writer, producer, and broadcaster (University of Texas Press, 1999), Edward Bliss Jr.'s comprehensive work, *Now the News: The Story of Broadcast Journalism*, devotes a fair amount of time to women's history in broadcasting (Columbia University Press, 1991) and Christine Craft, who broke open the issue of the discrimination of women in television news wrote *Too Old, Too Ugly and Not Deferential to Men*, Prima Publishing, 1988. Daniel Paisner followed up with a book that featured interviews with several prominent female broadcasters that addressed gender issues in the field in his book, *The Imperfect Mirror: Inside Stories of Television Newswomen* (William Morrow, 1989).

Biographies by women newscasters also offer insight into the topic: Barbara Walters's *How to Talk with Practically Anybody about Practically Anything* (Doubleday, 1970), Jerry Oppenheimer's best-selling, *Barbara Walters* (St. Martin Press, 1990), and Leslie Stahl's 1999 biography *Reporting Live* (Simon and Schuster), which offers insight into the professional rigors of life as a newscaster and the personal sacrifices of the demanding career. Connie Chung's paper "The Business of 'Getting the Get': Nailing an Exclusive Interview in Prime Time" was published by Harvard University's Joan Shorenstein Center for Press Politics and Public Policy in April 1998. In the paper, Chung describes what reporters must do to be successful in landing interviews with celebrities and other interviewees who may be difficult to reach. She also contends that the changing role of the anchor in television news has required them to pursue interviews to help them garner the biggest ratings. No longer is an anchor just a figurehead. In the immensely competitive world of television news, the anchor now functions as a draw for celebrities and heads of state. If the anchor can effectively convince the most desirable interviewees to appear on their network, it gives the anchor cache and job security. Andrea Mitchell wrote her gutsy autobiography, aptly named *Talking Back* (Viking, 2005), in which she outlines some of the most memorable 'gets' of her broadcasting career.

John Dickerson penned the book *On Her Trail* (Simon and Schuster, 2006), which is a personal account of his mother's life, including the considerable chauvinism she faced in the starchy 1950s and 1960s when she was one of a handful of women working in broadcasting. Erika Engstrom and Anthony J. Ferri look at the career perceptions of women TV news anchors in *Journalism and Mass Communications Quarterly*, 1998. Engstrom also examines the career barriers that women news anchors face in "Looking Through a Gendered Lens: Local U.S. Television News Anchors' Perceived Career Barriers" in the *Journal of Broadcasting*, Fall, 2000. Cindy J. Price and Shaun S. Wulff ask questions of gender balance in their 2005 *Women's Studies in Communication* article, "Does Sex Make a Difference? Job Satisfaction of Television Network News Correspondents." Thomas Smee asks "Does a News Anchor's Gender Influence Audience Evaluations of the Anchor?" in a Fall, 2004 media report to women. Craig M. Allen offers a complete look at the prominence of local news in his important book *News Is People: The Rise of Local TV News and the Fall of News from New York* (Iowa State University Press, 2001). *The News Interview: Journalists and Public Figures on the Air* (Cambridge University Press, 2002), by Steven Clayman and John Heritage carefully analyzes interviews by examining parts of the interviews, styles of questioning, adversarial questioning, and other areas relevant to broadcast interviews.

MEDIA PORTRAYALS OF TELEVISION NEWSWOMEN

Comic strip readers were intrigued with the adventures of Brenda Starr, who debuted in 1940 and portrayed a reporter's life as glamorous, mysterious, dangerous, and in need of a gutsy heroine ready to travel the world to get her story. In 1976 Sidney Lumet directed Faye Dunaway as the ruthless television producer in the Academy Award–winning film, *Network*. In the film she portrayed a woman that was so driven by her career her personal life was in shambles. The 1982 film *Broadcast News* similarly portrayed Holly Hunter as the all-business news producer whose personal life suffered as a result of her unfailing commitment to work. Actress Nicole Kidman caught the attention of critics for her edgy lead character Suzanne Stone, an ambitious and sexy woman who wanted nothing more than to be a big television news personality in the film *To Die For*. In 1996 actress Michelle Pfeiffer, in the film *Up Close and Personal*, portrayed a beautiful, neophyte journalist who was determined to build a career for herself in television news and falls in love with her first boss and mentor. In the 2004 film *Anchorman*, a woman broadcaster invaded the male dominion of a local news station set in the 1970s. While a satire, there are some truths to the film's portrayal of the three male anchors: sports, weather, and news. They were all white and more than a bit resentful of the woman trying to unseat their power. These less-than-flattering portrayals of women in broadcasting have contributed to the myth that to have a successful career, women in television must be workaholics lacking a personal life, who will go to any length, often becoming romantically involved, to get ahead in their careers or at the least to get a story.

On television for ten years, from 1988–1998, *Murphy Brown* showcased the fictional news program *FYI*, which was represented as a tough, talk-oriented investigative news program, and Murphy Brown, played by Candace Bergen, portrayed a more human than merely female reporter who was a tough interviewer. Bonnie Dow reports that "Murphy's style reflects the goal of gaining credibility in a male world."[35] The most media attention paid to the series, however, came when Murphy Brown became a single parent and gave birth, without having a spouse. Then vice president Dan

Quayle made a speech in California and criticized the television character's decision to have the baby and raise it without a father, calling it a "lifestyle choice."[36] The original ensemble included Corky Sherwood, played by actress Faith Ford, who was a Louisiana girl and former Miss America who took a few journalism classes in college but was mainly hired for her looks. Murphy Brown is reminiscent of the 1970s television show Mary Tyler Moore, but as Bonnie Dow deftly notes, "while Mary Tyler Moore was firmly within what Norman Lear called the 'emerging woman' genre, there is no doubt that Murphy Brown has made it. She is no struggling former secretary turned producer in local news, but rather, a powerful network co-anchor of a prime-time news magazine.[37] Most recently, in the summer of 2007, Fox television premiered *Anchorwoman,* a reality show that follows the travails of KYTX newsroom in Tyler, Texas. Desperate for ratings, the owner Phil Hurley hires bleach blonde Lauren Jones, a former beauty queen and professional wrestling diva, to become a news anchor. A television critic noted that although "Anchorwoman is only a summer show, it seems like Fox is using the show to degrade the value of television news and attach and humiliate anyone who takes journalism seriously."[38] In 2007, two Emmy award–winning actors, Kelsey Grammar and Patricia Heaton, star in another Fox program called *Back to You* about two former newscasters who find themselves paired together again and attracted to each other.

THE CHANGING WORLD OF TELEVISION NEWS

With the advent of Cable News Network (CNN) in 1980, the three major networks, ABC, NBC, and CBS, have less of a stronghold on the American public's news consumption. According to an annual report entitled "State of the News Media," 70 percent of the television sets tuned in to news prior to CNN's launch were tuned to one of the three major networks. In 2003, it was reduced to 40 percent.[39] While this statistic shows the reduction in the reliance on network news, it doesn't diminish the noticeable lack of women in the anchor seat. At the same time the three major networks are showing the evening news, CNN airs "Lou Dobbs Tonight" (EST). In 1996, Fox News Network was introduced to the country and in the same year MSNBC also presented itself as an alternative to CNN for viewers to receive news twenty-four hours a day. While the ratings prize being sought by the successors to the so-called Big Three is a fraction of what it once was, in an age when news is available instantly on the Internet and cell phones, the nearly 25 million viewers who collectively still watch the network news broadcasts each night are among those most valued by many advertisers.[40] Podcasts are also popular with younger news viewers, and this growing source of news is likely to continue with the expansion of handheld electronic devices. Authors Mark Halperin and John F. Harris contend that Matt Drudge, developer of The Drudge Report, an online publication has become the new Walter Cronkite. They note, "to put it mildly, [Drudge] will never be known as 'the most trusted man in America'" but in fact "Matt Drudge is the gatekeeper."[41] All of these alternate methods of getting the news impact the careers of broadcasters.

Before Katie Couric's historic CBS position, a few short stints by other women anchors include Jessica Savitch, who in 1977 became the backup anchor to John Chancellor. Savitch's notable broadcasting career ended with her sudden death in a car accident in 1983. Barbara Walters was brought in to coanchor the ABC Evening News with Harry Reasoner in 1976. Walter's appointment was an attempt to increase ratings, but Harry Reasoner wasn't happy about his cohost; their lack of camaraderie was visible on air and the arrangement was brief, lasting only two years. In 1993 Connie Chung sat beside Dan Rather briefly at *CBS Evening News*, and their antagonistic relationship has been well documented. From January to May, 2006 Elizabeth Vargas and Bob Woodruff filled in at ABC News after the unexpected death of long-time anchor Peter Jennings. Woodruff sustained injuries reporting on the Iraq war less than one month after the anchor team debuted and Vargas's second pregnancy was more difficult than anticipated. Both were replaced by longtime ABC anchor, the affable Charlie Gibson, from *Good Morning America*, who was named the permanent replacement for Jennings.

Women were rare in television news before the 1970s, even behind the scenes. Now in her late eighties, former news editor Marian Glick was, by her own description, "born a news junkie." As a very young girl, she remembers her uncle, who worked as a pressman for a newspaper, bringing her newsprint and it was then that her fascination in becoming a journalist was born. She graduated from Indiana University in 1942. Her father would have preferred that she majored in education, but her professor encouraged her that she "had it"—that is, the right skill set—to make a good journalist. Upon graduation she worked for UPI, then the DuMont network and eventually CBS, where she remembers the day the call came in from a young Dan Rather, who phoned New York from Dallas with the news that President Kennedy had been shot. Marian Glick was often the lone woman on the job, and out of courtesy men refrained from using curse words around her. She says, "I was accepted. I was considered a good newsman, but women in front of the camera were very slow to catch on. Maybe it was because the men did all of the hiring."[42]

OBSTACLES FOR WOMEN ANCHORS

The first question that comes to mind is: why has it taken so long for a woman to fill the anchor chair? Similar to the political phrase "All the President's Men" when news broadcasting started, there were "Murrow's Boys," and the feeling that anchoring the news is a man's job has persisted. Craig M. Allen in his comprehensive and seminal work *News Is People* found that people watch news when they can identify with an anchor who is like a "friend next door."[43] Allen has also put forth the notion that women pioneered successful local television anchor positions much more successfully than national ones. This too mirrors the slow rise of women in politics. The public may be willing to embrace a woman mayor, congresswoman, senator, even governor, yet the presidency remains elusive to women. Leslie Baldacci from *The Chicago Sun Times* observes incredulously: "It took thirty years—a generation—for women to fly solo in the network evening news anchor chair."[44] In 1987 Judy Woodruff lamented that "In television, they would say, "A woman doesn't have the credibility with an audience, or an audience isn't ready to hear news from a woman."[45] This chapter begins to ask: *why*?

Millions of people tune into the news every day, and among them are young girls who are shaping their ideas about what it means to be a working woman. According to Daniel Paisner, author of *The Imperfect Mirror: Inside Stories of Television Newswomen*, "the television newswoman is the most visible working woman around, working testimony that you can, in fact, have it all, or at least have a go at having it all. Newswomanhood is presented as a lifestyle first; journalism comes somewhat further down the list."[46]

Katie Couric's success on CBS is less important than the more penetrating question: why did it take so long to get her there? In a 1987 Phil Donahue television broadcast, Donahue assembled some of the most prominent women newscasters of the time, which included Jane Pauley, Maria Shriver, Leslie Stahl, Connie Chung, Joan Lunden, Rita Flynn, Mary Alice Williams, and Carole Simpson. He asked them "are women ornaments in television news or are their talents valued?" Back then he asked why a woman isn't a sole anchor of a major network broadcast. No solutions were provided, but the women spent the half-hour program discussing how new women are to broadcasting and that their presence there is important not only for parity in broadcasting, but that they also provide a visual image of women as leaders that could contribute to the successful election of a woman president.[47]

Erika Engstrom asked television news anchors about their perceived obstacles in her 2000 research article in the *Journal of Broadcasting and Electronic Media* and discovered that for women, physical appearance is the most significant news barrier faced by women.[48] Lana F. Rakow and Kimberlie Kranich echo this sentiment in their research when they observe, "Public controversies about double standards of appearance for women are no less the bearers of meaning, the object of male fantasy, than other representative of women. The double standard women newscasters thus face gives us insight into their difficulty satisfying a television audience."[49]

Kathleen Hall Jamieson contends that the absence of a legacy is part of the reason that women are unable to rise to the highest levels of leadership. Furthermore, she cites these obstacles to women achieving leadership positions on par with men:

- Women can exercise their wombs or their brains, but not both.
- Women who speak out are immodest and will be shamed, while women who are silent will be ignored or dismissed.
- Women are subordinate whether they claim to be different from men or the same.
- Women who are considered feminine will be judged incompetent, and women who are competent, unfeminine.
- As men age, they gain wisdom and power; as women age, they wrinkle and become superfluous.[50]

Naomi Wolf, in her groundbreaking book, *The Beauty Myth*, singles out the occupation of newscaster as one fraught with difficulties for the professional woman and what her image would project to the world. She writes, "The avuncular male anchor was joined by a much younger female newscaster with a professional prettiness level." [51]

Women as window dressing on the set? Johnathan Last notes, "There is no rising generation of young anchors. Extinction looms, and it's not clear who's to blame. Part of it must be our cultural fetish for youth, which pushes an endless line of tight-faced beauties at us. These days, looking older than fifty-five isn't just tragic; it's downright offensive."[52] Another reason that anchors are not what they used to be is that television news isn't what it used to be. The formal, stiff presentation that ushered broadcast journalism into our homes has given way to an image-driven conversational style of broadcasting that is more recognizable to viewers now. The same qualities that gave an anchor credibility in the past, a "Father Knows Best" orientation, has changed with the change in the workforce. Roderick P. Hart notes in *Modern Rhetorical Criticism* that verbal dimensions of credibility include power, competence, trustworthiness, goodwill, and similarity.[53] As women have entered the workforce in greater numbers since the days of early broadcasting when all the talking heads on television were male, the audience should be poised to accept women as "similar" since indeed there are more women working than ever. In addition, as more and more women gain access to the highest positions of power in America, in such positions as senator, secretary of state, governor, and eventually president, the perceptions of what it means to be powerful, competent, trustworthy, possessing goodwill and similarity will also shift. We are in a transitional state in broadcast history. The same qualities that viewers have embraced in their morning show hosts, such as friendliness and a warmth, have yet to reach the collective consciousness for our evening news broadcasters.

When Bob Woodruff's injuries prevented him from returning to *ABC World News Tonight* in a timely fashion, why wasn't Elizabeth Vargas appointed as the full-time solo anchor? Is one reason because the male anchor is really the star and the female sidekick an ornament, "window dressing," and someone to handle the softer, feature stories?

Although Vargas was pregnant, other women broadcasters have worked through their pregnancies, though Vargas admitted her second pregnancy was more difficult than her first. Was there was risk aversion from ABC to attempt to score high ratings with an anchor—Vargas—who, male or female, wasn't as well known as Gibson?

When Katie Couric joined then cohost Bryant Gumbel on *The Today Show*, she had been at NBC for just two years—as the deputy Pentagon correspondent and then as *The Today Show's* national correspondent—but she said she had no hesitation about telling Michael Gartner, then the news division president, that she wanted "a 50/50 split in hard news" with Gumbel. "Can you imagine?" she recalled with a laugh. "The gall I had. I'm sure they were probably like, 'Who is this person? Where does she come from?'" Gartner promised her 52/48, and Couric replied, "Well, I'll take that and I'll build from there."[54] Election Night 2000 included three NBC hosts, primarily Tom Brokaw and Tim Russert, with Katie Couric in more of a supportive role. As the election night turned into a bizarre twist of history and most Americans remained glued to their television sets overnight and into the morning, they noticed that Couric, who had little, if any sleep, was an astute, well-informed anchor explaining the historic election that remained unresolved for weeks ahead. A less competent, uninformed host couldn't handle the anchoring, but Katie Couric was able to tap into a deep reserve of Washington, D.C., experience that served her well then, as well as during the terrorist attacks of September 11, 2001.

While some women found success in television broadcasting because they looked attractive, the women who have had longevity in their careers have been able to bring a lot more than "window dressing" to the set. The trailblazer newscasters featured in this book are women who know American and world history and understand the delicate nuances involved in interviewing families who have experienced tragedies as well as explaining government policy to viewers. Most of them are as comfortable speaking with a head of state as they are with a five-year-old. Unruffled, confident, informed, and purposeful are the words that describe the most successful women in television broadcasting. Aristotle's concept of becoming fits well with the emerging woman in broadcasting. Aristotle held that the first concept is that of being and that is presupposed to the idea of becoming. That there are women in television is the concept of being and that they are emerging as anchors offers a glimpse of what they are becoming.

Who's talking is also an indication of who has the authority in television. In a study conducted by The White House Project, researchers likened the presence of women on Sunday morning talk shows as having the "authority-setting effect,"[55] similar to the overarching "agenda-setting"[56] concept introduced in the 1970s. The study asserts that since television is our most powerful medium, it has the ability to confer authority and set the agenda for the national debate, as well as establish the profiles and visibility of leaders. In 2006, The White House Project conducted an online poll to determine what kinds of press coverage Katie Couric has been receiving in anticipation of her role as anchorperson on CBS. The survey asked readers to determine whether or not the news coverage has been mostly about Couric's credentials or her appearance.[57] The result was that most of the coverage on Couric addressed her looks and not her experience as a journalist.

Katie Couric hadn't even finished her morning cohost assignment on *The Today Show* when reporters started to consider how she would need to change her wardrobe to appear more credible for her new assignment as CBS News anchor. A *New York Sun* reporter conjectured: "her impressive collection of strappy sandals, form-fitting tops, and shiny makeup may be gone for good. New York stylists surmise that the popular newswoman will tone down her wardrobe and makeup to cultivate a more serious image in line with her new gig as anchor of the *CBS Evening News*. Ms. Couric may trade her bolder outfits and hairstyles for tailored suits, classic pumps, pearl jewelry, stay-in-place hair, and matte makeup, observers say. "She can't deliver international news in a sweater set," a director of the marketing and consulting firm "Just Ask a Woman," Jennifer Drechsler, said.[58] The intense focus on the appearance and femininity of women on television has been an issue since the beginning of broadcasting and still persists today.

In an interview with Larry King in December, 2000, King repeatedly tried to talk to Katie Couric about her appearance. King introduced Katie Couric to his show by saying "We've got to begin with the most important question that all, everybody wants to know: your hair. What have you done with your hair?" She responded, "Very funny" and "Can we talk about *your* hair?" To which King asked "Does that offend you that no one would ask a man—no one would say to Dan Rather, let's talk about your hair?" Diplomatically, Couric responded, "I think that all women for whatever strange reason are fascinated by hair, particularly women. Because I was actually thinking about this the other day because there seems to be a bit of a national obsession lately. And I think that it's part of you that's easy to change and easy to play with. And it's not like losing ten pounds or going out and buying a new dress, but it's something you can do fairly easily to change the way you look."[59] Media scholar Ken Auletta notes: "Viewers had empathized with Katie Couric when her husband died, and then when her sister Emily died, of pancreatic cancer, but now her period of mourning was ending and her public image was changing. She even looked different. She closeted her conservative suits and replaced them with leather skirts and summer dresses that showed off her legs and arms, which had been buffed by a personal trainer. She streaked her hair blond and, it seemed, wore a different pair of colored glasses everyday. She appeared in fashion spreads for *Vogue*. She began to date, and the celebrity magazines and tabloids carried stories of a serious romance with Tom Werner, a Hollywood producer."[60] It seems that the more attention she paid to her looks and the more glamorous she had become, the less she was able to relate to the average viewer who felt comfortable with her. In anticipation of Katie Couric's new position as CBS anchor, *USA Today* reported: "her famously toned legs will probably be hidden by a news anchor desk—and, hence, from criticism. But if you ask some style mavens, a waist-up camera shot won't solve the problem of Katie Couric's hair color (too brassy) and cut (too long). Then there's her makeup (too dark), her clothes (too glam) and her skin (too tan). For the past few years, her look was "distracting," says Estee Lauder makeup artist Rick DiCecca. And in the context of delivering serious news, it would be even more so, experts say.[61] As Katie Couric moves into the evening anchor chair, she finds herself critiqued on everything from the cadence of her voice to the shade of her lipstick.

Former television news anchor Christine Craft commented on the changes that she has seen in the more than twenty years after her legal battle over her job as a news anchor. She says, "Things *have* changed for women in television news. You can now work past your fortieth birthday. The real impact in most television markets is that female anchors can stay on the air as long as men. However, they are required to have two facelifts for every single facelift of their male counterparts. Many news anchors faced with demotion because they are getting "too old" have raised the threat of litigation and "the Christine Craft syndrome" and have been able to keep their jobs. At the same time, the "new" trend known as the Faux News dumb blonde syndrome (Fox News) is operating against job tenure for women in TV news."[62]

An attractive appearance is an asset in almost any endeavor, especially television, since by its very nature it is a visual enterprise. Christine Craft's observation of women in television news is significant because it points to the differences in expectations for male and female appearance. While male news anchors have gone gray, gotten wrinkled and bald, women broadcasters, regardless of their age, have remained blond or brunette (mostly blond) with relatively smooth skin, regardless of their age. So even the women who have been in television for more than thirty years do not appear old. Lesley Stahl and Diane Sawyer, who are both over sixty years old, look youthful. Barbara Walters, who is nearing eighty, could pass for sixty.

AGEISM AND THE ANCHORWOMAN

The issue of anchorwomen being discriminated against based on their age was addressed in 1970 when the FCC promulgated a series of regulations prohibiting discrimination against women.[63] One of the regulations prohibited discriminating against women who are over forty years old. This issue is especially important to women in television since advancing age is more obvious in the visual medium of television than perhaps in any other occupation. Of course not all women on television are below forty years old. In fact many of the biggest stars are well over forty. Barbara Walters, Katie Couric, Diane Sawyer, Christiane Amanpour, and Candy Crowley, as well as others, remain fixtures on the national news scene and none of them is younger than forty. They are also major stars, and it is this distinction that is important to note. Between 1983 and 2002, men's tenure as correspondents on network news averaged eight years, versus five for women, according to a study conducted by Joe Foote, dean of the University of Oklahoma's Gaylord College of Journalism & Mass Communication. Of the thirty correspondents who reported during each of those twenty years—a measure of longevity—twenty-eight were male.[64] The lack of women decision makers, women overseas, pay inequities, focus on women's appearance, and insensitivity to women were issues that were addressed. Before the luncheon ended, the women presented a set of specific proposals. They wanted ABC to hire a full-time recruiter, to post job openings and institute employee evaluations, and they wanted Arledge to support their efforts to form a women's advisory board, to serve as a formal body to deal with women's issues.[65]

In 2003, network executives assigned younger and less experienced anchor Paula Zahn to take over many of the duties Judy Woodruff had. The leaders of Turner Broadcasting at the time—men—whose entire experience was in the world of entertainment, wanted to hire "younger and more attractive" anchors to jazz up newscasts with what they thought would be a more entertaining program.[66]

Many of the women who assert that their careers have been cut short because of their advancing age never make it to the national news scene. One of the first, and the most well known, newswomen who brought charges against her employer is Christine Craft, who sued Metromedia, Inc. in the 1980s for demoting her from anchor to reporter at the age of thirty-six after the station manager dubbed her "too old, too unattractive and not sufficiently deferential enough to men."[67] In her book with a similar title to the description of her, *Too Old, Too Ugly and Not Deferential to Men*, Craft explains that "They originally hired me saying they loved my "look," appreciated the fact that I was a seasoned journalist, and had no intention of changing me."[68] After nine months on the job, however, viewer research was conducted and the management at the Kansas City station, KMBC, informed her that because she didn't hide her intelligence, and she actually knew the difference between the American and National sports leagues, she wasn't making the men on the station look smarter and the ratings showed that the people of Kansas City didn't like her. She was removed immediately from the anchor chair. Craft's initial courtroom victory, which received a tremendous amount of press, was later overturned and her appeal rejected by the Supreme Court. Now a lawyer and a radio talk show host in Sacramento, California, Craft notes that although she wasn't successful in her lawsuit, "newsmen and newswomen all over the country have gone out of their way to tell me that my battle made a positive difference for them."[69] Linda Ellerbee, a former anchor for *NBC News Overnight*, noted that "No one ever said to Walker Cronkite, 'Gee, you're too gray.'"[70] In Ellerbee's 1986 autobiography she asks: "What happens as we [women broadcasters] age, our hair grays, our breasts sag? Will we be retired, as once was the custom with stewardesses? Will we be shifted from in front of the camera, in front of the White House, the Capitol, the explosion, the courthouse, the war zone—to more seemly assignments like covering cooking stories and one hundredth birthday celebrations of senior citizens?"[71] Judy Muller, a reporter for *World News Tonight, Nightline, 20/20,* and other *ABC News* broadcasts, described her meeting with an image consultant who told her she should soften her angular face by wearing scarves. Though she rejected the image consultant's suggestion, she did have plastic surgery to remove jowls on her face. She remembers the cadre of hair, makeup, and wardrobe assistants who helped Barbara Walters to look her best in between shots, while Muller struggled with minor accessory adjustments, such as making certain her pearl necklace was straight. Euphemistically she notes that "the best accessory is the string of words that, like so many pearls, can make for a beautiful story."[72] In 1982 Barbara Walters pointed out that she was generally considered the "grande dame" of television news when she was fifty. Dan Rather was considered the "brash young kid" who had replaced Walter Cronkite and he was also fifty.[73] Though Marlene Sanders and Marcia Rock contend that because Walters is not a conventional newswoman, the special qualities of her career have extended it beyond what is more typical for female broadcasters.[74] Bonnie Anderson, veteran news reporter and then vice president of recruiting for CNN, describes her wake-up call about the importance of younger anchors. Her boss, Garth Ancier, told her "we need younger, more attractive anchors (male and female) who project credibility." Anderson explains: "Not *have* credibility, earned through years of training and experience. Why didn't Ancier want anchors who had earned their stripes? Because those years of experience show—on one's face."[75] One of the questions to keep in mind is: are we allowing women anchors to age?

SOCIOLOGICAL IMPLICATIONS

When girls watch television, they are likely to form impressions of possible futures for themselves. L. Monique Ward and Kristen Harrison note that television viewing influences viewers' attitudes about jobs held by women, appropriate roles and behaviors for women, and their own personal preferences regarding the kinds of activities that interest them.[76] For many girls growing up in front of their television sets, the television newswoman stands as the most visible working woman around, working testimony that you can, in fact, have it all.[77] The image of beautiful newscasters who seemed to have everything contribute to the image of what it means to be a working woman in America. "The most emblematic working women in the west could be visible if they were "beautiful," even if they were bad at their work; they could be good at their work and "beautiful" and therefore visible, but get no credit for merit; or they could be good and "unbeautiful" and therefore invisible, so their merit did them no good. The double standard of appearance for men and women communicated itself every morning and every night to the nations of working women, whenever they tried to plug in to the event of 'their' world."[78]

Brian Lowry writes in *Broadcasting & Cable* magazine, "Too many younger women have become accomplices in undermining their hard-news credibility—particularly in local news, where flashing outfits and sexual come-ons mirror the poor sexuality-as-career advancement judgment consistently exhibited by female contestants on *The Apprentice*."[79]

Veteran news correspondent Maureen Bunyan sees a tie in the relationship between the political life and the public life and the public image in mass media. She believes that if we elect a woman president or vice president of the United States, then we will get a woman anchoring the evening news. She says, "When women achieve high political office in this country, it will be because the American public has said we accept top leadership from a woman."[80] This line of reasoning suggests that seeing women as leaders would awaken the public consciousness to the idea that women are capable as leaders. It shows the young girls watching television that being an anchor of a major network is a possible career option. In a similar way, having a woman president shows girls that it isn't a job only open to men.

INFOTAINMENT

Both this obstacle and next, "the bottom-line over real news" are not obstacles that only women in journalism face, and they may not be obstacles to some of the broadcasters who have embraced this form of journalism. However, they are indeed an obstacle to traditional journalists who wish to stay true to the doctrines of journalism. According to the Society of Professional Journalists, which was founded in 1909, journalism must be dedicated to the perpetuation of a free press as the cornerstone of our nation and our liberty. Furthermore, journalism must ensure that the concept of self-government outlined by the U.S. Constitution remains a reality into future centuries, the American people must be well informed in order to make decisions regarding their lives, and their local and national communities. It is the role of journalists to provide this information in an accurate, comprehensive, timely, and understandable manner. It is the mission of the Society of Professional Journalists:

- To promote this flow of information.
- To maintain constant vigilance in protection of the First Amendment guarantees of freedom of speech and of the press.
- To stimulate high standards and ethical behavior in the practice of journalism.
- To foster excellence among journalists.
- To inspire successive generations of talented individuals to become dedicated journalists.
- To encourage diversity in journalism.
- To be the preeminent, broad-based membership organization for journalists.
- To encourage a climate in which journalism can be practiced freely.[81]

The infotainment or "Hollywoodization" of journalism is significant to note, however, because it impacts the industry and thus is indeed faced by women who are attempting to rise in the field.

Ken Auletta complains that "an inescapable truism about journalism is that form dictates content. The form of journalism—gimme a headline, gimme a story in the next hour or two, and gimme it in 500 words or 250 words—subverts the context."[82] Clarence Page, a national columnist, regards infotainment as harmless. He says: "in the modern journalism era, there will be a hunger for accurate and reliable reporting as long as there is something newsworthy happening. There is also a need for the analytical and investigative role that holds the powerful accountable and keeps the rascals on notice."[83] He believes that sensational punditry, one that focuses more on the messenger than the news, only appeals to those less informed who want their own views reinforced. While this may be true, infotainment is hard to discern from news that is "accurate and reliable."

Bonnie M. Anderson, who was fired from her job at CNN as vice president of recruiting, describes the continuously eroding quality of journalism in her book, *News Flash*. Anderson recounts discussions with top level decision makers at CNN who wanted to attract as many viewers as possible, she says, putting journalistic standards in jeopardy. That journalism has given way to an entertainment-driven industry that is losing credibility and viewers every day, is the thesis of Anderson's book. She comments on the question: "How do serious women broadcast journalists proceed in their careers when they are faced with issues such as entertainment over news?" She answered: How does *any* serious broadcast journalist accomplish this in this day and age? There really isn't a gender issue here. She says that you could "cave in and prostitute yourself and the people's right to know. This will keep you employed and quite often help make you a star earning big bucks. But make no mistake; you are not practicing journalism, you are not a true, ethical and honest newsperson. You are a news whore, a news actor who cares more about what's in it for you rather than what you should be caring about: informing the American public as part of your public duty, as protected by the U.S. Bill of Rights.

Within the news organization, sidestep as much of the crap assignments as possible while simultaneously trying to work *within* the organization to foster positive change and a return to higher standards. You'll have to draw a line beyond which you will not cross. It isn't easy and it offers career dangers, but you will be able to look at yourself in the mirror."[84]

THE BOTTOM LINE OVER REAL NEWS

Author Ken Auletta notes that "the cultural gap between the business and news divisions at media companies is as wide as the gap between scientists and government that C. P. Snow wrote about nearly half a century ago. Media corporations prize teamwork to create a "borderless" company that eliminates defensive interior barriers among divisions, strive to use leverage to boost sales, and push synergy. But journalists are meant to prize independence, not teamwork, and to value distance from advertisers or sources, not synergies with them."[85] Bonnie Anderson writes: "The drive for increasing earnings on a yearly basis has a direct impact on what news is covered and how it is covered at a network like CNN. Everything, including programming and staffing, is affected. This conclusion has meant cheating American viewers of news they should have had immediately at times when the network could make more money renting its facilities and its services to others." She sites two firsthand examples of this, but she cautions readers that there are likely many more instances where profits supersede news. Anderson describes her coverage of Hurricane Andrew that was much worse in the town of Homestead, Florida, but went unreported to viewers because Newscourse, which is *CNN's* affiliate service, wanted live shots in the town of Cutler Ridge, even though the damage was much more severe in Homestead. Another example of this that Anderson describes is when, in 1996, leftist guerrillas belonging to Tipac Amaru took over the Japanese embassy in Peru, holding people hostage, but CNN's satellite was being used by TV Asashi to provide the Japanese network with international coverage, a service that provides between $11 million and $12 million annually to CNN. So again, American viewers had to wait for news because CNN was collecting rental money for its satellite.[86]

ONLY A FEW "WOMEN STARS" ON NETWORK NEWS

Since at least the early 1980s women at ABC News had been discussing the inequalities that faced women broadcasters at the network. At a luncheon held on the same day Barbara Walters was to be honored by the American Women in Radio and Television, in 1985, Carole Simpson, a well regarded correspondent and host of ABC's *World News Sunday*, spoke on behalf of her female colleagues in an effort to bring the inequalities she and her female correspondents perceived to the attention of Roone Arledge, president of ABC News. The issues that Simpson raised were described broadly as "institutionalized sex discrimination." The first issue was the inequality in airtime. While "women made up 18 percent of the correspondents—sixteen of the ninety—they contributed to just 9 percent of the spots on *World News Tonight*."[87]

TELEVISION BEAUTY QUALIFICATION

What Naomi Wolf dubbed the "PBQ" (professional beauty qualification) has grown in importance and obsession in the world of television since she introduced the term in 1991. There is increased pressure for women of all ages to be youthful and attractive, and I think that television anchorwomen, who may be a most visible image of a working woman to many girls and women, help to perpetuate the youthful and beautiful mandate for women, while male anchors continue to be gray, even bald and wrinkled. This increased emphasis on unnatural appearance, or "TBQ," television beauty qualificatio,n may be undermining women's progress as news anchors. Deborah Norville, who briefly replaced Jane Pauley on *The Today Show*, maintains that her career actually suffered because of her good looks. "The blue eyes, the blond hair, the gender, have been a handicap. They may have gotten me noticed, but they would have gotten me thrown out three times as fast if I hadn't busted my butt."[88] Katie Couric replaced Norville after a viewer backlash against Norville depicted her as the younger, more glamorous replacement of the longtime anchor, Pauley (see chapter seven). Christiane Amanpour, CNN senior international correspondent, describes how her appearance and voice were considered unacceptable to those whom she worked for early in her career: "Your hair is black, for heaven's sake, and very unruly. Don't you know that you have to be blonde to make it on television here? No, you've got a foreign accent."[89]

The increase in cosmetic surgery procedures and even TV shows that offer makeovers (*Extreme Makeover*, *The Swan*) have added to the beauty culture. More than a BFOQ (bona fide occupational qualification), television has added the mediated version, which is even more difficult to achieve for girls and women without limitless time and funds to support such appearance goals.

The levels of physical feature improvement that a host of reality television shows suggest, have made appearance even more important for women, not only on television, but in the lives of average people who do not appear on television. Some reality television shows cover a person or group of people improving some part of their lives. *The Swan* and *Celebrity Fit Club* are programs that introduce the subject or subjects in their natural environment, and shows us the less-than-ideal conditions they are currently in. Their appearance is the focus of these shows. Then the subjects meet with a group of experts, who give them instructions on how to improve things; they offer aid and encouragement along the way. Finally, the subjects are placed back in their environment and they, along with their friends and family and the experts, appraise the changes that have occurred. Examples of self-improvement or makeover shows include, besides the previously mentioned ones, *The Biggest Loser*, which focuses on weight loss, and *Extreme Makeover*, which attempts to alter the entire physical appearance of the subjects. *Dr. 90219* features Beverly Hills cosmetic surgeons who assist clients in improving their appearances through cosmetic surgery procedures. The most famous of the Beverly Hills' doctors, Dr. Rey, is also featured in his personal life. Even shows not classified as reality shows, such as *The Oprah Winfrey Show*, feature frequent programs dedicated to the enhancement of appearance. These programs, with their "appearance-driven" content and the focus on newswomens' appearances, have contributed to an atmosphere of heightened focus on looking good for women everywhere, but most importantly for those women who are looking at us from the television screen. How does an employer at a television network weigh the importance of looking good vs. journalistic efficacy? Even if a newswoman is attractive in her thirties, as she ages, her look will change, and if the current crop of television newscasters continue to "anti age" with cosmetic procedures, then the world may never see a naturally older professional woman.

This book will examine the careers and communication styles of the women who have made significant contributions in the dramatically changing world of television news, thus improving the opportunities for women in broadcasting and arguably in other areas that were once reserved only for men. Chapter one offers a look at the life and voluminous career of Barbara Walters. Her intimate interviewing style utilizes many of the strategies associated with interpersonal communication. She has built her reputation by interviewing show business celebrities and heads of state, perhaps instinctively knowing that journalism would become woven into the entertainment field despite the best efforts of those who warned against it. In chapter two, the impressive careers of Connie Chung and Elizabeth Vargas, who along with Barbara Walters have been coanchors on major news networks are discussed. Chapter three is devoted to Christiane Amanpour, who has become well known for her intelligent and daring war reporting. In chapter four the impressive careers of Dana Bash, Candy Crowley, Andrea Mitchell, and Judy Woodruff are revealed. Chapter five brings into focus three familiar faces: Diane Sawyer, Lesley Stahl, and Paula Zahn. Chapter six examines the meteoric rise of Katie Couric to the history-making position as the first women sole anchor of CBS News. Finally, chapter seven draws some conclusions about the future of women in broadcast journalism.

Journalism is communication in a market—a market of news, images, and stories.[90] Judy Holland, a congressional reporter for Hearst Publications, says, "The women who excel in this field have high emotional intelligence. They are just naturally curious people."[91] This book shows that there have been strategic rhetorical choices on the part of these broadcasting trailblazers. How they've managed their communication and the progress they've made in television news amidst the swirling change in the industry is a theme woven through each of the following chapters. Whether the person profiled has remained true to the tenants of journalism or has adopted the more modern infotainment practices will be evident in the analysis of her work. The importance of the news interview has made it a significant component of the contemporary public sphere, and hence worthy of social and scientific attention.[92] Thus, each woman's style of communication, including evidence of ethos, invention, disposition, memory, and how their capacity to ask questions that yield the most newsworthy responses will demonstrate the newswoman's ability to be seen *and* heard.

NOTES

1. Jonathan Last, "New Anchors Lack Stamina and Gravitas," *Philadelphia Inquirer*, September 24, 2006, C3.

2. Jeff Alan with James M. Lane, *Anchoring America: The Changing Face of Network News* (Chicago: Bonus Books, 2003), 145.

3. Ibid., 143.

4. Hal Boedeker, "PBS Celebrates Anchor's Career," *Daily Press* (Norfolk, VA), July 26, 2006, D-5.

5. Patricia Cohen, "Stop the Press, Boys! Women Claim Space on the Op-Ed Pages," *The New York Times*, March 15, 2007, www.thewhitehouseproject.org (accessed March 21, 2007).

6. Maurine H. Beasley, *First Ladies and the Press: The Unfinished Partnership of the Media Age* (Evanston, Illinois: Northwestern University Press), 2005, 6.

7. Mark Halperin and John F. Harris, *The Way to Win: Taking the White House in 2008* (New York: Random House, 2007), 33.

8. Ibid., 34.

9. Judith Marlane, *Women of Television News Revisited* (Austin: University of Texas Press, 1999), 75.

10. Roderick P. Hart, *Modern Rhetorical Criticism* (Needham Heights: Allyn and Bacon, 1997), 201.

11. Marlene Sanders and Marcia Rock, *Waiting for Prime Time: The Women of Television News* (Chicago: University of Chicago Press, 1994), 79.

12. Edward Bliss, Jr., *Now the News: The Story of Broadcast Journalism* (New York: Columbia University Press, 1991), 331.

13. Ibid.

14. Ibid.

15. Ibid.

16. Nancy Dickerson, *Among Those Present* (New York: Random House, 1976), 31.

17. Ibid.

18. Barbara Matusow, *The Evening Stars* (Boston: Houghton Mifflin Company, 1983), 181.

19. Leslie Stahl, *Reporting Live* (New York: Simon and Schuster, 1999), 47–48.

20. Cindy J. Price and Shawn S. Wuff, "Does Sex Make a Difference? Job Satisfaction of Television Network News Correspondents," *Women's Studies in Communication* 28, no. 2 (Fall, 2005), 208.

21. Daniel Paisner, *The Imperfect Mirror: Inside Stories of the Television Newsroom* (New York: William Morrow, 1989), 19.

22. Ibid.

23. Vernon A. Stone, "Trends in the Status of Minorities and Women in Broadcast News," *Journalism Quarterly* 65: 288–93.

24. Ibid.

25. Matusow, *The Evening Stars*, 180.

26. Janice Castro, "Women in Television: An Uphill Battle," *Channels*, January, 1988, 42–52.

27. E-mail correspondence with the author from Janet Vasil, October 10, 2007.

28. Martha M. Lauzen and David M. Dozier, "Recognition and Respect Revisited: Portrayal of Age and Gender in Prime-Time Television," *Mass Communication & Society* 8, no. 3 (2005): 241–56.

29. Ibid.

30. Judy Woodruff, *This Is Judy Woodruff at the White House* (Reading, Massachusetts: Addison-Wesley Publishing Company, 1982), 6.

31. http://www.tyndallreport.com/yearinreview2005.php3 (accessed July 12, 2006).

32. TV Guide, "Why Are There Still No Female Dan Rathers?" August 1, 1981, 1.

33. Deborah Potter, "Breaking the Mold," *American Journalism Review* 28, no. 3 (Jun–Jul 2006).

34. E-mail correspondence with the author from John Dickerson, January 18, 2007.

35. Bonnie J. Dow, *Prime-Time Feminism: Television, Media Culture, and the Women's Movement Since 1970* (Philadelphia: University of Pennsylvania Press, 1996), 140.

36. http://www.vicepresidentdanquayle.com/speeches_WSTL.html (accessed July 20, 2006).

37. Dow, *Prime-Time Feminism*, 136.

38. Kevin McDonough, "Catch This 'Anchor' Before it Sinks," *The Morning Call* (Allentown, PA), August 22, 2007, E5.

39. http://www.stateofthenewsmedia.org/narrative_networktv_audience.asp?cat=3&media (accessed June 19, 2006).

40. Jacques Steinberg, "ABC Rejects Dual Anchors in 2nd Shuffle," *The New York Times*, May 24, 2006 Wednesday, Section A; Column 5, 1.

41. Halperin and Harris, *The Way to Win*, 53.

42. Marian Glick, Interview with Nichola D. Gutgold, February 9, 2007.

43. Craig M. Allen, *News Is People* (Ames: Iowa State University Press, 2001), xiii.

44. Leslie Baldacci, "Anchor Juggles Life, Career Like Rest of Us," *Chicago Sun-Times*, May 26, 1996, F53.

45. Shirley, Biagi, *Newstalk II State of the Art Conversation with Today's Broadcast Journalists* (Belmost: Wadsworth Publishing Company), 1987, 55.

46. Paisner, *The Imperfect Mirror*, 27.

47. Phil Donahue Show, "Newswomen," 1987, distributed by "Films for the Humanities."

48. Erika Engstrom, "Looking Through a Gendered Lens: Local U.S. Television News Anchors' Perceived Career Barrier," *Journal of Broadcasting and Electronic Media* 44, no. 4 (September 1, 2006), 6.

49. Lana F. Rakow and Kimberlie Kranich, "Woman as Sign in Television News," *Journal of Communication* 41, no. 1 (Winter 1991): 8.

50. Kathleen Hall Jamieson, *Beyond the Double Bind: Women and Leadership* (New York: Oxford University Press, 1995), 11, 16.

51. Naomi Wolf, *The Beauty Myth* (New York: Perennial, 1991), 34.

52. Last, "New Anchors Lack Stamina and Gravitas," C3.

53. Hart, *Modern Rhetorical Criticism*, 222–23.

54. Matea Gold, "Moving Past 'Today': Katie Couric Shoots Down Skeptics Who Think She's Too Soft for the Evening News," *Los Angeles Times,* May 30, 2006, E-1.

55. "Who's Talking? An Analysis of Sunday Morning Talk Shows," The White House Project, September 5, 2001 (paper distributed at Forum for Leadership, Washington, D.C., 2001).

56. M. E. McCombs and D. L. Shaw, "The Agenda-Setting Function of Mass Media," *Public Opinion Quarterly* 36, no. 2: 176–87.

57. www.thewhitehouseproject.org. At this writing, the online poll was still in progress, August 24, 2006.

58. Gabrielle Birkner, "'Today' Is Couric's Last: Tomorrow, Her New Look," *New York Sun Times,* May 31, 2006, http://www.nysun.com/article/33587 (accessed July 11, 2006).

59. *Larry King Live*, transcript, December 18, 2000.

60. Ken Auletta, "The Dawn Patro:l The Curious Rise of Morning Television, and the Future of Network News," *The New Yorker*, August 8, 2005, http://www.newyorker.com/printables/fact/050808fa_fact1 (accessed August 22, 2006).

61. Olivia Barker, "Couric's Style Goes from 'Today' to 'Evening' New Job May Bring Subtler Clothes, Hair," *USA Today*, August 10, 2006, 1D.

62. E-mail correspondence with Nichola D. Gutgold, July 5, 2006.

63. Patti Buchman, "Title VII Limits on Discrimination Against Television Anchorwomen on the Basis of Age-Related Appearance," *Columbia Law Review* 85, no. 1 (January, 1985): 190–215.

64. Anne Becker, "An Age Old Problem: TV Newswomen Say Discrimination Persists. It's Just Harder to Prove," *Broadcasting and Cable* (October 31, 2005): 12–13.

65. Ibid., 202.

66. Bonnie M. Anderson, *News Flash: Journalism, Infotainment, and the Bottom-Line Business of Broadcast News* (San Francisco: Jossey-Bass, 2004), 26.

67. Christine Craft, *Too Old, Too Ugly, and Not Deferential to Men* (Rocklin, CA: Prima Publishing, 1988), 9.

68. Ibid.

69. Ibid., 207.

70. Becker, "An Age Old Problem," 12–13.

71. Linda Ellerbee, *And So it Goes: Adventures in Television* (New York: Putnam, 1986), 107.

72. Judy Muller, *Now This: Radio, Television . . . and the Real World* (New York: Putnam, 1999), 121.

73. Ellerbee, *And So It Goes*, 107.

74. Marlene Sanders and Marcia Rock, *Waiting for Prime Time: The Women of Television News* (Chicago: University of Chicago Press, 1994), 13.

75. Anderson, *News Flash*, x.

76. L. Monique Ward and Kristen Harrison, "The Impact of Media Use of Girls' Beliefs about Gender Roles, Their Bodies, and Sexual Relationships: A Research Synthesis," in *Featuring Females*, Ellen Cole and Jessica Henderson Daniel, eds. (Washington, D.C. APA, 2005).

77. Paisner, *The Imperfect Mirror*, 19.

78. Wolf, *The Beauty Myth*, 35.

79. Brian Lowry, "The Fluff Factor: Whether Male or Female, the Anchor Chair Isn't What It Used to Be," *Broadcasting & Cable*, December 13, 2004, 48.

80. Marlane, *Women in Television News Revisited*, 89.

81. http://www.spj.org/aboutspj.asp (accessed July 31, 2006).

82. Ken Auletta, *Backstory: Inside the Business of News* (New York: Penguin Press, 2003).

83. Clarence Page, Nieman Reports 58, no. 4 (Winter 2004), 57.

84. E-mail correspondence with Nichola D. Gutgold, July 5, 2006.

85. Auletta, *Backstory: Inside the Business of News*, xv.

86. Anderson, "News Flash," 167–71.

87. Marc Gunther, *The House That Roone Built* (New York: Little Brown, 1994), 197.

88. Jonathan Alder, "Looksism in TV News," *Newsweek*, November 6, 1989, 72.

89. Speech given by Christiane Amanpour, Spring, 2006, University of Michigan, http://www.umich.edu/newus/index.html?Vid/ca_sprcom06 (accessed October 20, 2006).

90. Mats Ekström, "Information, Storytelling and Attractions: TV Journalism in Three Modes of Communication," *Media Culture Society* 22 (2000): 465–92. Lowry, "The Fluff Factor," 48.

91. Judy Holland, phone interview with Nichola D. Gutgold, January 24, 2007.

92. Steven Clayman and John Heritage, *The News Interview: Journalists and Public Figures on the Air* (Cambridge: Cambridge University Press, 2002), 2.

2

FROM PERSISTENT TO POWERFUL

Barbara Walters

Figure 1.1.   Barbara Walters

> Wait for those unguarded moments. Relax the mood, and, like the child
> dropping off to sleep, the subject often reveals his truest self."[1]

Barbara Walters is as well known as the people she interviews. Her star-
dom is literally cemented with her 2007 star on the "Hollywood Walk of
Fame." She is so well known that her name and a brief biography are listed
in the American Heritage Dictionary.[2] Barbara Walters has interviewed

every American president and first lady since Richard and Pat Nixon. Many of the most controversial world leaders have sat down to tell their stories to her including Menachen Begin, Margaret Thatcher, Fidel Castro, Anwar Sadat, Vladimir Putin, Boris Yeltsin, King Hussein of Jordan, and Premier Jiang Zemin. When ABC offered her a five-year, $5 million contract to co-anchor the evening news in 1976, Walter Cronkite said at the time: "There was a first wave of nausea, the sickening sensation that we were going under, that all of our efforts to hold network television news aloof from show business had failed." He then tempered his criticism and said, "Her background is not what I would call well-rounded, but who is to say that there is only one route to a career in journalism?"[3]

Barbara Walters has been described as a pathfinder for those seeking an understanding of how news careers will be shaped in the years to come.[4] Long before some of the other prominent women in journalism profiled in this book were even out of grade school, let alone considering their career path, Barbara Walters was forging hers and considering how to build upon the business she grew up with—show business, and the business in which she wanted to make a name for herself—news. Barbara Walters' career is a provocative look and even a prophetic playbook for any woman or man considering a career in broadcasting.

A FAMILIARITY WITH THE FAMOUS

Barbara Walters was born on September 25, 1929 or 1931, depending on the source,[5] in Boston, Massachusetts, the third child of Louis Edward Walters and Dena Seletsky Walters, who had a son, Burton, and another daughter, Jacqueline. Burton died of pneumonia when he was less than two years old and Jacqueline was developmentally delayed.[6] Lou Walters became well known as a successful talent promoter and the creative genius behind a string of very successful nightclubs, known as Lou Walters' Latin Quarter in Boston, Miami, and New York City. Barbara's childhood was more comfortable than most of the children in the Depression. She enjoyed expensive toys and clothes, summer camps, trips to Europe, and the best schools.[7] She moved around a lot as a child because of her father's business. She started first grade in Brookline, Massachusetts, and later the family moved to Miami, where Barbara attended a private school in Biscayne Bay. When Barbara was twelve the family moved to New York, where her father opened a nightclub. Barbara Walters was enrolled in the Fieldston private school in Manhattan. Her family moved again to Florida for her father's business and Barbara attended school in Miami Beach, and when the family returned to New York, Barbara finished high school at Birth Wathen, a private school in Manhattan. Barbara Walters has credited her father's business with helping to give her a familiarity with the famous. She was not in awe of famous people, since her father's nightclub, The Latin Quarter, hosted some of the most famous names in show business at the time. "Mingling with the stars became second nature to Barbara."[8]

Barbara Walters had briefly considered acting as a career, but settled on teaching instead, and earned her bachelor of arts degree in English from Sarah Lawrence College, graduating in 1953. She married Robert Katz (the marriage was later annulled) and she began work on a master's degree in education, but her career took a significant turn when she took a job in television, first as a writer and producer at WNBC-TV in New York City, then at WPIX-TV for a job producing women's programming and a short stint a CBS's morning show writing for Jack Paar and Dick Van Dyke.[9] She credits her father's show business connections as her reason for being hired for her first job in television: "One of my early jobs was as the assistant to the director of publicity at NBC's local station, WNBC, because I knew all the columnists. I was Lou Walters's daughter. That's how I began in television. I wrote the releases for all the talk shows. I was then made a producer, the youngest producer at the time. I think I was twenty-four."[10]

That Barbara Waters immediately associated public relations, news, and entertainment as similar entities isn't surprising, since it was her father's entertainment contacts that provided her with her entrée into the world of broadcasting. She then moved on to a job at CBS where her duties were described as a "glorified gofer."[11] Actually, Barbara's job included booking guests on the CBS morning show, which attempted to compete with the formidable *The Today Show* on NBC. Charlie Andrews, who was producing the morning show for CBS, hired Walters. He said, "I was looking for a guest-getter. Barbara came up for an interview and she was obviously a sharp, aggressive, ambitious girl. Some people walk into a room and you know their wheels are spinning. Barbara was one of those people. She just created one great impression."[12] Barbara's timing for the job was excellent, since a young aspiring actress, Estelle Parsons, had just quit *The CBS Morning Show* to return to *The Today Show* where she had formerly worked as a production assistant and later a weather girl—the first of what would be a long line of so-called Today Girls. In 1963 Barbara married Lee Guber and together they adopted a baby girl, Jacqueline Dena. In 1973, they divorced. After CBS, Barbara worked for a public relations firm and then finally went back to *The Today Show* "not thinking I would be in front of the camera because, before me, they had used only actresses and models."[13]

She describes her writing assignments: "I was hired to write only feminine things: fashion shows, celebrity guests. My big breakthrough came when the producer, who knew me from CBS, said, 'she can write the same things the men can write.' So they began sending me out to cover all kinds of stories."[14] Her tenacity and perseverance paid off.

The very first time that Barbara Walters went on camera as a reporter was to cover the funeral of President John F. Kennedy in 1963. She and Hugh Downs cohosted a Saturday edition of *The Today Show* on the day following President Kennedy's assassination. They had the first of what William Manchester described in *Death of a President* as "the nonstop broadcasts of the weekend."[15] Hugh Downs and Barbara Walters covered the arrival of President Johnson back in Washington overnight, the bulletins on Governor John Connally, the arraignment of Lee Harvey Oswald, the arrival of the coffin at the White House, world reaction, and a complete recap of the events at the end of the week.[16] She explains, "After that, I did everything from a day in the life of a nun to interviews with murderers to being a Playboy Bunny."[17] During the Democratic National Convention in Atlantic City, New Jersey, in 1964 that nominated Lyndon B. Johnson for president, the actress Maureen O'Sullivan, who had been the "Today Girl," was no longer there, so Barbara Walters was named as her replacement. She was supposed to be on air for thirteen weeks. Walter's notes: "I stayed for fifteen years."[18] Barbara Walters insisted, however, when she was hired, that her title would not be the new "Today Girl" and instead simply started working without a title or special designation.

BARBARA WALTERS AT NBC

She applied for the job twice and was turned down both times, but now she had the plum job that she wanted at NBC and she wanted to be taken seriously. Barbara Walters was an interviewer and viewer response to her well-informed, professional presence was overwhelmingly positive,[19] although Elizabeth Peel in *Newsweek* writes that "even her own network, nearly a quarter of whose fan mail goes to *The Today Show*, admits that half the letters addressed to Walters run hostile. Walters is reviled for such qualities as aggression, tenacity and toughness that win plaudits for male interviewers."[20] Throughout the 1960s and the early 1970s, Barbara Walters developed her interviewing skills. "Her questions pounce and probe; whether tart or fiercely eager," notes Peel.[21] When interviewing Lady Bird Johnson, Barbara Walters confronted her with Lyndon Johnson's flirtatiousness, and Mrs. Johnson said, "he was a people lover and that certainly did not exclude half the people in the world, women." Audiences loved her probing, yet respectful, style with celebrities and political figures. Because of her popularity and growing ease in front of the camera, Barbara Walters's assignments increased in importance. In 1972, Barbara Walters was part of the NBC news team sent to cover President Richard Nixon's historic visit to the People's Republic of China. As the importance of her assignments increased, she gained credibility with viewers. She wasn't a common commodity, however, and indeed, an intelligent woman, traveling the world interviewing heads of states was rare. Almost always she was the lone female reporter among a pack of males. Hugh Downs described Barbara Walters as "the best thing that's happened to this show in a long time"[22] and Barbara said working with Hugh Downs was "a pleasure."[23] She notes that "his generosity was instrumental in my having a career. If Hugh [Downs] had not fought for my opportunity to appear regularly on *Today*, I wouldn't have happened in this business."[24] Other working conditions were less favorable for her, mostly because she was a woman working in a field largely dominated by men. Barbara Walters describes the rules that applied to her at NBC. "To give you an idea of the times, there was a host named Frank McGee. He had an agreement with the network that if there was a hard-news interview, he asked the first three questions before I could join in. The real reason I became very aggressive in going after interviews is, if I got the interview myself, and I did it outside the studio, I could do it myself."[25]

When Frank McGee died unexpectedly of cancer in 1974, NBC talked to Walters about who would be named as the show's new host, and she corrected them: "cohost."[26] Barbara Walters explains that "it was in my contract that, if Frank McGee ever left the show, I would be cohost. They never expected him to leave. He was relatively young when he died of cancer. Only then was I named cohost. Since that time, every woman has been called cohost on all the morning news programs."[27] After the death of Frank McGee, NBC named Jim Hartz, an affable and relaxed man who had been mentored by McGee, as cohost. Jim Hartz remembers the rising Barbara Walters fondly, "Barbara was and is a first-rate writer and reporter."[28] At this same time, ABC began broadcasting its own version of *The Today Show*, called *Good Morning America*, and it featured the male and female cohost team of Bill Beutel and Stephanie Edwards. Peter Jennings read the news on the program. *Good Morning America* was giving *The Today Show* competition in the ratings. The climate in broadcasting was changing for women and Barbara Walters was already an established, experienced, and well-known television broadcaster. That her style of mixing news with entertainment would become the prototype for news programming in the future makes Barbara Walters an important figure for study in broadcasting. Well-known dignitaries like Fidel Castro started to request that Barbara Walters interview them. "Where's Barbara?" Fidel Castro reportedly asked, when a contingent of fourteen reporters accompanied Senator George McGovern to Cuba in 1975.[29] Secretary of State Dean Rusk had chosen Barbara Walters to interview him when he left his post as secretary and the interview was aired for five days on *The Today Show*. She describes this as a breakthrough event in her career, since it was a hard-news interview, and it helped to establish Walters as a journalist who could do more than women's stories or celebrity interviews.[30] Barbara Walters cautions against women entering broadcasting because they think that only good looks are required. "I think you have to be able to write. We've had people who have come here from anchoring a program where writing skills weren't necessary and have not been able to prepare their own material. Then, it's very hard for them when they have to do magazine pieces. So these are skills you must get."[31] Working on her skills was advice that she had not only given to others who wanted careers in television, it was advice she followed herself. Her hard work and persistence were well known at NBC. *The Today Show* producer at the time, Stuart Schulberg, said that Barbara Walter's presentation was "better than anyone on the show. She reads every book she talks about."[32] From 1970–1974 *The Today Show* had won two Emmys and earned $10 million in annual profits, making it the most lucrative daytime venue and the envy of rival networks.[33]

On the January 24, 1973 broadcast, Barbara Walters's thoroughness and professionalism are evident. Meticulously groomed with ramrod-straight posture and slow, careful reading, Walters, seated next to cohost Frank McGee, announced:

> In our next half hour we will have the wife of an air force colonel listed as missing in action since 1967 and the sister of a naval flyer who has been a prisoner of war for five years. We would also like to mention that the photographs from Vietnam used for parts of our program this morning were taken by photography Larry Burroghs before he was killed in a helicopter crash there. Burroughs had been Saigon Bureau Chief for *Time* and *Life* magazines and we thank Time Life Books for permission to use those photographs.[34]

Though black and white, the video reveals a stylish, brunette Barbara Walters who frequently glanced at notes down on the desk, only looking up for sustained eye contact with the camera, although teleprompters were in use at the time. Her words were carefully scripted, and slowly read with emphasis and feeling and her trademark lisp. By sharp contrast, cohost Frank McGee sat back, leaning in his chair, with his pen in his hand, and offered what appeared to be impromptu commentary, in a fast, sharp-toned pace, as a response to Barbara Walters's statement. McGee noted, "The, uh, two senators, Scott and Mansfield, also said a while ago that, uh, have also said, uh, and its perhaps worth repeating, that the, uh, some prisoners of war will be returned soon. That clearly indicated that some of the arrangements, of which we know nothing about, have been worked out, and they know the point he'll be taken to and where they will be taken from there. Uhhh, the overriding point being that it won't be sixty days before they all come back, I suppose some will be back in a week to ten days. Great good news. A station break." Barbara Walters smiled politely, and the station went to a commercial break. The impression is that Frank McGee got the last word, almost as a correction to clarify Walters' report. It was clear that McGee was in the lead, and Walters was a careful underling, more polished and professional than McGee, although he had the upper hand.

BARBARA WALTERS AT ABC

Barbara Walters felt it was the right time to leave NBC, especially when she considered that the change would give her a better chance at having more time with her young daughter. She notes, "I came to ABC after a lot of thought. I had a seven-year-old daughter. I was always exhausted, and I thought the change would give me a better chance at having a normal life with her. I wanted to be able to see her at night and not always be tired. If there was a turning point, that was it."[35]

The year was 1976 and America was celebrating its bicentennial. For Barbara Walters, a new prestigious position at ABC, coanchor of *ABC News*, and host of *The Barbara Walters Special*, seemed to signal her independence from the drudgery and long hours she had put in to earn her stripes at *NBC*. "I was doing two, five-day-a-week shows [*The Today Show* and her syndicated program *Not for Women Only*] and it was killing me. I don't know how I did it. I did *Not for Women Only* because I wanted to prove that I could do my own show, that I didn't have to have a partner. It seems rather pathetic that I had to go out and prove that. A man wouldn't have had to. The other thing was that I would be able to lead a normal life. Being an anchor can be a very difficult job, but it can be the easiest job, too.

Nobody's going to know how much you do except you, yourself, and your producers, and they're not telling. You have writers who write the material. You can take it and rewrite it, or you can decide to write the headline every night, or the opening story. Or you can walk in at 3:00 p.m. every day, pick up the script, make a few changes, and read it. You also don't have to travel, which appealed to me. As the anchor, you are the automatic head. You are the one who does inaugurations. You are the one who does space flights. If the president goes on a trip, there's just no question who's going to cover it."[36] It makes sense to think that Barbara Walters thought her new position at ABC, after working so hard for so long at NBC, would feel like a big step up. Barbara Walters rose in broadcasting at a time when mostly pretty actresses were on camera. She put in years of work with sexist treatment and she persevered to eventually cover stories of world importance. She would be coanchor with Harry Reasoner of *ABC Evening News*, and she would be the host of four prime-time one-hour specials, bearing her name. These were important milestones for anyone in broadcasting, but for a woman, in 1976, these were monumental achievements.

Immediately, *The Barbara Walters Special*, produced by her own production company, was a hit, won rave reviews and quickly became a television institution. Still today, Barbara Walters' prime-time specials continue to draw large ratings for *ABC*. Stars and political powerhouses consider an interview with Barbara Walters an important media opportunity. Her position as coanchor of *ABC Evening News*, however, was much less successfully received than *The Barbara Walters Special*, and she would experience a much shorter tenure as coanchor.

Tremendous fanfare and public relations surrounded Barbara Walters's appointment as the first female coanchor of a network news broadcast. Much of the press focused on her million-dollar salary, dubbing Barbara Walters the "million dollar baby."[37] Barbara Walters points out, that while the salary sounded impressive, it was the same amount that Harry Reasoner, her cohost, received to coanchor the news: $500,000. The extra $500,000 was for her *Barbara Walters Special*, which garnered huge ratings and a lot of income for ABC. Barbara Walters explains: "ABC had a huge bargain in me. The specials alone made a tremendous amount of money then and have continued to do so."[38] *The New York Times* on April 21, 1976, described the news that Barbara Walters got an offer from ABC:

> *ABC News* offers *NBC-TV Today* cohost Barbara Walters a five year contract paying $1 million a year to become co-anchor of *The Evening News with Harry Reasoner*. Walters says she will decide this week whether to join ABC

or sign a new contract with NBC. Either decision will make her the highest-paid news personality in television history. Contest between ABC and NBC for Walters's services is significant in that it extends to news realm of television spectacular financial terms usually associated with entertainment stars.[39]

The article positions the pairing of Walters and Reasoner as ill-fated from the start: "Reasoner reportedly is displeased with the plan to team him with Walters."[40] "Doll Barbie to Learn Her ABC's," said the *New York Daily News*. *The Washington Post* called her "A Million Dollar Baby Handling 5- and 10-Cent News." Even the *Christian Science Monitor* cast Walters as a fickle woman, saying, "Barbara Leaves Jim for Harry."[41] Many of the news stories compare her salary to that of high-paid celebrities, although Jackie Reinhardt, then president of the Los Angeles chapter of Women in Communications, called it a breakthrough for women in the communications industry.[42] *Time* contends that "Salaries and network bidding wars entered a new phase in 1976, when Arledge lured Walters away from NBC for $1 million a year."[43]

A 1976 ad that appeared in *TV Guide* for the new ABC news team included the heading "Barbara Walters Joins Harry Reasoner on ABC" and a pleasantly surprised looking Barbara is shown with a cantankerous-faced Reasoner. In the photo, Reasoner looks like the older brother who was just told that he "had" to take his sister with him on his big night on the town.[44] But once the news that Barbara Walters would be joining Harry Reasoner on the *ABC Evening News*, Reasoner made this statement to his audience: "Some of you may have seen speculation about this in the papers. It's had more attention than Catfish Hunter, and Barbara can't even throw left-handed. Many of the stories said that I had some reservations when the idea came up. If I did, they've been taken care of, and I welcome Barbara with no reservation."[45]

On October 4, 1976 at 7:00 p.m. Barbara Walters officially became television's first network anchorwoman when she made her debut as coanchor of *ABC Evening News with Harry Reasoner and Barbara Walters*. This pairing and ascendancy created a tremendous upheaval in the nation's news media.[46] It seemed as though everyone in America wanted to see Barbara Walters as the first female anchor of a major broadcasting network. Author Oppenheimer noted, "It was the biggest television event since Jack Ruby shot Lee Harvey Oswald on camera."[47] Dressed in a red silk blouse with a navy velvet vest and a heart-shaped pin on the lapel, her hair lighter than it had been on NBC, Barbara Walters looked beautiful and credible. Her on-air presence had improved since her days on *The Today Show*. She looked more authoritative and confident. She sustained eye contact better and her cadence and tone had become smooth. Her lisp was slightly less pronounced and the formation of her "r" sound was better. Harry Reasoner looked dapper and well coordinated in a suit, tie, and checkered NBC shirt, and they were seated behind a large, gray news desk. Having a male-female anchor teamed was reminiscent of local news and it gave *ABC Evening News* a fresh look, compared to the male anchor counterparts of John Chancellor and David Brinkley at NBC and Walter Cronkite at CBS.

The first newscast went smoothly enough. After Harry Reasoner opened the broadcast: "Good evening, our major story tonight is that Agricultural Secretary Earl Butz has paid the price for telling an obscene racial joke on a commercial airline flight. Secretary Butz resigned today. The president accepted with regret, but immediately. Closer to home, I have a new colleague to welcome. Barbara?" Barbara smiled warmly and said,

> Thank you, Harry. Well, tonight has finally come for me and I'm very pleased to be with you Harry and with ABC News. Later I'll have a chance to comment on my duties. We'll tell you tonight about a Supreme Court action that allows the death penalty in at least three states. We will hear some unofficial but optimistic word on the Ford strike. We'll have a direct report. And our newsmaker tonight via satellite is Egypt President Anwar Sadat. He will reveal his plan to help end the fighting in Lebanon." As she announced her interview with President Sadat a video feed of the pipe smoking Sadat was shown with the smoke billowing through the air, almost obscuring the view of the president. Toward the end of the broadcast Walters told viewers that she imagined many of them tuned in because of "curiosity brought on by . . . my hourly wage." She invited viewers to continue to watch and promised that "Harry and I will try to bring you the best darn news program on the air. I'd like to pause from time to time as we shower news items on you and say, "Wait a minute. What does this mean to my life and to yours?"[48]

She also noted that there was some confusion about what she should be called: "anchorman, anchorperson, or anchorhuman," explaining that "titles don't matter."[49] At the end of the broadcast, Harry Reasoner joked, "you owe me four minutes."[50] While it sounded humorous, as the weeks and months wore on, the spirit of competitiveness between the anchors was noticeable, and the chemistry between them, which never was great, had turned to tension.

Initially after the *ABC Evening News* with Harry Reasoner and Barbara Walters debuted, ABC saw a small increase in the ratings, largely attributed to all the publicity. Then, the ratings plummeted. The day after Barbara Walters's ABC debut, David Brinkley began the *NBC Nightly News* with a wry comment about her opening-night performance, "Good evening," he said, in his clipped style, pausing slightly. "And welcome back."[51]

While Barbara Walters and Harry Reasoner were teamed up for the evening news broadcast, Barbara Walters was busy building her career as an interviewer of celebrities and politicians with her *Barbara Walters Special.* The first special aired on December 14, 1976. Millions of Americans tuned in and the program garnered a thirty-six share in the ratings.[52] The guests included legendary songstress Barbra Streisand, president-elect Jimmy Carter, and the new first lady, Rosalyn Carter. The interview with the Carters was personal, and it gave the American public a chance to learn more about its new president-elect. Rosalyn Carter, in her light and lilting southern drawl, told Barbara Walters that the only piece of furniture from her Georgia home that she was bringing to the White House was her sewing machine. President-elect Carter said that they would keep their double bed in Georgia and use whatever furniture the White House provided.[53] That wasn't the information that caught the attention of the critics. At the end of the interview, Barbara leaned forward and looked into the eyes of president-elect Carter and urged him to "Be wise with us, be good to us."[54] Barbara Walters's comment to the president was parodied by other news networks. CBS news correspondent Morley Safer, in a radio broadcast distributed to CBS affiliates, said that Barbara Walters "stopped being a reporter when she told Jimmy Carter to 'Be wise with us. Be good to us.'" He compared her to a talk-show host.[55] A few weeks after her interview with the Carters, NBC Board Chairman Julian Goodman gave a dinner at the Twenty-one Club in New York. The dinner was in honor of Herbert S. Schlosser, who was named NBC's chief executive officer. Toasting Schlosser at the end of the festivities, which were attended by the RCA and NBC boards, Goodman wound up by saying: "Herb, please be wise with us and be good to us."[56] The takeoff on Barbara Walters's advice for president-elect Carter a couple of weeks prior on her ABC TV special convulsed Goodman's audience. It was this type of fun-making of Barbara Walters that appeared throughout the press. Harry Reasoner may have initially rejected Barbara Walters as his cohost because he didn't want a partner; as Barbara Walters later described, "He was a man who didn't want a partner. It wasn't that he didn't want me in particular; he didn't want a partner, period. And I was forced on him."[57] It didn't help the situation that other news figures and the press were poking fun at Barbara Walters. There were problems with the *ABC Evening News* and Barbara Walters was taking the public relations brunt of it. In his 1981 book, *Before The Colors Fade*, Harry Reasoner reflected about the Reasoner-Walters pairing on the *ABC Evening News.* "I don't think Barbara and I made a very good anchor team; I don't think her talent is in anchoring. But that was sort of irrelevant. It just could not have worked because of the perception—not the reality, the perception—of what people thought ABC was doing. It didn't work; we didn't even work together very long. But it sure made an impression. It took me two years back at *60 Minutes* before, in a public appearance, the first or second question would not be: "What was Barbara Walters really like?"[58]

Veteran NBC reporter Sander Vanocur tried to put some of the problems in perspective for readers of *The Washington Post*: "The problem with the *ABC Evening News* is not primarily Barbara Walters. Nor is it Harry Reasoner. The problem with the *ABC Evening News* is ABC News."[59] In the article, Vanocur contends that ABC never invested in its news division as much as both NBC and CBS and because of that, the quality of the news program suffered. Speculation that Roone Arledge, the hard-driving visionary who shaped ABC Sports into the leading network in sports broadcasting, would come on board to head the news division gave Vanocur hope that Arledge would bring "the galvanizing energy which ABC News so badly needs."[60] In 1977, Roone Arledge, who was lauded on the Senate floor for the remarkable coverage of the Olympic games, took the initiative to produce a thirty-minute special report that documented the events leading up to the death of the Israeli athletes, taken hostage by terrorists. Arledge, who had scored a victory in sports programming, was brought in to head the news division at ABC, in the hope that he would score a victory with his take on how news should be presented. Marc Gunther, author of *The House That Roone Built*, explains: "Arledge had become a lightning rod for the concerns about the future of network news. Television critics who decried the beginnings of a star system, the incessant drive for ratings, and the sensationalism of local news viewed Arledge's appointment as another break with tradition. In a sense they were right: Arledge's arrival at ABC News meant that a whole new way of thinking about television news had taken hold at ABC."[61] Barbara Walters would bring to ABC the kind of combination of news and entertaining broadcasting that appealed to Arledge. He had added show business to sports with his flamboyant *Wide World of Sports* and "Monday Night Football." There was some anticipation about how he might add his flair for show business to the news, which had come from a more staid tradition than sports. Most of the big-name news broadcasters had come to television from print journalism backgrounds, that may not make them poised for success in the visual world of television, especially in one that purposely aims to add an element of entertainment to the news.

It didn't take long for the new president of ABC News, Roone Arledge, to make changes to *ABC Evening News*. In April, 1978, Arledge announced a new format for its lagging news program, by establishing Washington as the network's key "news center," dropping coanchor Harry Reasoner from the cast and putting WTOP anchorman Max Robinson in charge of the domestic desk in Chicago. In establishing four major news desks in Washington, London, Chicago, and New York, Arledge commented that Barbara Walters would handle "a special coverage desk" in New York where she would be doing little reading of the news and be more involved in "making the news herself."[62] In addition, Arledge quickened the pace of the show, hired more staffers, and made greater use of electronic gizmos.[63] Roone Arledge also ordered that Barbara Walters and Harry Reasoner not be seen in the same camera shot.[64]

With the new arrangement on the news and Barbara Walters handling a special desk in New York, there was no shortage of good stories, and her journalism credentials continued to increase with the many substantial stories she covered. While the difficulties with her pairing with Reasoner on the evening news were tough on Barbara Walters, she continued to work on her skills and she built a broadcasting reputation for herself in the tradition of legendary broadcast journalist Edward R. Murrow and the more modern-day Larry King, since she spent her time interviewing both heads of state and stars of television and film. While Edward R. Murrow is often described as "the preeminent broadcaster in America,"[65] his career wasn't much different from Barbara Walters considering that he, too, alternated reporting on serious news stories and interviewing celebrities. His well-received program *See It Now* featured such guests as Gloria Vanderbilt, Mary Martin, and fashion designer Valentina. Sometimes Murrow also interviewed political figures on *See It Now* and he once interviewed the newly elected young senator from Massachusetts, John F. Kennedy.[66] In a similar way, Larry King on his popular program *Larry King Live* on CNN alternates interviewing film and television celebrities with prominent political figures, including presidents. Walters's tenacity and hard work were especially evident on Sunday, November 20, 1977, when Barbara Walters was the first of the three big network news anchors to conduct a joint interview with Egypt's President Anwar el-Sadat and Israeli Prime Minister Menachem Begin. The picture of the two leaders sitting together for an interview with Barbara was more symbolic than what they actually said.[67] For Barbara, it was an important career moment. She had beaten the other two networks by interviewing the men first (Walter Cronkite interviewed them later that night and John Chancellor the following morning). *The Washington Post* reported that "ABC insiders claim that the mighty Cronkite, confidante of presidents, was infuriated at this development [that Barbara Walters got the first interview]. At the end of it [his interview with Begin and Sadat] Cronkite reportedly turned to the two world leaders and said, "Okay, now that it's over—did Barbara get anything I didn't get?"[68] The influence of Roone Arledge over ABC news is lauded: "Network news competition used to be a two-way tussle between CBS and NBC, but now ABC, under news and sports director Roone Arledge, and with Walters as the star performer, has become increasingly aggressive. So when ABC learned yesterday that Cronkite had also secured a joint Sadat-Begin interview, the network decided to go on the air at 5:50 p.m. with a six-minute excerpt from the Walters interview, which was not to air in its entirety until 10:45 p.m."[69] In her interview Barbara Walters was sure to stress that she had the first opportunity to interview the leaders together. She proudly stated, "This is the very first interview that the president of Egypt and the prime minister of Israel have done, and indeed, any president of Egypt with any prime minister. In that sense, it is historic."[70] In his memoirs, Cronkite acknowledged Barbara's scoop: "It looked like a clean beat. But we hadn't figured on Barbara Walters. A serious mistake." She had taken an earlier plane via a different route to Tel Aviv.[71] Although Barbara Walters has gained a reputation as an aggressive seeker of interviews, something evinced by her ability to get the first Sadat–Begin interview, she told Connie Chung, "The least pleasant part of the job is the competition. All of us [anchors] hate booking, I hate talking to people when friends and colleagues are going after them. It's debilitating."[72]

Throughout the next few years, Barbara Walters conducted occasional high-profile interviews and assignments for *World News Tonight*, but the kinds of stories that got her excited did not come along often. "She had to live as a correspondent rather than an anchor," said Victor Neufeld, her producer. "It was very difficult for her."[73] Still, she created a communication style that was not seen before on television. ABC producer Ene Riisna described it this way: "She invented intimacy on television. No one had done it before she came along."[74] This was evident in her first newscast on October 4, 1976, when she confessed to the viewers "I've missed you."[75] By observing many of her interviews with celebrities and politicians, there emerges some behaviors exhibited by Barbara Walters that could be described as those that promote self disclosure and intimacy. Researchers Weber and Patterson developed the Communication Based Emotional Support Scale (CBESS) with the goal of specifically measuring expressions of emotional support. These behaviors include listening, nonverbal immediacy, displays of caring, and offering advice.[76] In order for her guests to disclose intimate details of their lives, Barbara Walters enacts the behaviors that result in self-disclosure by her guests, something most viewers are hoping for. For example, routinely, Barbara Walters sits within three feet of her guests, if not closer, in a comfortable setting, usually in the interviewee's home or if not, in a very plush and cozy setting elsewhere. Simply by offering to interview the guest on national television is an offer to listen to that person and to allow the viewing public to listen as well, to their side of the story. Barbara Walters does not monopolize the dialogue. While she is as big a celebrity as most of her guests, they do most of the talking in every interview she conducts.

Getting a star to reveal when he lost his virginity, or when he stopped using drugs, or his sexual orientation were questions that other interviewers were not asking, and viewers tuned in to find out what Barbara Walters would ask next. "I care about what makes them tick," said Walters about her subjects, and in the early 1980s she conducted several interviews for the popular news magazine program, 20/20. 20/20 was started in 1978 by Roone Arledge and featured Time magazine critic Harold Hayes and former Esquire magazine editor Robert Hughes as the original hosts. Initially, ratings and reviews for the program were dismal. The initial reviews ranged from "dizzyingly absurd" from The New York Times to "the trashiest stab at candy cane journalism yet" from The Washington Post.[77] In an effort to give the enormously successful CBS 60 Minutes competition, President Roone Arledge then replaced Hayes and Hughes with Hugh Downs, who had been a Today Show host. With Hugh Downs's soothing voice and the compelling investigative stories that offered a consumer focus, 20/20 became a huge success for ABC. When Barbara Walters was invited to co-anchor the program in 1984, she agreed. After her disappointing stint as an anchor of the evening news almost a decade earlier, Barbara Walters had finessed her way back into the anchor chair, and this time, it was a resounding success. 20/20 proved to be the perfect program for Barbara Walters, who had shaped her career with the combination of interviewing celebrities and politicians. Although Hugh Downs was reluctant to share the anchor position with Walters at first, his longtime good relationship with her and Roone Arledge's considerable persuasive talents encouraged him to do so and when he did, viewers responded very favorably to the combination of Downs and Walters.

Since 1984, 20/20 has featured countless innovative and exclusive interviews with world-famous figures drawn from many different arenas of public life at the exact moment that the public wanted to hear more about these figures. Often controversial, they have ranged from politics and show business to sportsmen and even criminals. Barbara Walters, who had per-severed over the years and had convinced many of the most famous actors and politicians to sit down and tell their story first to her, would be an in-valuable part of the *20/20* success. Even as early as 1970, Barbara Walters considered herself an adept interviewer. In her book, *How to Talk with Practically Anybody About Practically Anything*, she advised anyone seek-ing a celebrity interview to find common ground before the actual inter-view starts in order to create a favorable communication climate. "I broke the ice with the usually aloof Barbra Streisand by asking how she chose the right nursery school for her young son Jason. Mrs. Mamie Eisenhower re-laxed before our long interview by talking of her favorite grandchild Susie. Former vice-president and Mrs. Hubert Humphrey enjoy talking of their grandchildren, and I spoke so often of my Jacqueline that they sent a can-did photograph to my home, autographed with affection, not to me but to Jacqueline."[78] Her tendency to disclose something about herself before-hand is an element of self disclosure known as reciprocity.[79] This ability to gain the confidence of her subjects by adopting behaviors that promote self-disclosure improved the quality of the interviews that Barbara Walters conducted.[80] She comments on why interviews are so interesting to view-ers: "People are fascinated by people. Are they happy? How do they live? Are they like me? Everyone's life is getting to know ourselves better or other people better."[81] As the years went by and her celebrity status rose, not only did the celebrities that she interviewed become more familiar with her, she felt on par with them, too. This was the case when Abbie Hoffman, the 1960s radical fugitive, telephoned Barbara Walters and agreed to give her an interview just prior to his finally surrendering to au-thorities. *20/20* producer Stanhope Gould explains that "Barbara's a 'movie star' journalist, so Abbie called up and said he would surrender only if Bar-bara did the interview."[82] Through the immediacy she created with her celebrity interviewees she gained a trust and the credibility that she would treat them with dignity. William Small, former NBC News president, noted, "If you were a celebrity, you wanted Barbara Walters to interview you."[83]

Some of the intimate questions asked by Barbara Walters may seem friv-olous, but the questions get audiences talking about Barbara Walters and tuning in to her show, and in the television world, that translates into effec-tiveness. For example, in 1981, Barbara Walters famously asked actress Katherine Hepburn: "If you were a tree, what kind of tree would you be?" This question became the brunt of many jokes, including a much-discussed and documented parody by comedienne Gilda Radner, who called herself

"Baba Wawa." Barbara Walters defended her asking of the "tree" question by explaining that in the interview, Hepburn herself had disclosed that "I feel like a tree."[84]

A question that comes to mind when considering the subject of celebrity interviews is: "Why do the celebrities do it?" Why would anyone subject themselves to the type of scrutiny that being interviewed by a savvy interviewer like Barbara Walters would lead? Carole A. Barbato found that people's motives for talking with others reflect both interpersonal function needs, such as self-confirmation, inclusion, control, and affection, as well as the needs found in mediated research, which are social utility, personal identity, and entertainment. The idea that Barbara Walters tries to achieve both with her guests, a nonmediated rapport before the camera rolls, and the kind of value that can be found in communicating in media, such as fame and positive attention, is a significant communication event.[85]

As the years went by, Barbara Walters became the person the politicians and celebrities sat down with, and often they would disclose information about themselves or the situation in which they were embroiled, in revealing ways. ABC promoted the exclusive interviews that Barbara Walters got to the greatest advantage. In 1988, Gary Hart was the democrat to beat in the presidential race, until he dared *Miami Herald* reporters to follow him, and they did. What they found was a romantic interlude between the married Hart and a beautiful young model, Donna Rice. On *World News Tonight*, Peter Jennings promoted Barbara Walters's upcoming exclusive interview: "It has been just six weeks since the former Democratic frontrunner dropped out of the presidential race. It seems much longer now. At the time he described Donna Rice as a casual acquaintance and a potential campaign worker. Well, Rice herself has said very little about her relationship with Hart until now. Now she has spoken to ABC's Barbara Walters."[86] In 1986 Barbara Walters married for the third time. She married TV mogul Merv Adelson, well known for his television show successes. It wasn't just because of *her* job that she was mingling with television and movie stars. In her husband's world, there were plenty of opportunities to meet and speak with big name celebrities. In 1992 Walters and Adelson were divorced.

In 1988 Barbara Walters's interview with boxer Mike Tyson and his then-wife Robin Givens revealed to the world a physically abusive Tyson. Givens told Barbara Walters, "He shakes, he pushes, he swings" and she was "very, very much afraid" of her husband because of his "extremely volatile temper."[87] Her disclosure to Walters in the national interview had news organizations around the country reporting that Givens may be in danger if she stayed with him, and soon after the interview, the couple separated and divorced. The risk of Givens's self-disclosure was great. She might not have been believed, or Tyson could have lashed out at her more because of her revealing comments. Why Givens chose to tell Barbara Walters on national television something that she might have told a marriage counselor in privacy is important to the dynamics of a celebrity interview and the ability for Walters to illicit highly sensitive information. While Cozby defines self-disclosure as the verbal communication of personal information about a sender with another person as the target,[88] the definition of self-disclosure also includes concepts of exclusivity, availability of information, and relational intimacy.[89] Because Barbara Walters was able to gain an intimacy with her guests, probably before the interview, they were more willing to give them information that they hadn't disclosed anywhere else. The interview with Givens and Tyson demonstrated that Barbara Walters interviews had the impact to create change. In this case, those watching, many in horror, realized that Mike Tyson was a physically abusive husband and that Robin Givens was in danger for her life. Another case of spousal abuse that monopolized the news was the O.J. Simpson trial, which was dubbed "the trial of the century" by the press. Although the jury found O.J. Simpson not guilty, he was found guilty in a civil case and many Americans believe he committed the crimes. Once again, Barbara Walters was able to secure some of the most coveted interviews of the story. Four months after the murders of Nicole Brown Simpson and Ron Brown, Barbara Walters talked in depth with close friends of Nicole Brown Simpson about Nicole's life as O.J. Simpson's wife and afterward, about O.J.'s jealousy and Nicole's fear of him. In her characteristically suspenseful way, Barbara Walter's introduced the program:

> Who really did know Nicole and O.J. Simpson? Many people have made that claim since the murders nearly four months ago, but tonight we bring you three people who, by everyone's measure, were really insiders. They will give you an intimate view of both Nicole and O.J. Simpson, including a startling revelation that could possibly shed new light on the case. Now, meet Nicole Simpson's closest friends.[90]

Even the defendant himself, O.J. Simpson, had a reaction to the Barbara Walters interview with Nicole Brown Simpson's friends. A confidante played an audiotape of the show to O.J. Simpson while he was being held in jail on murder charges and he responded to several of the comments by Nicole Brown Simpson's friends and he concluded by adding: "Tell Barbara that I didn't do those murders."[91] His first-name familiarity with Barbara Walters reminds us that Barbara Walters is able to gain a rapport with celebrities, partially due to her own fame. In many ways, these interviewees see her as one of them. Roderick P. Hart notes that one of the verbal dimensions of ethos is similarity. The speaker is seen as resembling the audience in important ways.[92] And from some of the comments she has made to interviewees, it seems as though she sees herself as one of them, too. In one of her several interviews with President Reagan, Barbara Walters felt comfortable enough with the president to complain about the shoddy condition of the Jeep he drove her around in on his ranch.

In June, 1992, Barbara Walters sat down with President and Mrs. Bush during his campaign for reelection. Note the first-name familiarity from the President:

Walters: Mr. President.

Pres. Bush: Hello, Barbara.

Walters: How nice to see you.

Pres. Bush: Good to see you.

Walter: Thank you.

Pres. Bush (again): Good to see you.[93]

Even though the interview was warm and cordial in the opening, Barbara Walters did not hold back once she got started questioning the president.

Walters: One of the criticisms, Mr. President, is that you waited too long before you attacked the economic problem, that it wasn't until January that you admitted there was a recession and talked about the country being in a fall. Why did you wait that long?

Pres. Bush: I don't—I haven't waited that long. I will concede I have had difficulty with an old-thinking Congress, but I must confess to a certain frustration over the last few years in terms of moving this country forward on the economic front. And the answer is not to go out and spend and tax and so, I'm fighting the battle there.

In a follow-up question, Barbara Walters is about to reference a previous interview with President Bush: "Well, you know you and I talked on the eve of your inauguration in 1989, and at that point, you said 'A lot of people in this country are hurting. . . .'[94] Barbara Walters's longevity in the broadcast field also raises her familiarity with guests because she has spoken with them before. The intimacy that Barbara Walters has with her guests has been cultivated over time, often, over years. Although author Kenneth Burke concentrated on the relationship between public speakers and their audiences, the concept of identification is also a way in which an audience member can perceive a communicator as being similar or having the same interests. Fraser and Brown[95] extend Burke's theory of identification to include the relationships that media viewers reconstruct with celebrities. I would further like to extend that theory to include the identification that celebrities and heads of state make with celebrity interviewers, such as Barbara Walters and several of the other women profiled in this book.

In 1996, First Lady Hillary Clinton's public image was in need of a makeover. She made history when she became the only first lady ever called to testify before a Grand Jury inquiry into "Whitewater," the scandal involving President Bill Clinton, the first lady, members of the Clinton administration, and private individuals and public officials in Arkansas. The focus of the investigation concerning a land deal was the question of whether the president and members of his administration participated in a cover-up. The role of Hillary Clinton in all of these events also became a target of investigators, and a media frenzy ensued.

On January 12, 1996, Hillary Clinton participated in an interview with Barbara Walters on *20/20*. Barbara Walters had already asked the first lady about her role in Whitewater and then said, "I have a tough question to ask you." Hillary replied, "Oh dear. All your questions." And then Walters continued: "Do you think that you're becoming more of the negative than a positive force for your husband? Are you becoming a political liability?" Brightening a bit, Hillary Clinton responded, "Oh I hope not because I love my husband and I really believe in what he's doing and I want to help him. But I have campaigned with him for, you know, gosh, ever since I've known him, and I'm going to do the same thing in this upcoming election. At the end of the day the American people will know we have nothing to cover up, there is nothing that we have done that should be of any concern to anyone. We've tried, maybe not as smartly as we could have, to answer peoples' questions, but we'll keep doing the best we know how." Later in the interview, Walters gets personal: "You've considered divorce?" Hillary Clinton: "No, never a divorce, but certainly I have thought hard about how a situation can escalate out of hand. You have to really be committed to it and you have to be willing to make compromises and bite that tongue from time to time."[96] These personal disclosures were provocative and revealing and the story of Bill Clinton's marital infidelities continues to interest viewers. Former White House intern and presidential paramour Monica Lewinsky gave an interview with Barbara Walters that drew 70 million viewers on March 4, 1999.[97] Enacting the role as "mother confessor" with Monica Lewinsky,

Barbara Walters tenderly looked into the eyes of the young woman and seemed to say nonverbally, "What were you thinking, sweetheart?" in the same gentle way a mother would address a confused daughter. In the interview, which was described as "the biggest television event since 'who shot J. R. on the 1980s blockbuster television drama, *Dynasty*,'"[98] Lewinsky talks about her childhood, lifestyle, her troubles, and the eighteen-month romantic affair that eventually led to President Bill Clinton's impeachment. "This was not a puff piece," Barbara Walters insisted to reporters. "This was not a huggy-kissy piece."[99]

Also contributing to *20/20*'s success with viewers has been its numerous health-related stories, one of the most personal involving Downs being shadowed by a crew who filmed him during his knee procedure and subsequent recovery. Encouraged by the strong showing of *20/20* and the continued popularity of rival *60 Minutes*, and spurred on by NBC's competitive bid into the newsmagazine forum with *Dateline*, ABC has created other news magazines over the years. With NBC's *Dateline* airing up to five times per week, in 1997 ABC decided to increase *20/20* showings to several nights a week. For the 1998–1999 season, combining all ABC news magazines (notably *Primetime Live*) under the *20/20* umbrella. Airing at least three times weekly, *20/20* expanded its original consumer focus to embrace the more investigative pieces and hard journalism that had marked *Primetime Live*, as well as to include more features on the day's top news. Additionally, Downs and Walters were no longer the sole anchors of the expanded program, but shared responsibilities with several other top ABC journalists, notably Sam Donaldson, Diane Sawyer, Charles Gibson, and Connie Chung. In August of 1997, Barbara Walters expanded her presence at ABC further when *The View*, a daytime talk show featuring Barbara Walters as a cohost and also executive producer, premiered on ABC. ABC News president David Westin told *The New York Times* that replacing Walters would be impossible, so instead, they plan to remodel the show to rely less on major interviews. Barbara Walters, who has interviewed almost every public figure worth interviewing and whose own celebrity matches many of her subjects, signaled that *The View*, her Emmy award–winning daytime television talk show she created along with Bill Geddie and Jessica Guff and featuring a panel of women as cohosts, would take a larger focus. The show is moderated by Whoopi Goldberg, with cohosts Joy Behar, Elisabeth Hasselbeck, Sherri Shepherd, and Barbara Walters. The concept of *The View* is to showcase women with a range of perspectives, as they speak with each other as well as with their guests. An early version of the show's opening credits, with a voiceover from Walters, captured the premise:

> I've always wanted to do a show with women of different generations, back-grounds and views: a working mother; a professional in her 30s; a young woman just starting out; and then somebody who's done almost everything and will say almost anything. And in a perfect world, I'd get to join the group whenever I wanted. . . .[100]

The show opens each day with "Hot Topics," in which the cohosts provide lightweight commentary on the day's top headlines in politics and entertainment; the segment's popularity soon led it to expand. Barbara Walters has come full circle in television broadcasting, from forging her way as an underling in a male-dominated world to the woman who calls the shots and "joins the group whenever she wants to."

Invention

When asked how she comes up with questions for an interview, Barbara Walters explains "I ask the questions that most people would like to ask."[101] She believes that if she does enough homework, she will know enough about the person to conduct the kind of interview that will be interesting to viewers. She says, "We don't pay people. We hope they will come on [the show] because that way they will set the record straight. When asked if she has ever been embarrassed by any questions that she asked she said: "It depends. Everyone is asked personal questions. I think they [the questions I ask] are tasteful. I will stay away from anything that I think is particularly painful. I did ask the Shah of Iran "you know it is said about you that you are a dictator. How do you answer this?" I don't say "You are a terrible dictator. What do you think about that?" Barbara Walters believes that asking interviewees about their childhood is an excellent way to get them to open up and expose a part of themselves that is very genuine. She likes to ask: "What was the best time of your life? What was the worst?" She notes, "I find people will talk with great sensitivity about their childhood." She recommends asking questions that will reflect on the interviewer's understanding of the person being asked about. For example, she says, "Don't ask, "What's your famous son really like?" Ask, "What qualities did you most want to instill in your children?"[102] She explains that her role as an interviewer is to "be curious" and "more interested in the person you are interviewing than in yourself." She commented that "the toughest interviews are young actors because they haven't had that much experience and there's not a lot to probe."[103]

Disposition

"I conduct interviews with show business people, politicians and everyday people. It's dealing with questions, it's getting people to open up. It's getting people to be wider and wider and wider as you get to know them or narrower and narrower if you are focusing on a subject. If you are trying to do a hard news interview you are trying to get something, a fact that hasn't been said before."[104]

Barbara Walters commented on how important editing is because if not done judiciously, it changes the meaning of a story: She says, "in order to make news, the stuff around it goes, which is a "boom boom boom" interview. I used to be very unhappy when I worked in news and I'd interview a head of state and it had to be edited down to four minutes. But you wouldn't get anything that made something make sense, or the qualifying statements."[105] The longer, in-depth interviews that Barbara Walters conducts for her Barbara Walters specials do not suffer the same aggressive editing fate as news stories. "It takes choreography so that you are careful about the order of questions and how you ask them. There is a point in an interview when something goes 'bing' and you realize you got something."[106] Notice how Barbara Walters organizes the questions in this 1996 interview with then first lady Hillary Clinton. At the time of this interview, the first lady was being called a liar and accused of illegal actions. Barbara Walters confronts the issue head on in the beginning of the interview: "Mrs. Clinton, instead of your new book being the issue, you have become the issue. How did you get into this mess, where your whole credibility is being questioned?" Her next question is directed at Hillary Clinton's personal state, "Are you distressed?" Then Barbara Walters gets specific about the news stories criticizing the first lady. "A 1993 memo by a former White House aide, David Watkins, was made public, in which he says that you were responsible for the firing of seven people in the White House travel office because you wanted to have an Arkansas travel agency take its place, and there would have been nothing illegal about your doing that. But you have said you had no idea how the decision was made and that you had nothing to do with it. Is he lying?" The first lady then admits to "voicing concern about the financial mismanagement that was discovered when the President arrived here in the White House travel office."[107] Even though her questions are specific and tough, she maintains a warm rapport with the first lady and then transitions into an interview about Hillary Clinton's book, *It Takes a Village*. Barbara Walters is not deferential to Hillary Clinton, but she is never rude or confrontational to the point that the first lady seems angry. In fact, the first lady seems to genuinely like Walters and answers all the questions, albeit pointed and tough, with warmth and composure. Veteran CBS *60 Minutes* host Mike Wallace says: "Barbara Walters really has the quality of reaching through to the person so she will get a person sufficiently at ease to reveal themselves to her."[108] That Hillary Clinton would say "I love my husband" and even confess that "I could have avoided some of the mistakes I made" is ample evidence that Barbara Walters is able to get her interviewees to open up in ways only a skillful interviewer could.

Style

Barbara Walters's typical use of language in her interviews—her rhetorical style—has several characteristics, including her use of personal and inclusive pronouns, sense of urgency with her delivery, direct sustained eye contact with her interviewees, and a sense of her own vulnerability and identification with the interviewees, by often using their first name, or disclosing something about themselves which gives them identification with the interviewee. For example, she often states a question as though she is the person she is questioning. When she interviewed Monica Lewinsky, she said, "Did you ever say to yourself, "I'm doing something wrong. This is bad for the president. This is bad for the country. Did you ever think about that?"[109] In the interview with Monica Lewinsky, she personified an aunt or mother figure, who was very compassionate, but had a tremendous curiosity—as did most of the American people—about what she was thinking when she engaged in a relationship with President Clinton. At another point in the interview, Barbara Walters asks, "Monica, are you still in love with Bill Clinton?"[110]

Another hallmark of Barbara Walters's style is her meticulous preparation for her interviews. She is able to readily quote passages from books, articles, and even her previous interviews with the interviewee to demonstrate her command of the material. For example, she recalled a previous interview that she conducted with President George H. Bush: "Well, you know, you and I talked on the eve of your inauguration in 1989 and, at that point, you said. . . ."[111] CBS broadcaster Bob Schieffer, who worked with Walters, noted that Walters "is nothing if not meticulous about preparing for interviews."[112] Barbara Walters demonstrated a competence that viewers recognized. Her many years in broadcasting gave her knowledge and experience that the audience does not have, which is one of the verbal dimensions of credibility Roderick P. Hart notes.[113]

Delivery

Barbara Walters brings a stack of index cards with her to her interviews. She carefully writes her questions on the cards and has them organized by subject. She is known for her meticulous preparation for interviews. She was known to read all the books that she spoke about on the air, and that "she knew the only way that she could be a star was by being well prepared" said NBC producer Julie Van Vliet Rubenstein.[114]

Throughout the years, Barbara Walters developed a distinctive broadcast voice, after overcoming a slight speech impediment. Still Barbara Walters will occasionally lisp on a few syllables. Her ability to overcome her original heavy lisp, evident in her early NBC broadcasts, makes her long career success as a broadcaster notable.

Conclusion

In many ways, Barbara Walters was way ahead of her time as a broadcasting pioneer. Whether it was tremendous foresight on her part, the luck of being the daughter of an entertainment agent, or serendipity, Barbara Walters combined celebrity and journalism at a time when very few broadcasters were. This caused her to initially be rejected by many in the established journalism community who felt that her particular brand of broadcasting, mixing celebrity interviews with important political interviews, wasn't true journalism. Through her tenacity and hard work, however, most of her detractors became allies and value her contribution to broadcast journalism. CBS broadcaster Bob Schieffer credits Barbara Waters for being the first female interviewer to impact broadcast news significantly enough to make the entry of more women more likely. "Success can make you go one of two ways. It can make you a prima donna, or it can smooth the edges, take away the insecurities, let the nice things come out."[115] Barbara Walters "let the nice things come out" when she said, I think the less we can hurt people, the better it is for all of us."[116] In a 2007 interview with Larry King, he asked Walters, "How is Katie [Couric] doing in your opinion? And how is she being treated, in your opinion?" Walters responded, "Well, I think there were similarities between Katie and me—and I'm very fond of Katie and I think she's doing so well. But that is all eyes are on them. When I came to ABC, I came to be the first female coanchor of a network news program with a partner, Harry Reasoner, who didn't want me. And it was very difficult. It still has been difficult for Katie. What is she wearing? How is her hair? I mean, things that are unimportant. I think she's done a very good job. I think it has been tough for her. I think she's getting better and better and that she's found her stride. But you know, to have that kind of a spotlight on you is very tough. And I think that Katie is a very special girl with a special talent, and I think all of us—I think—I don't know. I'm very supportive of other women on television. I always have been. While I was waiting to talk to you, Paula Zahn, whom I love, came in to give me a hug and a kiss. And not that I don't think that women have it much easier— I mean, when I think of my colleague, for example, Diane Sawyer, who's doing such sensational work now—but we had to work a little harder, we had to climb a little faster. Then we're called driven if we are obsessed, you know, things that they still never say about the men. So I think give Katie a little more time and you'll see, she'll just be fine."[117] Barbara Walters should know: she had been in exactly the same position as Couric, forty years earlier. Barbara Walters is indeed what Larry King described as a "living legend of television broadcasting."[118]

NOTES

1. Liless McPherson Shilling and Linda K. Fuller, *Dictionary of Quotations in Communication* (Greenwich, CT: Greenwood Press, 1997), 116.

2. http://abc.go.com/theview/hosts/walters.html (accessed August 1, 2006).

3. Joshua Lipton, "Barbara Walters," *Columbia Journalism Review* 40, no. 4 (Nov–Dec 2001): 80.

4. Jeff Alan with James M. Lane, *Anchoring America* (Chicago and Los Angeles: Bonus Books, 2003), 213.

5. Jerry Oppenheimer in his unauthorized biography lists 1929 as her birth date, as the 1930 Federal Census for the Enumeration District 41-184 shows her family on page 198, with father Louis Walters aged thirty-four, wife Dena Walters, aged thirty-three, Jacqueline, daughter, aged three years and eleven months, and Barbara, aged six months. This was recorded on April 21/22, 1930, so Barbara would have been born around October 1929 but other sources, including the Museum of Broadcast Communications (http://www.museum.tv/), list 1931.

6. Jerry Oppenheimer, *Barbara Walters: An Unauthorized Biography* (New York: St. Martin's Press, 1990), 5.

7. Ibid., 6.

8. Jacci Duncan, ed., *Making Waves: The 50 Greatest Women in Radio and Television* (Kansas City: McMeel Publishing, 2001), 272.

9. Ibid., 273.

10. Ibid., 275.

11. Oppenheimer, *Barbara Walters*, 112.

12. Ibid.

13. Duncan, *Making Waves*, 275.

14. Ibid.

15. William Raymond Manchester, *The Death of a President, November 20– November 25, 1963* (New York: Harper and Row, 1967), 329.

16. Alan, et al., *Anchoring America*, 220.

17. Ibid.

18. Ibid.

19. Ibid, 273.

20. Elizabeth Peel, "Barbara Walters: Star of the Morning," *Newsweek*, May 6, 1974, 57.

21. Ibid., 56.

22. Barbara Matusow, *The Evening Stars* (Boston: Houghton Mifflin Company, 1983), 169.

23. http://www.newyorkmetro.com/nymetro/news/people/features/2433/ (accessed August 2, 2006).

24. Louis Baldwin, *Women of Strength: Biographies of 196 Who Have Excelled in Traditionally Male Fields, A.D. to the Present* (Jefferson, North Carolina: McFarland Press, 1996), 108.

25. http://www.newyorkmetro.com/nymetro/news/people/features/2433/ (accessed August 2, 2006).

26. Alan, et al., *Anchoring America*, 221.

27. Duncan, *Making Waves*, 275.

28. Nichola D. Gutgold, e-mail correspondence with Jim Hartz, September 20, 2006.

29. Oppenheimer, *Barbara Walters*, 322–23.

30. www.shemadeit.org (accessed August 10, 2006).

31. Judith Marlane, *Women in Television News Revisited* (Austin: University of Texas Press, 1999), 50.

32. Peel, "Barbara Walters: Star of the Morning," 57.

33. Ibid., 56.

34. NBC news videotape from January 24, 1973, obtained from Vanderbilt University broadcast media archive.

35. Ibid., 276.

36. Matusow, *The Evening Stars*, 168.

37. Duncan, *Making Waves*, 276.

38. Ibid.

39. Les Brown, "Barbara Walters with ABC," *The New York Times*, April 21, 1976, 1.

40. Ibid.

41. Marc Gunther, *The House That Roone Built: The Inside Story of ABC News* (Boston: Little, Brown and Company, 1994), 42.

42. Fred Ferretti, "Barbara Walters on ABC," *The New York Times*, April 22, 1976, 66.

43. Richard Zoglin, "Star Power: Diane Sawyer, with a new prime-time show and a $1.6 million contract, is hot. But are celebrity anchors like her upstaging the news?" *Time*, August 7, 1989, 46–51.

44. Alan, et al., *Anchoring America*, 222.

45. Oppenheimer, 346.

46. Marlane, *Women in Television News Revisited*, 75.

47. NBC news videotape from October 4, 1976, obtained from Vanderbilt University broadcast media archive.

48. ABC news videotape obtained from Vanderbilt University broadcast media archive.

49. Vanderbilt TV News Archive, ABC News, October 4, 1976.

50. Ibid.

51. Ibid., 43.

52. Oppenheimer, *Barbara Walters*, 383.

53. Albin Krebs, "Notes on People," *The New York Times*, December 14, 1976, 34.

54. Richard F. Shephard, "Barbara Walters Gets the Interview," *The New York Times*, December 21, 1976, 67.

55. Ibid.

56. John Carmody, "Boston TV Job for Times' Lydon," *The Washington Post*, January 7, 1977, B8.

57. Duncan, *Making Waves*, 276.

58. Harry Reasoner, *Before the Colors Fade* (New York: Knopf, 1981), 186.

59. Sandy Vanocur, "Will Arledge Preside Over ABC News?" *The Washington Post*, March 9, 1977, B1.

60. Ibid.

61. Marc Gunther, *The House That Roone Built: The Inside Story of ABC News* (Boston: Little, Brown and Company, 1994), 27.

62. John Carmody and Lee Lescaze, "Anchors Away: The Crew's Changing at ABC News," *The Washington Post*, April 20, 1978, B1.

63. Oppenheimer, *Barbara Walters*, 375.

64. Bill Carter, "Chung to Join Rather as CBS News Anchor," *The New York Times*, May 18, 1993, C18.

65. Joseph E. Persico, *Edward R. Murrow, An American Original* (New York: Dell Publishing, 1983), 1.

66. Ibid., 345.

67. Oppenheimer, *Barbara Walters*, 395.

68. Tom Shales, "Covering the Big Story in Jerusalem: The News People as Newsmakers," *The Washington Post*, November 21, 1977, C1.

69. Ibid.

70. Haynes Johnson, "Historic Meeting of Heads of State—and a One-Eyed King: the Visit," *The Washington Post*, November 23, 1977, A3.

71. Walter Cronkite, *A Reporter's Life* (New York: Random House, 1996), 316.

72. Connie Chung, "The Business of Getting 'The Get': Nailing an Exclusive Interview in Prime Time," The Joan Shorenstein Center for Press, Politics and Public Policy, Harvard University John F. Kennedy School of Government, Discussion Paper D-28, April 1998.

73. Gunther, *The House That Roone Built*, 154.

74. Ibid.

75. NBC news videotape from October 4, 1976, obtained from Vanderbilt University broadcast media archive.

76. Keith Weber and B.R. Patterson, "Construction and Validation of a Communication-Based Emotional Support Scale," *Communication Research Reports* 13, no. 1 (1996): 69–76.

77. http://www.bookrags.com/history/popculture/2020-sjpc-04/ (accessed August 12, 2006).

78. Barbara Walters, *How to Talk with Practically Anybody About Practically Anything* (New York: Doubleday and Company, 1970), 11.

79. Paul C. Cozby, "Self-Disclosure, Reciprocity, and Liking," *Sociometry* 35, no. 1 (March 1972): 151–60.

80. Keith Weber, et al., "Construction and Validation of a Communication-Based Emotional Support Scale," 69–76.

81. Skip Blumberg, "Interviews with Interviewers . . . About Interviewing," videotape produced with grants from National Endowment of the Arts, 1985.

82. Oppenheimer, *Barbara Walters*, 409.

83. Connie Chung, "The Business of Getting 'The Get'," 4.

84. Steve Wulf, "Barb's Wired," *Time*, November 6, 1995, 68.

85. Elizabeth E. Graham, Carole A. Barbato, and Elizabeth M. Perse, "The Interpersonal Communication Motives Model," *Communication Quarterly* 41, no. 2 (Spring, 1993): 172–86.

86. ABC News transcripts, "World News Tonight with Peter Jennings," June 18, 1987. lexisnexis@prod.lexisnexis.com (accessed August 13, 2006).

87. Amy Walsh, "Life with Tyson Is "torture, pure hell" Says His Wife," *St. Petersburg Times* (Florida), September 30, 1988, 2C.

88. Paul C. Cozby, "Self Disclosure: A Literature Review," *Psychological Bulletin* 79, no. 2. (1973): 73–91.

89. Ronald B. Adler, Lawrence B. Rosenfeld, and Russell Proctor, *Interplay: The Process of Interpersonal Communication* (8th edition) (Fort Worth: Harcourt-Brace, 2001), 92.

90. ABC News transcripts, *20/20*, October 7, 1994. Transcript # 1440-3, lexis-nexis@prod.lexisnexis.com (accessed August 13, 2006).

91. ABC News transcripts, *20/20*, October 14, 1994. Transcript # 1441, lexis-nexis@prod.lexisnexis.com (accessed August 13, 2006).

92. Roderick P. Hart, *Modern Rhetorical Criticism* (Needham Heights: Simon and Schuster, 1997), 223.

93. ABC News transcripts, *20/20*, June 26, 1992, lexisnexis@prod.lexisnexis.com (accessed August 13, 2006).

94. Ibid.

95. Benson P. Fraser, William J. Brown, "Media, Celebrities, and Social Influence: Identification With Elvis Presley," *Mass Communication & Society* 5, no. 2: 183–206.

96. ABC News Transcripts, *20/20*, January 12, 1996. Transcript # 1602 lexis-nexis@prod.lexisnexis.com (accessed August 14, 2006).

97. http://www.cnn.com/ALLPOLITICS/stories/1999/03/04/lewinskyexcerpts/ (accessed August 14, 2006).

98. http://www.cnn.com/ALLPOLITICS/stories/1999/03/02/lewinsky/ (accessed August 15, 2006).

99. Ibid.

100. ABC transcript, *The View*, August, 1997.

101. Skip Blumberg, "Interviews with Interviewers . . . About Interviewing," videotape produced with grants from National Endowment of the Arts, 1985.

102. Barbara Walters, *How to Talk with Practically Anybody About Practically Anything*, 35.

103. Ellen Kelleher, "Queen of the Questioners: Barbara Walters Puts Her Success Down to Iron Will and Stamina," *Financial Times* (London, England), November 30, 2004, Media, 9.

104. Blumberg, "Interviews with Interviewers . . . About Interviewing."

105. Ibid.

106. Ibid.

107. ABC News transcript, *20/20*, January 12, 1996. Transcript # 1602, lexis-nexis@prod.lexisnexis.com (accessed August 14, 1996)

108. Ibid.

109. CNN, "Excerpts of Lewinsky Interview," March 4, 1999, www.cnn.com (accessed September 19, 2006).

110. Ibid.

111. ABC News transcripts, *20/20*, June 26, 1992, lexisnexis@prod.lexisnexis.com (accessed August 13, 2006).

112. Bob Schieffer, *Face the Nation* (New York: Simon and Schuster, 2004), 97.

113. Hart, *Modern Rhetorical Criticism*, 223.

114. Oppenheimer, *Barbara Walters*, 275.

115. Elizabeth Peer, "Barbara Walters," *Newsweek*, May 6, 1974.

116. CNN, *Larry King Live*, "Larry King Interviews Barbara Walters," November 28, 2005. http://transcripts.cnn.com/TRANSCRIPTS/0511/28/lkl.01.html (accessed 10/21/06).

117. CNN, *Larry King Live*, "An Interview with Barbara Walters," February 22, 2007. www.nexislexis.com (accessed 2/24/07).

118. Ibid.

3

ANCHORS AWAY

Connie Chung and Elizabeth Vargas

CONNIE CHUNG

Figure 2.1.   Connie Chung

Welcome to the world of "gets," newsroom parlance for the cutthroat competition for the big interview, the hot celebrity, the tell-all tattler *du jour*. It's where the supermarket tabloids, morning wake-up programs, afternoon talk shows, tabloid TV shows, and even the network news broadcasts collide in a mad scramble for an exclusive that will sell papers and draw viewers. It's the symbiotic world where it's hard to tell who is manipulating whom: the media or the newsmakers. And it is radically changing the way journalists and news organizations carry out their mission.[1]

This is the way that Connie Chung describes her profession in a paper she wrote at the Harvard University John F. Kennedy School of Government. In her long and varied broadcasting career, Connie Chung has gotten many "gets." Some of her most memorable interviewees include Claus Von Bulow, the British socialite who was accused of having attempted to murder his wife in 1980; the brother and mother of President Bill Clinton—Roger and Virginia Clinton—who were interviewed in 1993; and an exclusive interview with Joseph Hazlewood, the drunken pilot who steered the Exxon Valdez into a reef. The Joseph Hazlewood interview is a "get" she remembers with relish. Said Chung: "I got the one and only television interview. He didn't do any interviews before or after. It was of great interest."[2] She is remembered in the world of broadcasting for her exclusive interviews with Tonya Harding, the figure skater who schemed to injure fellow skater Nancy Kerrigan in 1994, and the audible one-word "whisper" from Newt Gingrich's mother, Kathleen, in 1995 that described what her son, Newt Gingrich, thought of Hillary Clinton. In 2001, more than twenty-three million curious viewers were glued to their television sets when Connie Chung interviewed Congressman Gary Condit about his connection to the missing young intern, Chandra Levy.[3]

She noted that while television broadcasting seems glamorous, throughout her career, "there was a lot of waiting for people to come out of the door. You just stood shivering in the cold with a little microphone in your hand; the person came out, you quickly asked a question and that was it. All you have to do is be aggressive; you don't have to be a good interviewer."[4] This style of quick interviews characterized Connie Chung's early career, but her career evolved into more in-depth interviews, and it was that style—the long and in-depth interview—that was not as successful for Chung as the initial "get" type of story that characterized her early career.

Early in Connie Chung's career she followed Watergate figure H. R. Haldeman to church to get an interview. She was known for her hard work ethic and tenacity. In his book, *The Boys on the Bus: Riding with the Campaign Press Corps,* Timothy Crouse notes:

> Few TV correspondents ever join the wee-hour poker games or drinking. Connie Chung, the pretty Chinese CBS correspondent, occupied the room next to mine at the Hyatt House and she was always back by midnight, reciting a final sixty-second radio spot into her Sony or absorbing one last press re-

lease before getting a good night's sleep. So here she was this morning, bright and alert, sticking a microphone into McGovern's face, asking him something about black ministers. The print reporters stood around and watched, just in case McGovern should say something interesting.[5]

Connie Chung's career in television journalism began to get noticed during the presidential campaign of 1972. CBS Correspondent Bob Schieffer remembered that "George McGovern used to say there wasn't a morning he didn't wake up to find Connie Chung waiting around the corner with a microphone. She was driven, always doing an extra spot late at night, never afraid to ask a tough question."[6] Schieffer noted that a few years earlier when he worked with Chung at WTTG, Chung was intent on moving up in her career. When Schieffer announced that he had secured a job with CBS, he notes that "The first question young Connie Chung asked was, 'Do you know if they need anyone else?'"[7]

Her tenacity paid off as her notoriety as an up-and-coming journalist was on the rise at one of the most newsworthy and significantly historic moments in political history: Watergate. She quickly moved up the journalism ladder and became one of the most prominent women in television news. From 1993–1995 she even occupied the coveted anchor chair opposite CBS veteran anchor Dan Rather.

Though an ill-fated and short-lived arrangement as coanchor, Connie Chung became known as a big-name, serious journalist. But just as her career grew, Connie Chung's serious journalistic traits became mired in the infotainment style of news that became increasingly popular and she conducted interviews that drew criticism for her type and style of questioning. This analysis will show that a confluence of occurrences worked to undermine Chung's reputation as a serious journalist, including her professional association with her husband, tabloid journalist Maury Povich, which concluded with Chung perched atop a piano in a parody torch song presentation that made her the object of ridicule on Internet blog sites.

Hard Work: A Family Tradition at the Chung Home

Constance Yu-Hwa Chung was born in Washington, D.C., on August 20, 1946, the youngest of ten children, five of whom died as infants before her parents emigrated from China. Her father, William Ling Chung, was a financial manager who had served as an intelligence officer under General Chiang Kai-shek. He and her mother, Margaret, moved their four daughters to Washington, D.C., in 1945, and the sisters named their new baby sister, giving her the Chinese "Yu-Hwa" middle name, which means "precious ivory."

Though quiet and meek, at the age of four, she started to use the metal tube from a vacuum cleaner as a make-believe microphone to "interview" friends.[8] The traditionally strict Chinese work ethic prevailed in the Chung household as well as the respect for education. Connie Chung and her sisters attended a very good public high school in Washington, D.C., which was attended by many gifted and talented students, including Carl Bernstein, the future Watergate reporter, and Goldie Hawn, the future actress.[9]

Connie came out of her meek shell in college at the University of Maryland. She obtained a job as a summer intern in the office of New York Congressman Seymour Halpern between her junior and senior years. He had been a newspaperman, and he encouraged Connie to try her hand at writing speeches and press releases. She discovered that she liked that kind of work. "That's when I got bitten by the bug. It was a lot of fun writing and watching reporters do their thing . . . it was the first time I sort of watched politics at work."[10] She said, "You can't grow up in Washington, D.C., and not be extremely aware of news and what's going on on Capital Hill."

She started at WTTG-TV in Washington, D.C., part time while she was still in college. When she graduated from college, with honors, in 1969, she was determined to make her mark in her chosen field of journalism. At first, she stayed on at WTTG as a copy clerk and then took the job as newsroom secretary, though at the small station there was often an overlapping of duties. She worked with her future husband, Maury Povich, at WTTG and eventually became a full-fledged reporter. She left WTTG, however, when she was hired by CBS's Washington bureau as a reporter. This was her first job with CBS, which included working with broadcasting great Walter Cronkite from 1971–1976 as a Washington correspondent, where she covered Watergate, Capitol Hill, and the 1972 presidential campaign. She commented about her hiring at CBS. She said, "They only had one women at CBS News at the time and they wanted to hire more. So they hired me, they hired Lesley Stahl, they hired Michele Clark and they hired Sylvia Chase . . . in other words, a Chinese woman, a black woman, a nice Jewish girl and a blond shiksa. Perfect. And so they took care of years of discrimination.[11] It's unlikely that any of these qualified journalists was hired because she was a certain race, in addition to being female. This quote says more of Connie Chung's slightly sarcastic sense of humor than it does about hiring practices at CBS. The time of their hiring, however, does coincide with the government's mandate to hire more women in broadcasting. As this chapter and all chapters in this book demonstrate, however, women were hired, but they had to perform at an excellent level to be promoted in their jobs. Connie Chung's career is a fitting example of a female who had to cautiously watch her public image in order to stay at the top of her career. Her career has significantly changed over the years, and it is now all but null. She left for an anchor position with KNXT-TV (now KCBS-TV), a CBS affiliate in Los Angeles, working on both local network broadcasts, where she stayed for seven years. While she was in Los Angeles, she co-anchored three daily newscasts, and was a substitute anchor for *CBS Morning News* and CBS News's weekend and evening broadcasts. She also anchored *CBS Newsbriefs* for Pacific time zones. In 1981 Connie Chung earned $600,000, making her the highest paid local news anchor in the country at the time.[12] But the East Coast native missed her old stomping grounds and Connie Chung's former boss at CBS, Neil Small, was now with NBC news. He welcomed her to NBC in 1983 and she stayed on until 1989. Though it meant a $200,000 salary drop to move from her position at KNCT-TV to NBC, it also meant "coming home" for Connie and getting back to her first love, political reporting.[13] The other big plus was that the move put her closer to Maury Povich, her longtime boyfriend, and in 1984 they were married. At NBC, Chung anchored the Saturday edition of the *NBC Nightly News*, *NBC News at Sunrise*, which aired right before the popular *Today Show*, *NBC Digests*, several prime-time news specials and the newsmagazine, *1986*. She also served as a political analysis correspondent and podium correspondent during the 1988 presidential campaign and political conventions. Steve Friedman, an executive producer at NBC, said at the time, "Connie's career will rise or fall on how well she does on *Early Today*. If it does well, that career could rise a long way."[14] Since the networks began programming news before 7:00 a.m. there was a lot of competition for ratings among ABC, CBS, and NBC. Connie produced excellent ratings for NBC and her clout with the network began to rise. In 1986 she signed a new, three-year contract with NBC that offered her a $2 million salary and an opportunity to host specials on in-depth topics for the network. The first episode, which aired in 1987, was called "Life in the Fat Lane." It featured celebrities like Oprah Winfrey and Tommy Lasorda describing their battles with weight loss. Critics complained that it wasn't real news—it was infotainment. Tom Shales, *Washington Post* reporter, noted about Chung's special on stress: "Here's Connie Funn with another of her prime-time popumentaries. This one is called "NBC News Report on America: Stressed to Kill," and if you learn anything new about stress from it, you haven't been keeping up with your copies of *Reader's Digest*. Our Gal Con (whose real last name is Chung) not only anchors the report, at ten tonight on Channel Four, she frolics through it. She plays pool with a North Carolina businessman who had a stress problem, she plays chess with a military man who went through emotional hell, and she sticks her hand in a bucket of ice water as part of a test to measure her own stress quotient."[15] He went on to complain that "more intriguing aspects of the subject—why stress seems to take a greater toll in the computerized 1980s, what the chemical causes and possible chemical treatments of stress are—are only flirted with as Mistress Connie treks on to her rendezvous with the next gimmick. In the end, the pretty schoolmarm [Chung] has words of advice. "We can learn to limit hostile feelings," she says. One way would be by not watching any more of these glib and shallow Connie Chung elementaries."[16] The once-serious journalist had to deal with critics who saw her made-for-television type of programming and thought that she had "sullied her good name"[17] by doing them. In 1990 Connie Chung made an announcement that she was curtailing her twelve-hour daily work schedule so she and Povich could work on having a child. "I now need to take a very aggressive approach to having a baby," she stated in a press release. Late-night comedians and tabloid magazines found her announcement amusing, as did much of the general public who kept watching Connie Chung to see if her "aggressive approach" resulted in pregnancy.

She left NBC for CBS where she hosted *Saturday Night with Connie Chung* and was then paired with Dan Rather as coanchor of the *CBS Evening News.* While hosting the *CBS Evening News,* she also hosted a side project on CBS, *Eye to Eye with Connie Chung.*

Coanchor of CBS Evening News

Chung became a member of the most exclusive sorority in evening news when, in 1993, she was tapped to coanchor the *CBS Evening News* with Dan Rather. Although there was considerably less fanfare for Connie Chung than there was for Barbara Walters when she became an anchor on a national evening news network, her debut marked the first time an Asian-American, of either sex, was an official anchor of a weeknight evening news program.

On June 1, 1993, she took her place beside Dan Rather, in an effort to help CBS News "redefine the role of the anchor," according to then CBS news president Eric Ober.[18] *USA Today* called the hiring a "preemptive strike" on the part of CBS, based on a hunch that NBC News might pair either Katie Couric or Jane Pauley with Tom Brokaw to try to pull No. 3-rated

NBC Nightly News ahead of *CBS Evening News.*[19] Connie Chung and Dan Rather kissed and embraced before they were introduced to reporters. Chung noted, "I have a lot of challenges ahead. I'm thrilled. She also thanked newswoman Barbara Walters for "blazing the trail."[20] Of the pairing, Dan Rather said, "What you're looking at today is a very happy, very excited Dan Rather," he said, with his arm around Connie Chung. "I know when I get to go out to report on stories, I understand what's happening much better. Why wouldn't I be excited at the chance to work with the charismatic, energetic, terrific Connie Chung? Connie is a tremendously experienced network correspondent, and she is also a big-time anchor talent. In addition to that, Connie is Miss Congeniality. She could win a Miss Congeniality Contest in any language on any continent."[21] Dan Rather was also adamant that the decision to bring Connie Chung to his broadcast was not made because it was suffering in the ratings (the broadcast was, at the time, in third place behind ABC and NBC).

CBS's research department conducted research that found that Connie Chung was already more familiar to television viewers than anyone else in network news, including Dan Rather and the anchors at the other network newscasts at the time, which were Peter Jennings at ABC and Tom Brokaw in NBC.[22] The June 1, 1993, broadcast was historic, with the announcer reading for the first time: *The CBS Evening News with Dan Rather and Connie Chung.* Chung and Rather sat center-set for the on-camera opening, sitting next to each other. Chung, impeccably groomed and poised read the first item, "For President Clinton, a lurch to the center. An exclusive CBS poll shows the president having to scramble to regain popularity lost." Dan Rather reported, "The killing fields of Bosnia, shelling kills children on a soccer field in Sarajevo while the world watches in horror." Dan Rather, leaned over to touch her hand and said, "Good evening and welcome, Connie." Chung warmly responded, "Thank you, Dan." [23] At the end of the inaugural broadcast, they gave a nod to the first network coanchors, Chet Huntley and David Brinkley. Dan Rather closed by saying: "Part of our world tonight, and what a different world it is." This was Dan Rather's effort at tying it all together: the broadcast, history, and the stories of the day. Connie Chung responded, "Thank you for joining us, and for all of us at CBS News, good night." With a gleam in her eye, she continued, "Good night, Chet," and Rather played along, "Good night, David. Good night, everybody. See you tomorrow." [24]

Connie Chung's meticulously well-groomed appearance, strong and commanding voice, and excellent command of her news reading were evident as coanchor. She and Rather looked like a strong professional team of two news professionals at the top of their game. But just seven weeks after the duo debuted, Connie Chung was receiving criticism in the press as being the broadcast's "show pony—the little woman who minds the New York anchor desk while "Big Dan" jets off to a summit in Tokyo or flooding in the Midwest. Chung commented on the criticism: "After twenty some years in this business, in hard news, I was very surprised at that, but it comes with the territory, it really does, and I can't dwell on it."[25] Six months into the Chung-Rather pairing, ratings for CBS Evening News were in a disappointing third place to ABC and NBC. CBS President Ober was undaunted by the low ratings and confidently stated: "TV news reflects the culture, and the one thing that may be outmoded is the middle-aged white anchorman."[26] And Erik Sorensen, executive producer, explained that without the coanchor format, CBS might have been unwilling to let Rather go to Des Moines the previous week and anchor the news from a river levee, a helicopter, and waist-deep water inside a flooded house. "It takes a lot of time for an audience to readjust and recalibrate. In a year or two, if we aren't making rating progress, we're not going to feel good. But today we don't feel bad."[27]

Six months later and continued low ratings resulted in news reports declaring that the anchor duo would be getting the ax. NBC News was clobbering CBS News in ratings, and *USA Today* noted that "Virtually everyone at CBS News—Rather and Chung included—think the double anchor experiment has bombed in its 1-year run and is embarrassing. Many think viewers are flocking to *Nightly News* not because it's so improved but because the Rather-Chung team is a turnoff to viewers."[28] Media critics also did not respond favorably to the use of news simulations in her program *Saturday Evening with Connie Chung*. Critics branded Connie Chung's use of simulations "a travesty." Though other newscasters were less chastised, it seems that Chung's journalistic behavior was held to a higher standard and she got criticism for participating in news stories that used simulations similar to those that Lesley Stahl and Diane Sawyer, among others, did. In addition, shortly before she left CBS, Chung drew criticism for her questions during two of the interviews she conducted for the network. In January, 1995 Connie Chung interviewed Newt Gingrich's parents and in May 1995, she was in Oklahoma City, Oklahoma, covering the bombing at the Murray Federal Building when she questioned the Oklahoma City Fire Chief: "Can you people in Oklahoma handle something this big and disastrous?" Steve Yandell, a doctor who administered to the injured during the emergency, noted the backlash against Chung's question: "As if we [in Oklahoma] lived in a different era. She then crashed the media line and tried to get up closer than the rest of the media. She was escorted back and even threatened to be arrested. Tee shirts were made up with 'Who the hell is Connie Chung?' on the front and something I can't repeat on the back. We noticed the next day that Connie was gone and Dan Rather was in her place."[29] Shortly afterwards, on May 18, 1995, Chung was removed as coanchor of *CBS Evening News* and her magazine program *Eye to Eye with Connie Chung*.

After her unsuccessful coanchoring pairing with Dan Rather ended, Chung moved to ABC News where she cohosted *20/20* and began independent interviews. In 1995 she and her husband, Maury Povich, adopted a son, Matthew Jay. The trajectory of Connie Chung's career shows that she kept moving from network to network and she never found a home at any of them for very long. Connie Chung stayed at ABC long enough to land some significant interviews, including the interview with Congressman Gary Condit, but before long she was lured to CNN in 2002 for yet another short-lived position.

Connie Chung's Changing Channels

In 2002 Connie Chung joined CNN to host her own show, *Connie Chung Tonight,* an hour-long, prime-time news and interview show based in New York. Of her new position, Chung noted, "I'm delighted to be part of an organization of dedicated journalists whose sole mission is to report the news every minute of every hour every day."[30] But in 2003 her show was preempted by Iraq War coverage and never put back on the air. CNN hoped a Chung-anchored program could compete with the Fox News Channel, but ratings were never spectacular and early on Chung struggled with the live format.[31] Connie Chung was hired by Walter Isaacson, the former chairman of CNN who, during his tenure, focused on hiring well-known personalities to anchor shows. This move frustrated some old-timers because when Ted Turner founded CNN the motto was: "News is the star."[32] Although CNN offered Connie Chung a chance to remain at the network in a different on-air capacity, she declined. *Connie Chung Tonight* was criticized by CNN veterans as overly tabloid and lacking in journalistic heft. Even CNN founder Ted Turner said, "Connie Chung's just awful."[33] Whenever Connie Chung's persona revealed anything less than the "Miss Congeniality" figure that Dan Rather admired, her audience responded by shutting off their televisions. Unlike Barbara Walter's tendency to reveal a bit of herself to her interviewees, Connie Chung often questioned whether or not the interviewee was telling the truth by asking "really?" It made it seem as though she were making fun of her subject or, worse, accusing them of not telling the truth.

In 2006, Chung and Maury Povich began hosting a show titled *Weekends with Maury and Connie* on MSNBC. Lizz Winstead, cocreator of the Comedy Central's very successful *The Daily Show with Jon Stewart*, served as executive producer. The network promised that the two hosts would "cut through the spin and get to the truth, exploring all sides of a story as only two people who have been married for twenty years can do."[34] It was Connie Chung's first appearance as a host since 2003, and the first time the veteran broadcasters worked together on a national news program. The show was cancelled due to poor ratings and aired its final episode on June 17, 2006. Connie Chung gave an unusual "swan song" to mark her departure from the show. Atop a piano, dressed in a strapless evening frock, she sang, rather poorly, "Thanks for the Memories" to her husband, Maury Povich. The two-minute-forty-eight-second video of her serenade took on a life of its own on the Internet site YouTube, and it was viewed by more than 413,000 people, almost 200,000 more than watched her show with Maury Povich.[35] Ultimately, Chung was unable to transcend the complacent newsreader position and has all but vanished from television.

Significant Interviews by Connie Chung

In 1993, Connie Chung appeared on the CBS morning program with Paula Zahn and Harry Smith to discuss her interview with President Clinton's mother and brother, Virginia Kelly and Roger Clinton. Paula Zahn opened the interview with: "Topic A this morning, *Eye to Eye With Connie Chung*. Lately, Connie's been making news as well as reporting it with her appointment as coanchor of the 'CBS Evening News.' Well, starting tonight, hey—and look at all this other news she's generating." Harry Smith, coanchor, noted: "Is there a magazine in the hierarchy you're not on?" Paula Zahn came back: "Yeah, I wonder. I wonder if Connie Chung even saves those covers. But her brand-new CBS News program starts tonight, *Eye to Eye with Connie Chung*. And thank you for gracing us this morning." Connie Chung said, "Thank you for having me." Zahn asked, "Do you keep those all in the room, all those magazine covers?" Chung's wry sense of humor was evident: "In the bathroom. Right." Paula Zahn transitioned: "So tonight's big debut, you start off with the—President Clinton's stepbrother. . . . " Chung corrected her slightly, "Brother, yes. Uh-huh. Roger Clinton, who is a bit outrageous, a bit out of control, but at the same time, he's rather endearing. I think there is some sympathy for him, you know. He's thrust into this situation." Harry Smith interjected: "We haven't really seen him since this inauguration." Zahn added: "He's kind of hidden." Connie Chung noted: "Right.

That's right. The—he's—the lid has been kept on him, I think. And this is his first prime-time interview. The only, actually, previous—the only previous television interview he . . . " Smith said exaggeratedly: "I know what show he was on." Enthusiastically, Connie said, "Yes!" Smith teased a little, as though he couldn't remember the show's host: "That guy—that guy—that guy . . . " Paula Zahn continued, "All in the family, that good looking guy, Mar—Ma—Ma—Maury Povich!" Connie Chung admitted, "Right. That's right." After a little more banter, Chung tells a little bit about her interview: "Roger Clinton talks about his relationship with his brother. He—his brother was clearly his guardian, his parent, his—his close friend, his best friend, his patron. Everything. He was everything to this little Roger, ten years older. They grew up with an abusive alcoholic father and Roger needed—needed something. And—and it was Bill who gave it all to him. I think we have a clip. It shows you a little bit about it." In the excerpt of *Eye to Eye with Connie Chung,* Connie Chung addressed Virginia Kelly: "Roger's life has obviously changed a great deal since his brother became president. How do you think he's handling the limelight? Which is not easy." Mrs. Kelly said, "No it isn't. And I was really concerned about this." Chung encourages the completion of the statement: " You were afraid that he might . . . " Mrs. Kelly, Clinton's mother clarified: "He might start drinking too much. I really believe if—had he had not been an alcoholic, he would not have had the drug problem. Roger may have a different story. I don't know." Roger Clinton says: "I don't think I was an alcoholic and I don't think I am an alcoholic. I could go in there and drink—a light beer, or a glass of wine. It would be no problem." "Were you ever worried that you may have inherited alcoholism directly from your father?" Tearfully, Roger Clinton answered, "Yes, ma'am. Yes, ma'am."[36]

USA Today television critic Matt Roush complained that the "thin interview with Clinton is one of the reasons the magazine show isn't called *Mind to Mind.* The show is playing the only game the networks trust nowadays: quick-hit news features that require little commitment or thought."[37] It was true that Connie Chung did not illicit new information from the president's brother. Her treatment of him was condescending, too. Unlike most interviewers who cleverly disclose a little about themselves in order for the interviewee to open up, Chung doesn't do that. Alternatively, she frequently chides her guests or seems to be making fun of them. For example, she asked Roger Clinton, "You honestly don't think that was embarrassing? Come On! Don't you know by now you shouldn't act this way?"[38] Connie Chung was referring to Roger Clinton's physically attacking a fellow Knicks game attendee who criticized his brother. That she leads Virginia Kelly, Bill and Roger Clinton's mother, into finishing her sentence by just starting off the statement: "You were afraid that he might . . . " gives the viewer the impression that Connie Chung wants her guests to reveal weaknesses and that she doesn't over-empathize with them. Certainly that is the case when, in 1994, she interviewed Tonya Harding, an Olympic ice skater accused of being implicated in a plot to injure a fellow skater. Harding gave Chung an exclusive network interview. Tonya Harding said, "I believe now that I have a real family. Stephanie's parents are going to adopt me soon. . . . " Connie Chung questions her: "Really?" Tonya Harding explained, "and so I can have a real family and a real sister and brothers and—I mean, it's wonderful. I mean, I've never had anything like that." Connie Chung asked, "Is that something you've always wanted?" Harding said, " Yeah. I've always wanted to have a family. I always wanted to—somebody to love me for me." Connie Chung asked, "But don't you think your father loves you for you?" Tonya replied, "Yeah, I do." Chung asked, "This is a—is this going to hurt him at all?" Tonya Harding said, "No." Connie Chung questioned, "You sure?" Tonya. Harding explained: "Because we're all kind of—all big—one happy family." Connie Chung asked: "And what about your mother?" Tonya Harding said, "I don't see my mother that very much." Chung asked, pointing to her head: "Are you a little better up here if you don't see her that much?" Tonya said, " I'm a little better if she doesn't put me down. I mean, you know, right—recently, she's been really good, and she says that, you know, I look good and I'm skating great and—but most of my life she always told me I skated like crap; I was too fat; I'm never—I'm never going to win; I'm never going to beat these people; I'm never going to do anything. And so it was really hard, and I think that that had a lot to do with the hate relationship that I had for her."

Connie Chung's interview style is not sympathetic to Harding. She patronizingly asks Harding about her feeling better off mentally if she doesn't talk to her mother. Connie Chung then explained her impression of the interview to the public after Tonya left by saying, "This interview was obviously Tonya's attempt to make her case to the American public. Both she and Nancy Kerrigan stand to make big money from book, movie, or television deals. Harding says she intends to use some of the money she receives from her current notoriety to set up a trust for Special Olympics children."[39] By communicating with the audience that Tonya Harding had a hidden agenda by giving the interview breaks the confidence with her subject that suggests she wants to present her in a good light. It is similar to a friend gossiping to another about something that the friend thought she told you in confidence, a lot like the comment Mrs. Gingrich though she was just whispering to Connie Chung.

While interviewing Bill Gates for *Eye to Eye* in 1994, Chung presciently likened Gates's business tactics to knife-fighting, a comparison she picked up from a Microsoft competitor. "A lot of people make the analogy that competing with Bill Gates is like playing hardball," she said. "I'd say it's more like a knife fight." The usually polite Microsoft chairman tore off his mike and stormed off the set, even though Connie Chung followed up warmly, "Can I just ask you one more question, Bill?" Before he stood up and walked off, curtly, Bill said, "No, I don't think so."[40]

In 1995 Connie Chung interviewed the parents and sisters of the newly installed speaker of the house. She said, "You have a nickname for your son. He is the first Republican speaker of the House in forty years and perhaps the most powerful Republican in the nation." Mrs. Gingritch said: "Newtie." Connie Chung asked, " Does he mind that you call him Newtie?" She said, "He's never said anything about it." Surprised, Connie Chung asks, "Really?" Mrs. Gingrich: "Mm-hmm." Connie Chung pressed: "Even now?" Mrs. Gingrich confirmed, "Even now." Connie Chung said, "I mean, he's over fifty." Is he a true Southerner? Both Mr. and Mrs. Gingrich replied, "No." Mr. Gingrich went to explain that Newt was born in a Harrisburg hospital: "He was born in Harrisburg Hospital and he lived there until 1953." Connie Chung said, "So he's kind of a Yankee. Newt's a Yankee." Mrs. Gingrich whispered "I think so," and Connie Chung whispered back, "But we won't tell anybody." Then Connie Chung played a little "word" game with the Gingriches. She said, "These are some of the things that are said about your son. 'A very dangerous man.'" Mrs. Gingrich said " No." "Visionary," said Chung, and Mrs. Gingrich said "Yeah." Chung said, "Bomb-throwing guerrilla warrior." Mrs. Gingrich said, "No." Chung said, "Abrasive." And Mrs. Gingrich conceded, "That could be." Mrs. Gingrich added, "Especially if you don't like him. Then he becomes very abrasive." Mrs. Gingrich wondered: "Yeah, but who doesn't like him?" Mr. Gingrich commented, "Yeah, right." Chung asked, "Do you think that Bill Clinton and Newt Gingrich can ever become friends?" Mr. Gingrich said, "I don't think so." She asked: "Mrs. Gingrich?" Mrs. Gingrich commented, "I don't think so either." Chung then asked, "What does Newt tell you about President Clinton?" Mr. Gingrich said, "The only thing he ever told me—that he's smart, that he's an intelligent man and he's not very practical, but he is intelligent. That's all he's ever told me." She then asked: "Mrs. Gingrich, what has—what has Newt told you about President Clinton?" Mrs. Gingrich said, " Nothing, and I can't tell you what he said about Hillary." Chung asked, "You can't?" Mrs. Gingrich said: "I can't." Connie Chung then offered, "Why don't you just whisper it to me, just between you and me?" Mrs. Gingrich whispered, "She's a bitch. About the only thing he ever said about her. I think they had some meeting, you know, and she takes over." Chung said, "She does?" Mrs. Gingrich said, "Oh, yeah. Yeah. But when Newtie's there, she can't."

Many people interpreted Chung's suggestion that Ms. Gingrich whisper this statement as a promise the statement would be off the record. When the statement aired, viewers felt Chung had compromised her journalistic integrity. (It has been suggested that CBS, by this time looking to drop Chung from her contract with them, made no defense of the incident.) Ellen Hume, director of the Democracy Project at the Public Broadcasting Service said, "When Connie Chung goads the relatives of a public official [Gingrich] into name calling, it calls into question what is the difference between news, entertainment and propoganda is hard to define."[41] In her article, "The New Paradigm of News," she thought that Chung had crossed the line and as a result, her career was on the wane.

In 2001, after months of silence, Representative Gary Condit, who was under investigation for his possible involvement in the disappearance and murder of Chandra Levy, a young intern in his employ, sat down with Connie Chung for his first television interview since Chandra Levy disappeared. They talked at the congressman's home in Modesto, California. While the congressman was criticized throughout the investigation for behaving in a rigid and defensive manner, Connie's Chung's closed-ended questions made the interview stilted and pointed to a lack of interviewing savvy on the part of Chung. She began by asking Congressman Condit: "Congressman Condit, do you know what happened to Chandra Levy?" Condit replied, "No, I do not." Again, Chung asked a question that could easily be answered with one word: "Did you have anything to do with her disappearance?" The congressman fully answered the question with, "No, I didn't." Once again, Connie Chung asked a closed-ended question: "Did you say anything or do anything that could have caused her to drop out of sight?" Condit responded with: "You know, Chandra and I never had a cross word." This evasive and self-serving response wasn't even an answer to Chung's question, and she never called him on it. If she had, it might have given her an opportunity to break the chain of closed-ended questions. Chung asked another question that produced a short response: "Do you have any idea if there was anyone who wanted to harm her?" He said, "No." Chung asked: "Did you cause anyone to harm her?" Again, Condit said, simply, "No." Finally, Connie Chung asked, "Did you kill Chandra Levy?" To that, Condit said, "I did not." Then Chung got one of the longest answers of the interview from Condit when she asked: "Can you tell us, did you have a romantic relationship with Chandra Levy?" He answered: "Well, once again, I've been married thirty-four years. I have not been a perfect man. I have made mistakes in my life, but out of respect for my family, out of a specific request by the Levy family, it's best that I not get into the details of the relationship." Chung then asked a question that is pure tabloid fodder: "Can you tell me this: Was Chandra Levy in love with you? Were you in love with her?" He responded, "Well, I—I don't know that she was in love with me, she never said so, and I was not in love with her." Questions that really mattered to the viewers were answered with a couple of unemotional words from Congressman Condit. Those things that were irrelevant, such as how long Mr. Condit was married and other issues, were answered in length. Each question that Chung asked began with a verb followed by "you"—two solid indicators that a questions is closed-ended and likely to yield a "yes" or "no" answer.

Invention

Connie Chung describes the great lengths that she has gone to get "the get" in her paper, "The Business of Getting 'The Get': Nailing an Exclusive Interview in Primetime." Less attention is paid to what to do once she has secured the interview. Her interview with Gary Condit is an example of her interviewing skills at the worst since she did nothing with her questioning to allow her subject to expand. Almost as though all of her energy was spent just securing the interview, the fact that she had the golden opportunity to contribute news to a top story eluded her. Her efforts to get other subjects to disclose sensitive information made them angry (Gates, Harding) and her "whisper" request to Mrs. Gingrich was arguably a career breaker. Though intelligent, telegenic, and hardworking, Connie Chung thrived as an anchor and faltered as an interviewer because her questions did not illicit the responses that viewers craved.

Disposition

Connie Chung was condescending in her interview with Tonya Harding when she asked: "Do you realize that the whole world is talking about you now?" Harding said, "I think they're talking about all of the Olympics." Chung said, "You aren't deluding yourself into believing that the world is talking about you because of anything but the controversy, right?" Harding appeared annoyed and said, "I don't understand the question." Chung continued, "People are not—the world is not talking about you because of your figure skating, you know that, don't you?" As Chung continued Harding became increasingly annoyed and announced fifteen minutes into the interview, "I'm done with this." A similar scenario occurred between Chung and Bill Gates when Gates became annoyed with the questioning. Connie Chung does not hold back when she wants to press an interviewee. This idea that she snagged the interview seems enough. She is often abrasive in her questioning or she pulls back completely, as in the case of the Condit interview, and gets nothing of value. In all cases both she and the interviewee look bad.

Style

Connie Chung's typical use of language in her interviews—her rhetorical style—has several characteristics, including questioning whether or not the interviewee is being completely honest with her by asking, "really?" For example, she asked Tonya Harding this follow-up question and also asked it of Bill Gates. It sounds as though she tries to get the interviewee to say that they were less than honest with their first reply. Another example of this is when she questions Harding by asking, "Honestly, you didn't notice?" In addition, she seems to stick to script and is not successful when she is more spontaneous. Instead, her attempt at identification with her guests is more patronizing than effective at getting them to reveal information. Instead, her "just whisper it to me" remark to Mrs. Gingrich and her patronizing question to Tonya Harding, "Are you better off up here. . . ?" revealed a disingenuous nature to viewers that made the audience question whether or not she had compassion for her guests or was just fueling ratings. Connie Chung's style includes a cool and unflappable delivery. Initially in her career, Connie Chung demonstrated a competence that viewers recognized, her no-nonsense, serious delivery of the news gave the network and Connie Chung a certain gravitas. When she appeared in the less serious, magazine, type of news story, her style adapted to the situation; however, many viewers and colleagues thought that she had reduced her credibility. Her ethos was further diluted by her tendency to move from network to network. As a series of controversial questions gave her negative attention, her faithful viewers began to dwindle.

Delivery

Connie Chung usually brings a legal pad with notes and questions prepared for her interviews. When she worked as an anchor, she didn't write stories, but she did edit them to suit her delivery style. Connie Chung cultivated a strong following early in her career and then a series of interviews showed Connie Chung's more aggressive style. This style turned off many viewers, who thought she was rude to her guests, even arrogant.

Conclusion

Connie Chung is an important woman to consider in broadcast news. The early trajectory of her career was a steady rise and she was determined to make a name for herself by getting exclusive interviews. She landed many important interviews, and she became one of the most recognizable faces on television. A series of miscalculated questions on her part and her tendency to move from network to network decreased her viability as a reliable figure in broadcasting.

ELIZABETH VARGAS

Figure 2.2. Elizabeth Vargas

We're way overdue on a woman sitting in one of those Big Three chairs.[42]

It wasn't because she grew up watching the likes of Barbara Walters or Connie Chung that made Elizabeth Vargas want to become a broadcast journalist; her family rarely, if ever, even watched television. Instead, it was her "insatiable curiosity" in the world—fostered by her military father's constant relocating, that made young Elizabeth Vargas, a self-described "army brat" decide that journalism would be her chosen field. She was born to a Puerto Rican father and Irish-American mother; her father was then a colonel in the United States Army. She spent her youth moving from base to base in Germany, Belgium, and Japan. A competitive gymnast, she graduated from an American high school in Heidelberg, Germany. Her mother notes that the "nomad life" served her children well, showing them first hand at a young age that "there's more to the world than the backyard of a small town."[43] Elizabeth Vargas graduated with a Bachelor of Journalism degree from the University of Missouri in Columbia, where she made her debut broadcast as a reporter and anchor for KOMU-TV. The university-owned commercial television station is an NBC affiliate that utilizes its newsroom as a working lab for students. The school's website proudly boasts Elizabeth Vargas of *ABC News* as one of its most accomplished alumni.[44] After that, she spent a year at KTVN-TV, the CBS affiliate in Reno, Nevada, and then moved on to KTVK-TV, the ABC affiliate in Phoenix, Arizona, where she worked from 1986–1989 as a lead reporter. Elizabeth Vargas then spent four years as a reporter and an anchor for WBBM-TV, a CBS affiliate, known as CBS 2 in Chicago. Edward Marshall, a producer at WBBM, said Elizabeth Vargas "really took ownership of a story once she was on it."[45] From Chicago, Vargas went to NBC News in 1993 as a correspondent for the NBC news magazine, *Now with Tom Brokaw and Katie Couric.* For the next three years, she worked as a correspondent and substitute anchor, mostly for *Dateline NBC* and *The Today Show*, and served as a substitute anchor on *NBC Nightly News* on the weekends. After NBC, Vargas made the move to ABC news where she wore many hats, including filling in for Diane Sawyer at *Good Morning America*, anchoring on *Primetime Live*, and filling in for the late Peter Jennings on the evening news. Phyllis McGrady, a senior vice president at ABC, said, "Elizabeth is one of the most flexible talents I've ever worked with. She could do hard interviews, and do hour-long specials that make you think, and then she'll do a great interview with P-Diddy. She is that versatile."[46] In 2001 she married Marc Cohn, whom she met at the 1999 U.S. Open after being introduced by Andre Agassi. In 2003 the couple had their first son, Zachary Raphael Cohn, and in August, 2006, Samuel Wyatt Cohn was born.

Elizabeth Vargas has reported on some of the most controversial stories in recent times, including a 2003 special based on the best seller *The DaVinci Code* and the role of Mary Magdalene, which helped to fuel a national debate. Her provocative questioning on why the Laci Petersen case merited more attention than two other similar cases, one involving a black woman and the other involving an Hispanic woman, drew attention to her journalistic skills. Laci Peterson was the pregnant California woman who was killed by her husband Scott in 2003. "I was really proud of that special; proud that I was able to give these other women their story."[47] The story that has received as much attention as some of her most significant journalism, however, is the one that involves Elizabeth Vargas's abrupt removal from the *ABC World News* anchor chair after her coanchor Bob Woodruff was injured covering the Iraq War and Vargas's pregnancy became complicated. *New York Magazine* described Vargas as "collateral damage" that ABC could afford.[48] Says Vargas of her symbol of how tricky it is for a working mother to perform at a high level on the job:

> The struggle is the same no matter what kind of job you have, and even sometimes [no matter if] you're a mom or dad. But you're right . . . I was the first network news anchor who was the mother of a young child and when I got pregnant, it became overwhelming. . . . When we did make the decision just to anchor *20/20* for now—the debate it ignited took me by surprise. There are a lot of women who think I did the wrong thing and that this is sending the wrong message: that working women aren't as good and can't do it.[49]

In *New York Magazine*, Vargas describes her reaction [to being replaced on ABC News by Charles Gibson] as "complicated," but says her pregnancy had caused her to reevaluate her life and career. "I hope I get another chance to do this job, maybe at another time," she adds. "It doesn't mean it might not work out in a few years."[50]

In December, 2005, ABC News President David Westin announced that the anchor team of Elizabeth Vargas and Bob Woodruff would replace the late anchor Peter Jennings at *World News Tonight* because "you need more than one anchor. One person can't do all of this."[51] At that time ABC also noted that *World News Tonight* would be the first network evening newscast to broadcast live for three different time zones—Eastern, Mountain, and Pacific. Its anchors would travel frequently to the site of major news and update stories during the day on the Internet and for cell phone users. The pairing made Elizabeth Vargas the first network news anchor of Hispanic heritage. On her new position as anchor, Vargas said, "I'm so proud. I know what this means to Hispanics in this country . . . to have people who look like you and talk like you in positions of importance."[52] The idea behind the dual anchor team echoed the pairing of Chung and Rather, in that ABC intended to have one anchor on the scene covering a major story while the other anchor would stay in the studio and report the evening news. A difference, though, is that the Vargas-Woodruff pairing was more egalitarian than the Rather-Chung pairing, since it was clear that Rather would be out covering the stories and Chung's role was always to be the one "anchored" to the desk. On one of Woodruff's "on the scene" reporting duties—in war torn Iraq— he was gravely injured, less than one month into his coanchoring paring with Vargas. This made Elizabeth Vargas the first de facto solo woman evening news anchor, since after Woodruff's injury she anchored almost every broadcast alone, albeit for a brief period she coanchored the evening news with either Charlie Gibson or Diane Sawyer. Her tenure as coanchor of *World News Tonight* was brief, just January through May, 2006, though her impact and importance in the world of network news was made.

Vargas as Coanchor

The morning of their inaugural telecast as coanchors on January 3, 2006, Bob Woodruff and Elizabeth Vargas appeared on Good Morning America. Woodruff reported from Iran: " You know, this is what you'll be seeing a lot more of. My trip here to Iran, Elizabeth Vargas's reporting last month from Iraq, are examples of what we hope to do. One or both of us will be on the road quite often. We want to dig deep into the issues that may not get attention they otherwise deserve. We also want to get to where the big stories are breaking. We'll be up close, reporting, connecting viewers to the world because there's nothing quite like being at the heart of the story just as it unfolds. It is certainly the place to be. Back to you guys." Diane Sawyer noted, "So, Bob, out in the field tonight. And among other things, you have two, not one, but two new live feeds to the West Coast broadcasts? How does that work?" Elizabeth Vargas said, "Yes, we do. You know, for years all three networks have just ignored the, the West Coast viewers. You are often live to the West Coast, but the evening newscasts rarely are. So, we're going to begin, you know, many of our viewers on the West Coast have complained that they would see news on their local news that was more up-to-date than what, what they were seeing on the network news. So we finally decided to do live shows to the West Coast. So that involves two different time zones. So, it will be one live at nine, 8:30, and then, again at 9:30 East Coast time." Charlie Gibson asked: "And it will be different to the West Coast?" Elizabeth explained: "Sometimes it will be. A great example of this was when the Patriot Act was renewed for another five weeks. And this happened after we all went home for the day, the week before Christmas. We updated the West Coast version of *World News Tonight*, but if we had actually had a chance we would have redone the broadcast. That was a significant political development. We would have covered the story differently than we had just in updating it."

One of the most provocative stories Elizabeth Vargas reported was the controversy behind the blockbuster best-selling book, *The DaVinci Code*. In her serious, intelligent voice she previewed her story: "There is a legend that sometime in the first century, just after the death of Jesus, a boat full of refugees from the Holy Land arrived in the south of France. The story says the group included some of the closest followers of Jesus, Lazarus, whom Jesus had raised from the dead, and the repentant prostitute named Mary Magdalene." She then asked her viewers: "But what if we told you there was more to the story? What if we told you that some people think Mary Magdalene was not a repentant prostitute but instead Jesus's wife? That she bore his child? That the truth was suppressed by the church but handed down through a secret society whose most famous member was Leonardo Da Vinci? And that Leonardo encoded the truth in some of his most famous paintings?" Her reporting on the story took her to southern France, England, Italy, and Jerusalem. She interviewed Dan Brown, the author of *The DaVinci Code*, as well as scholars such as Father Richard McBrien of the University of Notre Dame, Elaine Pagels of Princeton University, Jack Wasserman of Temple University, and Henry Lincoln.

Even her parents felt unsettled by her delving into the topic of *The DaVinci Code*. Vargas felt that her story was important and she pressed on: "*The DaVinci Code* was selling millions of copies. People were reading about what the church had done to Mary Magdalene, describing her as a prostitute from the year 400 to 1960."[53] A week after her story aired, *Newsweek* followed with a similar analysis of *The DaVinci Code*. "It was a risky thing to do, but I was proud of that show because we sparked a debate on religion."[54]

Elizabeth Vargas revisited the Holy Land in 2005 during a *20/20* special where, once again, she spoke with scholars, writers, and theologians about the mystery at the heart of the Christian faith. "These are topics that are near and dear to people. I think there's nothing better in the world than a spirited discussion about the Bible and Jesus and God and the Catholic faith, or the Jewish faith, or the Muslim faith—any religion."[55]

In 2004 Vargas drew praise from *New York Times* writer Virginia Heffernan, who described Vargas's *20/20* story on the killing of Matthew Shepard in 1998 as "intellectually brave."[56] In October 1998, Mr. Shepard, a twenty-one-year-old student at the University of Wyoming in Laramie, was found tied to a fence on the outskirts of town. He had been pistol-whipped and left shoeless in near-freezing temperatures and was left for dead. A few days later he died, and his funeral drew media from around the world who told the same story: Matthew Shepard was killed because he was gay. Elizabeth Vargas's notable interviewing skills were evident in her pointed questions of Shepard's killer: "Did you kill Matthew Shepard because he was gay?" Aaron McKinney said, "No, I did not." Elizabeth Vargas isn't afraid to put her subjects on the spot. When she asked one of the experts on her show about two other women missing under similar circumstances to Laci Peterson why Peterson got such a disproportionate amount of media attention, he said: "Laci Peterson was a beautiful, attractive, white, well-off girl who disappeared."[57]

Invention

Elizabeth Vargas's insatiable curiosity is evident in how she interviews her subjects. Though always polite, she doesn't hesitate to ask the most pointed questions that will get her interviewees to reveal significant reasons why something happened. Almost as though she is seeking stories that will get the audience talking about the most provocative subjects, such as antigay sentiment, religion, discrimination, and more hot-button topics interest her. She researches deep topics even deeper than they have been researched. Her special on the book *The DaVinci Code* reinvigorated the debate about the role of women in the Catholic church. Her logos, or logical argument, is evident in her quoting of experts who have studied the Bible and hold various views on the meaning in it. Her daring expose on the death of Matthew Shepard told a part of that story that wasn't told before as she courageously suggested that the media got the story wrong the first time. Again her logical proof—this time the personal experiences of those who knew Shepard—strengthened her thesis of the story. Her questions are tough and sharp, yet calm, measured, and polite. They reveal the level of research that has been done on the story. For example, in 2001 her interview with the owners of two vicious dogs charged in the death of a San Francisco neighbor, defendant Marjorie Knoller, appeared arrogant and remorseless as Vargas pressed her for answers. She asked, "Can you understand why people might say you were unable to control this large dog, larger than the victim? The victim is dead after a several-minutes-long attack?" The interview was shown by the prosecution repeatedly during their trial and the family of the victim credited Vargas with helping to convict Knoller of the murder.[58] Another example is her interview with Steve Thomas, the lead detective in the JonBenét Ramsey murder investigation. JonBenét Ramsey, a six-year-old daughter of prominent Boulder, Colorado, businessman John Ramsey and his wife, Patsy Ramsey, was found brutally murdered on Christmas Day, 1996, in their stately home. Vargas asks the detective: "Do you think Patsy Ramsey killed her daughter?" Thomas replied, "I do. People want to have this inherent belief that a parent cannot do something like this, that some three-eyed, six-fingered, stub-footed, intruder came—some monster came in the house and did this." Vargas follows up: "What makes you believe that Patsy Ramsey is a killer?"[59]

Disposition

Elizabeth Vargas's questions have always been specific and well considered. Her research for the topics she has presented is obvious. For example, her research on the history of the Christian faith is evident in the story she presented for *Primetime Live* on *The DaVinci Code*. She remarks about Leonardo DaVinci: "The little we know comes mostly from notebooks he began writing at the age of thirty. Thousands of pages covered with his reversed left-handed script . . . he believed that men could find a way to fly, five centuries before the invention of the airplane." She asks Dan Brown, "And you think this is the kind of man who would hide information in his paintings?" Dan Brown says, "Absolutely, because he was living at a time when this information, you couldn't just stand on a street corner and proclaim how you felt on a topic that way contrary to the church." This interview continues to raise contradiction to Dan Brown's view as Vargas gathers the opinions of several theologians and scholars. This type of in-depth, detailed, research-heavy reporting is typical of Vargas's career.

Another example of her keen questioning came when she covered the Elian Gonzalez story. She asks the reporter on the scene whether or not President Clinton anticipated that the "enforcement action would be as stunning and aggressive as it was."[60]

Style

Elizabeth Vargas's typical use of language in her interviews—her rhetorical style—has several characteristics, including her use of direct and sustained eye contact and pointed, specific questions. She doesn't take as much time to "warm up" to a subject, instead, she gets right to the most salient issue of the interview. She directly confronts the author of a book about the JonBenét Ramsey murder and asks, "what makes you believe that Patsy Ramsey is a killer?" Notice that she requests specific evidence versus a more vague question such as "Why do you think Patsy Ramsey killed her daughter?" Her style of questioning is almost confrontational, yet her delivery, which is calm and measured, suggests an earnest curiosity that solicits an earnest reply. Her forceful and robust use of questioning assists in the development of the thesis that she puts forward in her stories.

Delivery

Elizabeth Vargas's delivery helps to maintain her ethos as a news anchor. Although English is her first language, she speaks fluent Spanish. Her delivery is authoritative and she modulates her voice to help sustain interest in her stories. Her passion for her investigative stories is conveyed through her facial expressions of curiosity and concern about her topics.

Conclusion

Elizabeth Vargas became one of the few women to hold the coveted position of network news anchor in the United States. Her intelligence, drive, and experience served her well. The "insatiable curiosity" fostered by her travels as a young girl were requisite for her career in broadcasting and aided her rise to the top of the field. As one of her former editors noted, Vargas "did everything well. She's a good writer, live reporter and anchor."[61] As she continues as a correspondent for ABC we may likely see her role expand because of her deft reporting and compatibility with viewers.

NOTES

1. Connie Chung, "The Business of Getting the 'Get': Nailing an Exclusive Interview in Prime Time," The Joan Shorenstein Center for Press, Politics and Public Policy, Discussion Paper D-28, April 1998.

2. Judith Marlane, Women in Television News Revisited (Austin: University of Texas Press, 1999), 116–17.

3. David Bauder, "Chung-Condit Interview Lures Viewers to ABC," *The Milwaukee Journal-Sentinel*, August 30, 2001.

4. Mary Malone, *Connie Chung: Broadcast Journalist* (Hillside, New Jersey: Enslow Publishers, 1992), 48.

5. Timothy Crouse, *The Boys on the Bus: Riding with the Campaign Press Corps* (New York: Random House, 1972), 15–16.

6. Malone, *Connie Chung*, 36.

7. Bob Schieffer, *This Just In: What I Couldn't Tell You on TV* (New York, NY: G. Putnam and Sons, 2003), 122.

8. Ibid., 13.

9. Ibid., 14.

10. Ibid., 15.

11. Ibid., 23.

12. Craig M. Allen, *News Is People: The Rise of Local TV News and the Fall of News from New York* (Ames, Iowa: Iowa State University Press, 2001), 198.

13. Ibid., 75–76.

14. Ibid., 80.

15. Tom Shales, "Connie Chung, Stressing The Obvious," *The Washington Post*, April 25, 1988, B1.

16. Ibid.

17. Malone, *Connie Chung*, 96.

18. Gail Shister, "Chung and Rather—A Surprise TV Pairing," *Philadelphia Inquirer*, May 18, 1993, F1.

19. Peter Johnson, *"CBS's Big Gamble—News Head Ober Defends Anchor Team,"* *USA Today*, November 29, 1993, 1D.

20. "Adding Chung Not a Ratings Ploy, Rather Says," *Pittsburgh Post-Gazette*, May 18, 1993, D7.

21. Bill Carter, "Chung to Join Rather as CBS News Anchor," *New York Times*, May 18, 1993, C18.

22. Ibid.

23. CBS news transcripts, June 1, 1993, CBS Evening News, 6:30 p.m., www.lexisnexis@prod.lexisnexis.com (accessed November 12, 2006).

24. CBS news transcripts, *CBS This Morning*, June 2, 1993, www.lexisnexis.com (accessed November 12, 2006).

25. Tom Feran, "Chung and Rather: A Team on the Go," *Plain Dealer* (Cleveland, Ohio), July 20, 1993, 13C.

26. Johnson, "CBS's big gamble," *USA Today*, November 29, 1993, 1D.

27. Feran, "Chung and Rather," 13C.

28. Peter Johnson, "Viewer Slide Spills onto CBS' Rather-Chung Team," *USA Today*, August 3, 1994, 3D.

29. Steven Yandell, "Caring in the Midst of a Crisis," *Dynamic Chiropractic*, May 22, 1995, Vol. 13, Issue 11.

30. "Connie Chung Joins CNN," *People's Daily* (Beijing), January 24, 2002, http://english.peopledaily.com.cnn (accessed November 8, 2006).

31. Richard Huff, "Chung Done at CNN as Network Pulls Show," *Daily News* (New York), March 26, 2003, 98.

32. Caroline Wilbert, "Connie Chung Show Canceled: Veteran Anchor to Leave CNN," *The Atlanta Journal-Constitution*, March 26, 2003, 1D.

33. Scott Collins, "Chung Quits after Show Cancelled," *The San Diego Union Tribune*, March 27, 2003, E-7.

34. "Chung and Povich, On Screen and Off," *St. Louis Post-Dispatch* (Missouri), November 9, 2005, E6.

35. Amy Sara Clark, "Connie Chung's Serenade Gag a Web Hit," June 20, 2006, http://www.cbsnews.com/stories/2006/06/20/entertainment/main1736320.shtml (accessed November 12, 2006).

36. *CBS This Morning*, June 17, 1993, "Connie Chung Talks About Her Program's Debut and Her Chat with Roger Clinton."

37. Matt Roush, "Bleary Opening for Chung's 'Eye to Eye,'" *USA Today*, June 17, 1993, 3D.

38. Ibid.

39. *Eye to Eye with Connie Chung*, February 10, 1994, "Olympic Hopeful Tonya Harding Speaks Out; Hard Evidence Explained; World Reaction Examined."

40. CBS news transcripts, *Eye to Eye with Connie Chung*, May 19, 1994, "Bill Dollar Bill; Microsoft's William Gates Discusses His Life and Business."

41. Ellen Hume, "The New Paradigm of News," *Annals of the American Academy of Political and Social Science*, Vol. 546 (July 1996), pp. 141–53.

42. Joe Hagan, "ABC News' Vargas Girl Asks: Why So Few Women in Prime Time?" *New York Observer*, December 12, 2004, http://www.observer.com/node/50209 (accessed September 23, 2007).

43. Elinor J. Brecher, "Elizabeth Vargas: Tuning in at the Top," *Puerto Rico Herald*, June, 2002, www.puertorico-herald.org/issues/2002.vol6n24 (accessed November 15, 2006).

44. http://www.komu.com/satellite/SatelliteRender/KOMU.com/ (accessed December 7, 2006).

45. Brecher, "Elizabeth Vargas," *Puerto Rico Herald*.

46. Liz Liorente, "Talent, Versatility, Class: ABC New Personality Elizabeth Vargas Finds Balance as a Mother, a Wife and a Super-Journalist," *Hispanic Magazine*, December, 2004, www.hispanicmagazine.com (accessed December 12, 2006).

47. Ibid.

48. Joe Hagan, "Charlie the Conquerer," *New York Magazine*, June 19, 2006, http://nymag.com/news/media/17255/index.html (accessed December 17, 2006).

49. "Year of the Mother: Elizabeth Vargas Sees *20/20* When it Comes to Career and Family," TVGuide.com, November 16, 2006, www.tvguide.com (accessed December 12, 2006).

50. Hagan, "Charlie the Conquerer," *New York Magazine*,.

51. "Vargas, Woodruff to Share Anchor Desk at ABC," MSNBC.com, December 9, 2005, www.msnbc.com/id/10335483 (accessed November 15, 2006).

52. Ibid.

53. Liorente, "Talent, Versatility, Class," *Hispanic Magazine*.

54. Ibid.

55. Ibid.

56. Virginia Heffernan, "Was Killing of Shepard an Anti-Gay Hate Crime?" *The New York Times*, November 26, 2004, E, 34.

57. Liorente, "Talent, Versatility, Class," *Hispanic Magazine*.

58. Brecher, "Elizabeth Vargas," *Puerto Rico Herald*.

59. *20/20*, April 12, 2000, "Who Killed JonBenét? Former Lead Detective of the JonBenét Ramsey Murder Investigation Believes Patsy Ramsey is the Murderer," ABC News.

60. ABC news transcripts, "Elian Gonzalez Successfully Reunited with His Father; President Clinton Comments; Live Coverage Continues of Protestors and Rioters in Miami," ABC News Special Report: Elian Gonzalez, April 22, 2000.

61. Brecher, "Elizabeth Vargas," *Puerto Rico Herald*.

4

THE WORLDLY WONDER

Christiane Amanpour

Figure 3.1. Christiane Amanpour

Remember the movie *Field of Dreams* when the voice said, "Build it and they will come." Well somehow that dumb statement has always stuck in my mind. And I always say, "If you tell a compelling story, they will watch."[1]

What was Osama bin Laden like as a teenager as he played soccer in his neighborhood? When, how, and why did Osama bin Laden became more and more of a religious fundamentalist, a holy warrior, and then an extremist? And why, although he was born the son of a billionaire, did he choose a life of austerity and adopt a mission to kill?

These provocative revelations about the elusive Osama bin Laden were made during the CNN program, "In the Footsteps of bin Laden," hosted and reported by Christiane Amanpour. The two-hour program, which was a year in the making, was produced in conjunction with the book, *The Osama bin Laden I Know*, by CNN terrorist analyst Peter Bergen. For this production, Christiane Amanpour traveled to ten nations on four continents to get a better, more intimate picture of the world's most wanted man.[2] This intensive and cerebral news program told much about Osama bin Laden, the "quiet boy" who became the "angry voice of the holy war,"[3] but also revealed the depth and experience of the reporter, Christiane Amanpour, who is known for her expertise and daring in covering world events. As the world has become increasingly dangerous and complex, Amanpour's profile has been raised and devoted CNN viewers have come to expect intellectual, educational journalism from this world-class correspondent. Her impact on covering world events has had what media scholar Todd Gitlin has described as having "omniscience, and having the need to become the viewers' earliest and best source of information."[4] Indeed, when something of global magnitude occurs, many viewers have come to expect to see Christiane Amanpour on the scene telling the story. Oprah Winfrey told her: "You are the international spokesperson, you're the most known international reporter there is. You know that all of the good guys and the bad guys are watching you. I hear a lot of the troops watch CNN to see where they're going to be deployed next by seeing where you are."[5] True that *The New York Times* coined the phrase that sums up her career: "Where There's War, There's Amanpour."[6] The *Washington Post* noted that "Amanpour, with her near continuous coverage on CNN's world-wide beam, is a special concern. A determined reporter with a nose for death and destruction, Amanpour figures in the worst nightmares of generals and diplomats alike."[7] Her unique background suggests an unusual and specialized training—some from birthright and some from her education—both which have prepared her exquisitely for the custom career in journalism she has created for herself.

Although many of the highest paid and famous broadcast journalists have incorporated infotainment into their careers, Christiane Amanpour conspicuously has not. Her reports as CNN's Senior International Correspondent are robust, intellectual, and important. Reese Schonfeld, CNN's first president, said that CNN's news coverage "has become worldwide and skin-deep . . . its coverage splashes over everything and saturates nothing."[8] This could not be further from the type of reporting that Christiane Amanpour has brought to CNN. Though certainly "worldwide," her serious, in-depth coverage in the world's most dangerous places is what has made Christiane Amanpour stand out in a world of television broadcasting that often glosses over instead of penetrating. Another vast difference in Amanpour's style of journalism from that of others is her missionary zeal for the complex stories she tells. Christiane Amanpour feels that she doesn't have an option. "The politically correct thing is to say that it's not a journalist's role to be an advocate, to have an agenda, to agitate on behalf of any kind of political position. But in my work, basic matters of life and death are on the table—whether it's genocide in Africa and the Balkans or violations of human rights. I'm not just a stenographer or someone with a megaphone; when I report, I have to do it in context, to be aware of the moral conundrum. If I'm talking about genocide, for instance, I have to be able to draw a line between victim and aggressor. It would be irresponsible of me and CNN to tell you what the person being gang-raped says, what the rapist says—and to give each equal time and moral equivalence. I can't do that because it means being neutral in the face of unspeakable horror. When you're neutral, you're an accessory."[9]

Christiane Amanpour was born in London in 1958, the oldest of four daughters. Her father, Mohamed, was an Iranian Muslim airline executive; her mother, Patricia, a British Catholic housewife. Before she was one year old, the family moved to Tehran where they enjoyed an affluent lifestyle that included Arabian horse racing and vacations in Switzerland. Her comfortable lifestyle was in place until the Shah was deposed in 1979. The Islamic awakening that occurred in 1979 impacted young Christiane's family. Her cousins fought on the front line in the Iran–Iraq War. Her uncle, who was the director of the military police hospital, was arrested and died in jail.[10] As commencement speaker in 2006, she described some of her biography for University of Michigan graduates:

I came from what you might call a privileged background. I grew up in Iran very comfortably, very safely, surrounded by a warm and loving family, fabulous friends, great schools and great fun. And then, when I was about twenty, a revolution hit my country and overnight we were strangers in our own homeland. We lost everything . . . home, possessions and people. We watched in horror as our friends and family members were arrested, jailed, tortured and some even executed. My world and my worldview turned upside down. But I quickly decided to turn loss and failure into my driving force. And I would say, never be afraid of failure or loss. Use it.[11]

She amplified those sentiments when she declared: "The revolution was the best thing that ever happened to me,"[12] maybe because it forced her out of her comfortable life. The historic changes were preparing the young future journalist in a way that no career booklet could possibly describe. Her family fled the fundamentalist revolution and resettled in London. "I knew I wanted to be at the center of important international events and I wanted to record them. The best way, I thought, was through journalism."[13] Christiane moved to America to study journalism at the University of Rhode Island, where she was elected to the Phi Beta Kappa and graduated summa cum laude. Amanpour started her professional career as a reporter, anchor, and producer for WBRU-Radio in Providence and then became an electronics graphics producer for NBC affiliate WJAR in Providence.

Christiane Amanpour had an edge over other journalism school graduates since the history lessons she was offering her audience weren't just those she had read about in books; indeed she had lived many of them. She reflects on the events that changed her life and the lives of so many others, including Osama bin Laden's, in the program, *In the Footsteps of bin Laden*. In her self-assured, deep, and distinctive tone she dramatically declares: "In 1979 Ayatollah Khomeini overthrew the Shah of Iran and Americans were taken hostage at the American embassy; the Grand Mosque in Mecca was seized and Saudi government sent in troops; and the Soviet Union invaded Afghanistan. One year; three monumental events that would change bin Laden forever. The once shy boy would enter the world of the Jihad, and he would never look back again."[14] She notes, "The story of militant Islamic fundamentalism, which led to bin Laden's ascendancy, did not begin with September 11, 2001. The beginnings can be traced to the late 1970s. Our family witnessed the beginning of Islamic fundamental politics during the takeover of the U.S. embassy in Tehran. That's when fundamentalist Islam awoke as a movement in the Middle East. The entire world is feeling its shock waves today."[15]

This in-depth, scholarly look at the world of Islam and the life of Osama bin Laden is representative of the kind of hefty programs that Christiane Amanpour has built her reputation upon. Edward R. Murrow told us that the television could be used to educate, and Christiane Amanpour's television career has exemplified this. Instead of entertainment-oriented, image-conscious journalism, which has become standard fare on television in the age of the sound bite, Christiane Amanpour's reports are narrative, and often lengthy. She unfolds the stories she tells in provocative ways that invite the audience to learn about events that are impacting the world in the most important ways. For example, shortly after the terrorist attacks on the

United States on September 11, 2001, Christiane Amanpour hosted a special presentation called "An In-Depth Look at Islam." In this program, she served as teacher for many Americans who did not understand Islam and the rationale behind the attacks on the United States. In her trademark intense and dramaturgic tone, Christiane Amanpour tried to describe life for Islams to her American audience: "Extreme like the Taliban regime that includes a ban on television, music and keeps women hostage in their own homes." She asks provocative questions for which many viewers want to know answers: "Islam forbids suicide, so how does Islam rationalize suicide missions?"[16] In her favored style of dress, a safari-style jacket and her raven, shoulder length, often unkempt hair, Christiane Amanpour describes what the Koran, the holy book of Islam, says about violence: "Like the Bible, it's a book of both compassion and vengeance. For example, one verse says, slay the idolaters wherever you find them, and take them captive and besiege them, and lie in wait for them in every ambush." She also explains that "The Koran also teaches tolerance of other religions. It includes some of the same teachings as Abraham, Moses and Jesus, a belief in one God, the creator— in this case, Allah."[17]

Christiane Amanpour first appeared in American homes as an international correspondent during the Gulf War in the early 1990s. Since then she has been a key conduit between millions of Americans safe in our homes and the war torn areas around the globe. "In TV, she's the best. She knows what she wants and how to get it," said Walter Rodgers, one of her CNN colleagues.[18] Interviewing presidents and prime ministers have become regular assignments for Amanpour, although she describes how she chose to apply to the fledgling (it was only three years old) CNN and how arbitrarily she was put on the international desk at CNN when she first arrived in the early 1980s. "My friends [at the local television station in Rhode Island] said that they had heard English accents on CNN and suggested I check it out."[19] She was hired over the phone to work for CNN and "because I am foreign I was assigned to the foreign desk. I kid you not, it's true. I was really just the tea boy to begin with, or the equivalent thereof, but I quickly announced, innocently but very ambitiously, that I wanted to be, I was going to be, a foreign correspondent."[20] Ed Turner, a CNN vice president (no relation to Ted Turner) remembers Amanpour's determined spirit when he met her. "I tried to dissuade her and tell her gently that it didn't seem to be in the cards [for Amanpour to become a foreign correspondent]. She just looked at me and gave me this Henry Higgins answer: 'You just wait, Ed Turner, you just wait.'"[21] She earnestly built her own launching pad by coming in on weekends to practice scriptwriting and paying her own way to the 1984 Democratic National Convention to help with the coverage. In 1986 she was promoted to producer-correspondent in the New York Bureau. Less than a decade after she started at CNN, she had become a presence in the homes of Americans who wanted to learn more about what was going on around the world, and in particular what was happening during the Persian Gulf War in 1990–1991. "In the spring of 1990, when a slot opened up in the Frankfurt bureau and no established correspondent claimed it, she grabbed it. The day the Iraqi Army invaded Kuwait, August 2, 1990, Amanpour immediately volunteered for that assignment. She arrived in Dubai with a week's worth of clothes and ended up staying five months.[22] In her 2006 University of Michigan commencement speech, she reflected on her early career days at CNN:

> I loved joining that new, upstart channel back then, CNN, for my first ever bottom-of-the-rung job. It was twenty-three years ago. I traveled down to headquarters in Atlanta with my bicycle, with my suitcase and $100. I came in on weekends and I worked nights to practice, practice, practice and to plow my way up to being what I wanted to be. . . . a foreign correspondent roaming the world, telling stories on somebody else's dime, taking risks and having fun doing it. To do it, I had to lose the ability to hear the word "no." "No," as in, "Your name is too unpronounceable to be on television. No, your hair is black, for heaven's sake, and very unruly. Don't you know that you have to be blonde to make it on television here. No, you've got a foreign accent. No, you can't say that." I still hear that sometimes and I'm still a little hard of hearing. You, too, may have to battle "Fortress No," and you will have to go a little deaf sometimes. But I was thrilled with the way it turned out eventually and I soon knew that I was in a position of unique privilege. But I started to understand that position was also one of unique responsibility. I began to ask, "Why am I doing this. What is the platform for? What am I doing with it? What should we be doing with it?"[23]

In 1996 she became the first broadcast journalist to begin work simultaneously for two major networks. She was also under contract to CBS where she worked as a *60 Minutes* correspondent for occasional stories.[24] Her debut story on *60 Minutes* was about the women of Kabul, especially the doctors, teachers, and other professionals who have been consigned to domesticity in accord with Taliban doctrine. Ms. Amanpour delivered a quick, pointed history of the still mysterious Taliban. By her account, the young fighters, who seemed to descend from nowhere "armed with the Koran and the Kalashnikov," are the spawn of endless war in their country. Indoctrinated and trained in Pakistan, they are determined to impose what they deem to be the laws and punishments of Islam.[25] Though critics responded favorably to her substantial reports, her contract with *60 Minutes* expired in 2005, and she did not renew it.[26]

Her passion to cover the world makes her job more of a mission than a way to earn a paycheck. About the dangers of being a war correspondent, and why she has distinguished herself, she said, "I think I have an impact, because I'm a woman doing what is ostensibly a man's job, going to war and I really mean going to war. When we go out, we go to the front, we stay for lengthy times on a story. I think I've covered Bosnia, for instance, much longer than any soldier is deployed there."[27]

Her ability to win interviews with heads of states suggests an intimate communication advantage. Fraser and Brown[28] extend Burke's theory of identification to include the relationships that media viewers reconstruct with celebrities. This study extends that theory to include the identification that celebrities and heads of state make with celebrity interviewers, and Christiane Amanpour has gained a profile as an international correspondent with notoriety that is on par with the celebrity of the heads of states whom she interviews. Further, her Middle Eastern and British heritage make her a comfortable choice for those leaders who hail from the parts of the world where she knows intimately from her British and Iranian heritage. Also having lived in America, she has a full understanding of American sensibilities.

In May, 1994, President Bill Clinton participated in a global forum organized by CNN, which featured 160 foreign journalists inside the Carter Center in Atlanta, Georgia, and satellites piping to the wide-screen TV onstage the questions from journalists planted in four cities: Sarajevo; Johannesburg, South Africa; Jerusalem; and Seoul, Korea.[29] Christiane Amanpour, who participated by satellite from Sarajevo, asked a pointed question of the president: "Mr. President, it is a privilege to address you from Sarajevo. You tonight just said that Bosnia was just a humanitarian catastrophe. Surely, sir, you would agree it is so much more than that, a fundamental question of international law and order. You also said that it is clearly in your national interest, the U.S. national interest. So my question is, as leader of the free world, as leader of the only superpower, why has it taken you, the United States, so long to articulate a policy on Bosnia? Why, in the absence of a policy, have you allowed the United States and the West to be held hostage to those who do have a policy—the Bosnian Serbs—and do you not think that the constant flip-flops of your administration on the issue of Bosnia set a very dangerous precedent and would lead people such as Kim Il Sung or other strong people to take you less seriously than you would like to be taken?" Looking visibly upset by Amanpour's question, Clinton stared directly into the screen featuring Amanpour and snapped back, "No, but speeches like that may make them take me less seriously than I'd like to be taken." He stiffened his jaw and added, "There have been no 'constant flip-flops,' madam." Amanpour did not have a chance to respond, since the next question was taken from another journalist. At the end of the program, Clinton returned to what Amanpour had initiated: "I was waiting for my lecture from Sarajevo tonight, and I rather enjoyed it," he said. "That poor woman has seen the horrors of this war, and she has had to report on them." The moderator, Judy Woodruff, clarified to whom he was referring when she interjected, "Christiane Amanpour." Clinton responded, "Yeah, she's been fabulous. She's done a great service to the whole world on that. I do not blame her for being mad at me. But I'm doing the best I can on this problem from my perspective." The audience erupted into applause. Clinton added, when he saw Christiane Amanpour's image on the screen. "I didn't know I would have to look at her; you now blush." The audience burst into laughter. Clinton said, "Anyway, go ahead." On the monitor, Amanpour bundled again in the predawn Sarajevo chill, smiled and shook her head without a verbal response.[30] Judy Woodruff summed up the program by saying, "That's a good note to end on. Thank you very much, Mr. President. Clinton said, "Thank you very much, all of you. Thank you." Woodruff concluded, "On behalf of CNN, goodnight."[31]

President Clinton felt obligated to bring up Christiane Amanpour's question at the end of the program. "The nervousness with which Western officials talk about CNN's star [Amanpour] is a reminder of the fact that two very different wars are being fought around the former Yugoslavia. The media savvy President Clinton may have known all too well what The Washington Post conjectured in its article titled "The Amanpour Factor": "There is the war in Bosnia itself, a messy, tragic war, in which tens of thousands of people have been killed and hundreds of thousands driven from their homes. And then there is the war for Western public opinion."[32] President Clinton acknowledged Christiane Amanpour because he knew she wasn't just any reporter asking a question. She is, The Washington Post described, "the worst nightmare of generals and diplomats alike," since she "shows up and shows it all on CNN."[33] President Clinton felt it important to his image and the credibility of his administration to acknowledge Amanpour's influence, gained mostly from her coverage in Bosnia. "While many other print and television reporters have distinguished themselves in Bosnia, no one has achieved the visibility of Amanpour. Her reports are beamed to Serb militia leaders, Pentagon generals, NATO bureaucrats and U.S. marines sitting on warships in the Atlantic."[34] "She is a particular obsession with the

military," said one Pentagon planner. "We routinely sit around and try to figure out how to react when she shows up at the scene of some tragedy."[35]

In 2006 she reflected on why she sees her profession as a mission:

> A much more experienced colleague said to me when we were covering the
> first Gulf war in 1990 . . . sixteen years ago . . . you graduates were probably
> about six years old then . . . he said to me, "Christiane, you have to find your
> voice." I didn't really understand what he meant then, but two years ago I
> found my voice in Bosnia. I had landed in the middle of the worst bloodlet-
> ting in Europe since World War Two, and in the age of "never again," in cities
> like Sarajevo and Srebrenica, slaughter was committed in broad daylight for
> all of us to see. The carnage could have left me speechless. Instead, that is
> where I found my voice and so did many of my colleagues, not only as re-
> porters, but as citizens of the world.
>
> When our world leaders wanted to shrug away and call it a terrible civil war
> for which all sides were equally guilty, we said, "No." Genocide against Mus-
> lims in Europe was being committed and this had to be stopped. For me, to
> this day, it remains the proudest achievement of my generation of journalists
> and I know my colleagues at the time feel the same way . . . that we played a
> small part in making our leaders confront the reality of what happened there
> and hopefully of finally causing them to intervene and stop it. And it is an in-
> tervention that has worked.[36]

In 1998 she interviewed Iranian President Mohammad Khatami. She
bagan: "Mr. President, a month ago you announced that you had a historic
message to deliver to the people of America. I understand that message will
take the form of a short address and then we'll discuss the issues." President
Khatami then presented a brief message stating his feelings about America
and his respect for the American people. Then, Christiane Amanpour
asked: "If you were provided with the proof that an Iranian official had used
any kind of Iranian funds to reward or finance any group or individual that
was involved in an act of terrorism, would you punish that person or that organization?" President Khatami said: "Certainly if I learn of any instance of
such assistance to terrorism, I shall deal with it, so will our Leader, and so
will our entire system. At the same time, supporting peoples who fight for
the liberation of their land is not, in my opinion, supporting terrorism. It is,
in fact, supporting those who are engaged in combating state terrorism."
Christiane Amanpour: "Regardless of the motive, do you believe that killing
innocent women and children is terrorism, as for instance what happens on
the streets of Israel?" The President stated: "It is definitely so. Any form of
killing of innocent men and women who are not involved in confrontations
is terrorism; it must be condemned, and we, in our term, condemn every

form of it in the world." Christiane Amanpour noted: "Americans say that they have reports that Iranian officials abroad regularly engage in acts of surveillance against Americans, the sort of surveillance that could be interpreted as preceding an attack. Do you think that is appropriate?" President Khatami said: "I deny this categorically. On our part there has been no new move, no special measures with regard to the United States in external fields; this is another false rumor spread by those who bear a grudge against us."[37] In September, 2005 Amanpour landed an interview with Iranian president Mahmoud Ahmadinejan, which she points out remains his only television interview with a Western news organization.[38]

From interviewing heads of state to putting herself in the middle of a war zone, Amanpour's contribution to journalism has been substantial. She comments on why she puts herself in harm's way: "I have a huge passion, and I really believe in this. I don't want to allow this to become an endangered species and to contribute to the endangerment of my species, which is the serious coverage of international events. The notion that Americans do not know what goes on around the world, particularly in places where they are deeply involved, is just an unacceptable notion to me."[39] More humorously she notes, "It's like being a doctor. If you are going to scream every time you see blood, you are not going to be able to do your job."[40]

In 1998, she married James Rubin, who at the time was spokesman for the United States State Department. A son, Darius John Rubin, was born in the year 2000. The family resides in London where Rubin works for Sky TV.

Because of her unique assignment in the world of journalism, Christiane Amanpour is a frequent speaker at forums throughout the world. She speaks about her passion for good journalism and publicly eschews the flashier, entertainment style of journalism that has become popular. In September, 2000, Amanpour spoke at the Edward R. Murrow Awards Ceremony in Minneapolis. She describes her commitment to uphold the traditions of journalism excellence:

> I remember once doing a live shot from a so-called famine camp in Ethiopia—
> and actually in Somalia as well. I was showing a man and telling his story and
> explaining how ill he was, and it was a live camera and all of a sudden I realized that he was dying. And I didn't know what to do, I didn't know how to
> break that moment, how to get the camera away, what to do that would not
> sully what was happening in real life. And then there's always the crying and
> the weeping that we hear—children, women, even men. And these images
> and these sounds are always with me. And I have often wondered why I do it,
> why we do it. After a few seconds the answer used to come easily: because it's

worth it, because it matters, because the world will care once they see our sto-ries. Because if we the storytellers don't do this, then the bad people will win. We do it because we're committed, because we're believers. And one thing that I always believed and that I knew for certain was that I could never have sustained a personal relationship while I worked this hard, or while I was that driven this intensely by the story.[41]

Indeed, Christiane Amanpour's style of journalism has been that of a sto-ryteller and an educator. In 2001 Christiane Amanpour offered this beefy report about Slobodan Milosevic:

Just as allegations of corruption, election fraud, political killings and money laundering have brought Slobodan Milosevic to the attention of prosecutors at home evidence of an array of wartimes crime has earned him indictments by international prosecutors. In May 1999, Louise Arbour, who was then chief prosecutor at the War Crimes Tribunal in the Hague, indicted Milosevic and four of his lieutenants for crimes committed during the war in Kosovo that year. Milosevic made history that day, becoming the first ever sitting head of state to be indicted by an international court. The charge of crimes against hu-manity being the second most serious crime, after genocide, under interna-tional law. But by the end of this year, he could face the genocide charge, too. The current chief prosecutor, Carla Del Ponte, is working on bringing more indictments against Milosevic for crimes committed during the Bosnia and Croatia wars from 1991 to 1995. Throughout the 1990s, in the name of pre-serving Yugoslavia, Slobodan Milosevic instead presided over its destruction. He led Yugoslavia into three wars that left hundreds of thousands dead, first in Croatia, then in Bosnia and finally in Kosovo. Civilians were primary tar-gets, a violation of the laws of war handed in the Geneva conventions after World War II. The term ethnic cleansing became synonymous with Bosnia, as Serb forces there loyal to Milosevic tried to carve out a separate state by forcibly moving the non-Serb civilian population. They unleashed heavy ar-tillery against multi-ethnic cities like Sarajevo, and laid siege to towns and vil-lages throughout the state.

Snipers targeted men, women and children. Markets full of people shopping were shelling, and in scenes unknown in Europe since World War II, there were concentration camps, mass rape, and the forced prostitution of women and very young girls. And almost every day, deportations, which added to the millions of refugees. The climax came with the Bosnian Serb assault on the tiny Muslim village of Srebrenica. To this day, the International Red Cross says that about 8,000 Muslim men and boys remain unaccounted for there. The top Bosnian Serb leaders, Radovan Karadzic and his military chief, Radko

Mladic, were twice indicted for genocide and crimes against humanity. But after NATO conducted bombing raids to stop the Bosnian Serb rampage, Slobodan Milosevic became the West's partner in the peace that was forged at Dayton in November 1995. Four years later, Milosevic launched what was to be his final military campaign in Kosovo. NATO again went to war to stop him, and just as the West was considering a negotiated cease-fire, Milosevic was indicted by the War Crimes Tribunal. Two years on, Slobodan Milosevic is no longer president of Serbia or Yugoslavia. He is no one's peace partner, and the tribunal says it's ready to present what it calls a solid case against him.

The tribunal has always said that it will go after the architects of the Balkan wars, not merely the foot soldiers. With top figures such as Milosevic, Mladic and Karadzic still at large, skeptics doubted the tribunal would succeed. But recently, it has brought in key figures, such as former Bosnian Serb senior officials Momcilo Krajisnik and Bilijana Plavsic. And it's handed down heavy sentences to three Bosnian Serb soldiers accused of mass rape as well as a senior Bosnian Croat wartime leader.[42]

She offers these reports, because, she says, she is "trying to make sense of the world."[43]

While she has also reported many breaking news stories, her longer, documentary-style programs give her the opportunity to teach lessons that are not quickly digested. She comments, "It's kind of rare in today's traditional news world [to have documentaries]. I think that people really want to be able to sink their teeth into information and get it in a way that's compelling and interesting and done differently than just as a small short segment somewhere."[44] For example, her CNN special "Where Have All the Parents Gone?" was likely to be the first in-depth television program for many viewers on the subject of AIDS orphans in Africa. While celebrities like Angelina Jolie and Bono have embraced the cause of Africa, it is Amanpour who tells the story that "holds her audience spellbound."[45] Her gripping telling of the grim realities for life as a child whose parents are dying or have died of AIDS rivets: "I'm Christiane Amanpour. Join me as we travel to Kenya to hear the children's stories. In Isiolo, Kenya, just where the northern highway turns to dust, we met eleven-year-old Muktar trying his best to be just like all the other children in school. Studying hard in class. Having fun with his friends in the playground. But try as he might, he can't escape the tragedy that is bearing down on his family. Here, in this small room, his eyes burning with sorrow, Muktar watches over his father, who is slowly slipping away. Another little African boy wonders whether he too will become one of the million AIDS orphans in Kenya. Muktar, can you tell me what you are thinking right now, what you are feeling?" Muktar says: "I am feeling but I—if I go to school I just remember my father." Christiane Amanpour clarifies her young interviewee's sentiments: "So you are just thinking about your father all the time?" She goes on to educate her viewers: "Every day, 1,400 children die of the disease, even though there are, by now, life-saving drugs. But so few people have access to them. Africa is by far the hardest hit. Here, the legacy of AIDS is 12 million orphans and counting!"[46] Amanpour punctuates this statement with persuasive indignation, as if to ask: "what are we going to do about this?" She asks a woman who is surrounded by rail-thin boys: "Do you have enough food?" The woman answers incredulously: "The children are dying here, don't you see?"[47] Christiane Amanpour realizes that her work is different from that of other correspondents. She says, "There may have been a shift in the environment in regard to serious news and foreign news, but I have not—nor have I been under pressure to—change the way I do my work. I pretty much do it the same as I used to do it when I started—hopefully getting better. For instance, I've just come back from Africa where I've put together an hour on the effect of AIDS on the children, who are the hidden victims of this disease. We've told some very compelling stories. It's important that we keep doing this kind of work, whether it's that kind of personal, human story, or the international crises such as the Middle East."[48] Robert A. Hackett, in a journal article about media bias, notes that the newscaster has a unique position with respect to objectivity. He writes: "The newscaster's or reporter's voice is that of truth. Only he or she is accorded the privilege of introducing or concluding news items, of direct address to the camera, of sustained voice-over narrative."[49] This has been especially true for Amanpour, whose narrative style of reporting lengthier stories in the form of documentaries, and ongoing stories, such as war, have given her special recognition from viewers who see her as the voice of the Middle East, for example, or children in Africa whose parents have died of AIDS. No other broadcaster profiled in this study has had a career that has so consistently been the voice of world events as Amanpour's has been. This is also the reason that she commands the respect and attention from the military and heads of state, such as President Clinton, who took the time during the global forum to acknowledge that Christiane Amanpour had done a "great service to the whole world" with her reporting. Veteran journalist Mike Wallace has called her "the best-known foreign correspondent in the world" and Pentagon officials once gave her a world map decorated with push pins representing her various reporting campaigns. They called it the "Amanpour Tracking Chart."[50]

In 2002 Christiane Amanpour was the first woman and the youngest person ever to be awarded the Edward R. Murrow Award for Distinguished Achievement in Broadcasting. Later that year, she voiced some of her concerns about her profession in a speech before the Los Angeles World Affairs Council.

> Those of us who've been reporting from around the world, my colleagues and I who have toiled, sweated, bled, died and even cried many, many times for twenty years in far and distant lands, will continue to provide a home for anybody in this country, and around the world, who is still interested in what is happening in our world. I do not believe that enough foreign news or international news is provided to the American people, and for me that's something that I feel is not only wrong but ultimately dangerous. I remember being horrified when I was reporting after September 11th at some of the basic questions coming from this country. People were asking, "Who are these people? Why do they hate us? Who is Osama bin Laden?" We've been reporting on Osama bin Laden, but obviously not enough and our reports were not getting enough air in this country.[51]

In 2005 Christiane interviewed British Prime Minister Tony Blair about his activism in Africa. She asked him: "What motivates you to take up the cause of Africa?" Prime Minister Blair responded: "There's a strong moral reason because there are thousands of children dying every day from preventable diseases, there are millions of people who have died from circumstances that are preventable over the past few years, through conflict, through famine and through disease. And I think there is a very strong reason of self-interest as well. Africa is a continent of mixed religion and mixed races and if we end up with the continent continuing to get poorer and its people devoid of any hope, I think that could cause us huge problems in the future. So I think there are reasons of self-interest but frankly, the moral causes are upper most in my mind." Christiane Amanpour followed up, seeking clarification: "Do you mean a war on poverty could also be a war on terrorism?" Blair answered: "I think you've only got to look at the conditions that give rise to terrorism. Now sometimes people who become terrorists are people who are well-off, and for various reasons get drawn into terrorism and, and you can't really say it's their social conditions or poverty that's given rise to that. On the other hand, I think it's very clear as we saw with Afghanistan, if you have an immensely poor country without any economic infrastructure, without any hope that people have for the future then it's in those conditions that terrorists can recruit, and can train and if you look at Africa, you've got Christians and Muslims living side by side. It's important I think that for those reasons too, that we try and make progress in Africa. But, again, as I say, in a sense, I think they're always long term reasons of enlightenment, self-interest for doing these things. The most immediate reason is how many people die in circumstances of tragedy and preventing it." Taking the role of agitator, Amanpour pressed: "Columnists being derisive, is this about Africa lifting the poor into the middle-class?" Blair said: "I think the first thing it is about is stopping Africa from declining as a continent and things like HIV, AIDS are affecting the population to such an extent that some countries can't teach children properly because the teachers are dying of AIDS. Now, there's an urgent need to act in these areas that I think, that I hope is obvious to everybody. But we are not saying that AIDS is the only thing. Opening up markets and tide is important, too conflict resolution is important but we've got sitting on our desks for the past two years, a report from the United Nations that describes how we should build an African peace-keeping force and peace enforcing force that will allow the African union to go into various conflicts, for example the Sudan, and manage to keep people apart so the political process can work. There's also measures to do with building capacity in those countries, capacity for governors, proper judicial systems, proper commercial and legal systems. There is a lot more than simply aid but without aid it is difficult to make progress. And, you know, it's important to look at some of the countries like Mozambique or Botswana and you can actually see tremendous progress has been made. It's not true in Africa things have gone backwards. Even in Ethiopia and even with the problems you will have seen that there is significant progress."

In a speech Christiane Amanpour gave at the University of Michigan Spring Commencement in March, 2006, she said:

> Nearly thirty years ago, like so many refugees, I came here to America. where I had heard and I had read that if you have a dream, if you have a goal, if you work hard, you can make your way in this world. And I loved every hard-won step along the way. I loved being at the University of Rhode Island in the United States, where I learned so much about American values and culture. I got only slightly miffed, only slightly upset, when, to the tune of "Barbara Ann," fellow students would sing "Bomb, bomb, bomb, bomb, bomb Iran." Let's hope that that song doesn't become popular here again.[52]
>
> I recognized for the first time then that I had to use the gift that I was given to tell stories, to reach people, to make use of CNN's privileged platform and its global audience in the service of truth. And that has made all the difference to my career and to my life. Whatever you decide to do, whether you go into business, politics, arts or science, do well for yourselves and your

families. But I ask you to consider also doing good for your communities, your countries and for our world. Consider giving your business, whatever it may be, a social face. As well as passion and commitment, find in yourselves tolerance, open-mindedness, understanding, patience as you look at your world and your place in it. "We, I believe, are in the fight of our lives to save this profession which we love. I believe we can do it, and I believe we can win this battle."[53]

Christiane Amanpour's communication style is full of passion. She notes: "At CNN, I have witnessed most of the epoch-making events of the end of the twentieth century and the dangerous new world that the twenty-first century has ushered in. As we teeter towards a more perilous and complex world, my passion for telling these vital stories from overseas has not dimmed. Rather, I feel a renewed sense of urgency and commitment to bringing the world home for our viewers."[54] She notes, "I am satisfied that I have been able to keep the idea of the foreign correspondent alive in an era, regrettably, in the United States, where foreign news is almost invisible these days. I grew up hearing about Edward R. Murrow and Eric Sevaried, all of these great foreign correspondents, the legends of our business. To-day it's celebrity journalism, trivial journalism, stock-market-mad journal-ism. I have been able to give a human face to crises and disasters, whether a famine, an earthquake or a war. I think that I've been able to get beyond the bang-bang, get beyond the heavy weaponry, get beyond the sort of techno speak of war, and relate in a human way to what's going on wherever I happen to be."[55]

Invention

Christiane Amanpour reflects on why she is determined to continue to report on the world's most important issues: "Because even though my pro-fession is awash in a sea of sensationalism and shortage of seriousness, I do it because I remain convinced that good journalism still matters. And, as a good colleague put it, 'Our historic role is to report the world, not to over-enrich our shareholders.' I do it by saying to myself that a strong and robust democracy, yes, even this one here in the United States, needs strong, in-dependent journalists of integrity who are committed to reporting without fear nor favor and who report the good and the bad, never exaggerating, but never shying away from it. I do it because I respect the American people and their right and their need to know. I do it because I am convinced that we can be a strong and a positive force in our world and that good journal-ism most definitely can make a difference. I do it because I believe we must always speak the truth, whether it is in vogue or not. And how I wish there were more voices raised earlier on the Iraq issue earlier in defense of the facts and truth, rather than politics and ideology."[56] At Stanford University in October, 2006, speaking in honor of the late journalist Daniel Pearl, she said, "I believe strongly that in this uncertain world our profession has a particular and important role and a particular and important place in our societies and our democracies," Amanpour said. "Without robust journalists, we as a society are weaker because we can't tell the stories that we absolutely must be able to tell."[57]

Disposition

Her ability to orient her material to reach the interviewee is impressive. For the young children whose parents have died from AIDS, her questions are simple, but powerful: "Do you remember what it was like, in your family before your father was ill?"[58] This brief question is in sharp contrast to the lengthy and well-researched questions she has posited to more well-known subjects. For example, she opens the interview with Syrian president Bashar al-Assad: "Mr. President, it's not just with the United States that you're having trouble right now. It is potentially with the whole world. As you know, in two weeks, the U.N.'s investigation into the assassination of Rafik Hariri will be published, and there are well-informed U.N. sources who say that Syria will be implicated."[59]

She describes her method for telling the stories: "I connect with people because my instinct is to be a human being. I think that I tell the stories, or at least I try to tell the stories that I do, in a way that everybody can connect with. For instance, a war like Bosnia wasn't the traditional army against army on a battlefield. It was a war of ethnic cleansing, of racism, of one army against civilians. I was able to tell the story of the women who were affected, the children who were affected, the old men who were affected. People who could have been your brother and sister, my parents, it was that basic, and I try to tell every story in that manner.[60] She says, "I see myself as a storyteller and a news person; someone who is out there to gather information, to report without fear or favour."[61]

In her public speeches she speaks both from manuscript and sometimes without notes, as she did in October 2006 at Stanford University. Speaking without notes to a standing-room-only audience, Amanpour offered insights, not only from her experience as a prolific foreign correspondent, but also as a critic of her own industry and a first-hand observer of world conflicts. Her subject matter ranged from diminishing international support for the War on

Terror to her view that journalism has become too heavily beholden to profits and, consequently, too trivial. "The age that we are in right now is the age
of serious, but what we are given is about the most banal and frivolous diet
you can imagine," she said. "I don't know where it's coming from, or why the
networks are peddling this kind of frivolity when we desperately need to get
to the bottom of these matters."[62]

Style

Christiane Amanpour's typical use of language—her rhetorical style—has
several characteristics, including a sense of urgency in her dramatic delivery, identification with her interviewees, direct, sustained eye contact, and
a serious tone. For example:

> Imagine your religion is your life. Your faith is your foundation. Now imagine
> your faith under attack. On the one hand, from a dominant, modernizing
> United States culture. On the other hand, from militants within, determined
> to resist that culture, even violently. [63]

The topics she chooses demand a serious and urgent delivery. In 2007
she went face to face with religious zealots for her special "CNN Presents:
God's Warriors." In the provocative special, Amanpour examines the intersection between religion and politics and the effects of Christianity, Islam,
and Judaism on politics, culture, and public life. Her topics demand a vast
knowledge of her topic, an ability to communicate in multiple cultures and
the ability to make understandable to the audience, complex, intellectual
topics. For instance, in the special "God's Warriors" Amanpour interviews
Noa Rothman, the granddaughter of Israeli Prime Minister Yitzhak Rabin,
whose 1993 peace treaty with the PLO upset many in the proreligious settlement movement. A militant Jewish fundamentalist assassinated Rabin in
1995. Because of her extensive experience in international affairs, Amanpour is able to orient the viewer to this intellectual topic with the connection of the role of religion in American politics.

Delivery

Well prepared, she takes no shortcuts in getting the story as fully to the
audience as possible. Traveling to ten countries to get the best picture of
Osama bin Laden for the "In the Footsteps of bin Laden" special is typical
of her preparation. When her voluminous research is finally edited down to
the script, her delivery is dramatic and exclamatory, zeroing in on the most

salient features of the story. For example, in the CNN special "An In-Depth Look at Islam," Amanpour begins:

> They are images that will probably forever be etched in our minds—the World Trade Center, the Pentagon, thousands of people buried in the wreckage. The suspected mastermind behind those grotesque acts, Osama bin Laden, is an extremist who thinks he can rid the Muslim world of America's presence, American influence.[64]

In her urgent and serious voice Amanpour states as narrator of the HBO documentary *The Journalist and the Jihadi: The Life of Daniel Pearl*: "The film was horrific. Daniel Pearl was beheaded. After refusing to be forcibly sedated, Daniel Pearl was held down by four of his captors and slaughtered. Omar Sheikh is found guilty and has been sentenced to hang."[65] Chosen as the narrator for the film, Amanpour's familiar voice lends credibility and weight to the program, which tells the story of *The Wall Street Journal* reporter held captive and murdered by Islamic extremists in 2002.

Conclusion

Her well-traveled, global approach to news equaled the need for global understanding to make sense of the events leading up to the twenty-first century and beyond. Mary Robinson, former president of Ireland, notes "Christiane Amanpour is very good. She offers an education on world events with her programs."[66] While other newswomen were considering what to wear to look good, Amanpour was considering whether or not a flak jacket would be required. She has put herself in harm's way to make CNN viewers aware of the events she covered. Her unique look, style, and rapid-fire delivery quickly gave her a distinctive place in the world of news broadcasting. In 2007 Christiane Amanpour, chief international correspondent for CNN, was named a commander of the Order of the British Empire by the Queen of England. In an interview with CNN, Christiane Amanpour noted that she was honored that a journalist would receive such a designation and that her mission has always been and will continue to be: "to report without fear no favor and to give a voice to those who don't have them."[67]

NOTES

1. Christiane Amanpour, speech before the Los Angeles World Affairs Council, "While America Slept: Bombs, But Then What?" December 6, 2002, http://www .lawac.org/speech/amanpour (accessed September 22, 2007).

2. Dana Gee, "War Journalist Would Grill bin Laden: CNN Documentary: Christiane Amanpour Traces Footsteps of Most-Wanted Terrorist," *The Vancouver Province*, July 16, 2006, C7.

3. Virginia Heffernan, "A Mastermind of Terror and Allure," *The New York Times*, August 23, 2006, E6.

4. Roderick P. Hart, *Modern Rhetorical Criticism* (Needham Heights: Allyn and Bacon, 1997), 181.

5. http://www.oprah.com/tows/pastshows/tows_2002/tows_past_20020220_b .jhtml (accessed October 19, 2006).

6. Stephen Kinzer, "Where There's War, There's Amanpour," *The New York Times*, October 9, 1994, 57.

7. Michael Dobbs, "The Amanpour Factor: How Television Fills the Leadership Vacuum on Bosnia," *The Washington Post*, July 23, 1995, C2.

8. Bonnie M. Anderson, *News Flash: Journalism, Infotainment, and the Bottom-Line Business of Broadcast News* (San Francisco: Jossey-Bass, 2004), 6.

9. Oprah Winfrey, "The O Interview," *O: The Oprah Winfrey Magazine,* September, 2005, 209.

10. Jacci Duncan, *Making Waves: The 50 Greatest Women in Radio and Television* (Kansas City: McMeel Publishing, 2001), 8.

11. http://www.umich.edu/newus/index.html?Vid/ca_sprcom06.

12. Ibid.

13. Rob Harris, "How to Be Christiane Amanpour: TV News Correspondent," *The Guardian* (Manchester, UK), May 30, 2005, 28.

14. CNN special presentation, "In the Footsteps of Bin Laden," August, 2006 (recorded from television August 23, 2006).

15. Dusty Saunders, "CNN Digs Deep on bin Laden," *Rocky Mountain News*, August 22, 2006, 2D.

16. CNN special presentation, "An In-Depth Look at Islam," October 13, 2001 (obtained from Pennsylvania State University Library).

17. Ibid.

18. Kinzer, "Where There's War, There's Amanpour," 57.

19. Harris, "How to Be Christiane Amanpour," 28.

20. http://gos.sbc.edu/a/amanpour.html (accessed October 10, 2006).

21. Kinzer, "Where There's War, There's Amanpour," 57.

22. Ibid.

23. http://www.umich.edu/newus/index.html?Vid/ca_sprcom06 (accessed October 29, 2006).

24. Richard Huff, David Bianculli, and Helen Kennedy, "CNN Calmly Brings Attack to the World," *Daily News*, December 17, 1998, 46.

25. Walter Goodman, "A Reporter's Debut on '60 Minutes,'" *The New York Times*, November 4, 1996.

26. Jacques Steinberg, "'60 Minutes' May Be Too Few For All the Stars," *The New York Times*, June 3, 2005, C1.

27. Judith Marlane, *Women in Television News Revisited* (Austin: University of Texas Press, 1999), 20.

28. Benson P. Fraser and William J. Brown, "Media, Celebrities, and Social Influence: Identification with Elvis Presley," *Mass Communication & Media* 5, no. 2 (2002): 183–206.

29. Drew Jubera, "Clinton, Reporter Trade Jabs," *Atlanta Journal and Constitution*, May 4, 1994, B1.

30. CNN transcript, "A Global Forum with President Clinton," transcript #320-6 (accessed October 19, 2006).

31. Ibid.

32. Michael Dobbs, "The Amanpour Factor: How Television Fills the Leadership Vacuum on Bosnia," *The Washington Post*, July 23, 1995, C2.

33. Ibid.

34. Ibid.

35. Ibid.

36. http://www.umich.edu/newus/index.html?Vid/ca_sprcom06 (accessed October 31, 2006).

37. http://www.cnn.com/WORLD/9801/07/iran/interview.html (accessed October 10, 2006).

38. James Silver, "She Doesn't Do Froth," *The Independent* (London), July 10, 2006, 10.

39. Gee, "War journalist would grill bin Laden," C7.

40. Duncan, *Making Waves*, 7.

41. http://gos.sbc.edu/a/amanpour.html.

42. CNN, March 31, 2001, "Milosevic's Legacy Still Scares Balkans," http://trascripts.cnn.com/TRANSCRIPTS/0103/31/smn.14.html (accessed October 20, 2006).

43. Patricia J. Williams, "Guaranteed Authentic," *Oprah Magazine*, March 2007, 214.

44. Glenn Gavin, "She's Not Just the Host—She's Also the Story's Main Reporter," *Miami Herald*, August 23, 2006.

45. Alex Strachan, "The Truth Chaser: Christiane Amanpour Never Lets up Her Pursuit of the Story," *Ottowa Citizen*, July 29, 2006, K1.

46. CNN Special Presents, 8:00 PM EST, September 24, 2006, "Where Have All the Parents Gone?" http://web.lexisexis.com.ezaccess.libraries.psu.edu/universe/document (accessed October 14, 2006).

47. Virginia Heffernan, "Asking Simple Questions of AIDS Victims and Getting Simple, Powerful Answers," *The New York Times*, September 23, 2006, B10.

48. Alex Strachen, "Christiane Amanpour: Serious, Fearless and Fiercely Intelligent: CNN Stalwart Does News the Old-fashioned Way—Without Apology," *Edmonton Journal* (Alberta), July 18, 206, c1.

49. Robert A. Hackett, "Decline of a Paradigm? Bias and Objectivity in News Media," *Critical Studies in Communication* 1, no. 3 (September, 1984): 229–259.

50. Duncan, *Making Waves*, 7.

51. http://www.lawac.org/speech/pre%20sept%2004%20speeches/amanpour%202002.htm.

52. http://www.umich.edu/newus/index.html?Vid/ca_sprcom06 (accessed October 31, 2006).

53. Anderson, *News Flash*, 23.

54. Christiane Amanpour, "Commentary," *The Quill*, Chicago, 2005, 40.

55. Duncan, *Making Waves*, 10.

56. http://www.umich.edu/newus/index.html?Vid/ca_sprcom06 (accessed October 31, 2006).

57. Janet Kim, "Lecture Honors Daniel Pearl," *The Stanford Daily*, October 17, 2006, 1.

58. Ibid.

59. CNN presents "Christiane Amanpour Interviews President of Syria," http://www.cnn.com/2005/WORLD/meast/10/12/alassad.transcript/index.html (accessed August 22, 2007).

60. Duncan, *Making Waves*, 11.

61. Strachan, "Christiane Amanpour," C1.

62. Kim, "Lecture Honors Daniel Pearl," 1.

63. CNN presents, "An In-depth Look at Islam: The Realities and the Rhetoric," October 13, 2001, http://transcripts.cnn.com/TRANSCRIPTS/0110/13/cp.00.html (accessed October 28, 2006).

64. Ibid.

65. HBO Special: *The Journalist and the Jihadi: The Life of Daniel Pearl*, transcribed from television, October 29, 2006.

66. Mary Robinson in interview with Nichola D. Gutgold, November 1, 2006.

67. Transcribed from CNN broadcast, June 18, 2007, 7:18 Eastern Time.

5

POLITICALLY SPEAKING

Dana Bash, Candy Crowley, Andrea Mitchell, and Judy Woodruff

DANA BASH

Figure 4.1. Dana Bash

"You can play back, almost verbatim, Democrats . . . saying almost exactly what you all just said, so is there a little bit of hypocrisy in you saying that you want minority rights?"[1]

One of the newest faces, and perhaps the most likely to ask the question on everyone's mind, belongs to Dana Bash, who is CNN's congressional correspondent. Based in CNN's Washington, D.C., bureau, she covers the activities of both the U.S. House and Senate. Dana Bash's extensive knowledge of the political process and the issues facing the House and Senate are obvious when she offers impromptu and thorough responses to anchors' questions. The quote above is Bash's response to Republican senators who were demanding that the new Democratic majority give the new Republican minority all the rights that Republicans had denied Democrats for years.

On another assignment, Dana Bash answered an anchor's question with this impressive utterance:

> On the floor of the United States Senate, senators are voting to confirm the man who will be in charge of U.S. forces, multi-national forces actually, in Iraq, General David Petraeus. When he gets confirmed, and it is certainly expected he will get confirmed overwhelmingly, he will be boosted from lieutenant general to general and he will have a role that the Senate Armed Services chairman on the floor just now said, "will be the single most important command in the national defense establishment." He is somebody who is highly regarded for his education and also for things that he has done in recent years. For example, writing the Army and Marine Corps training manual for counter insurgency.[2]

Bash represents the second generation of women broadcast journalists who are schooled knowing that they will be expected to speak well, look good, and have a competence about political affairs on par with their male counterparts. Bash is not a weather-girl-turned on-air personality, like several of the women profiled in this book who came of age when few women were on air. Prior to her on-air position, Dana Bash was the Capitol Hill producer for CNN, where she had primary editorial and newsgathering responsibility for the network's coverage of the U.S. Senate. She covered every major story on Capitol Hill, including the Republican dominance in the 2002 elections, the war on terrorism, campaign finance reform, the Florida recount, and the impeachment of former President Bill Clinton. Frequently cited on air by anchors and reporters, she also provided live reporting during the evacuation of the Capitol in the days after the September 11, 2001, attacks. She was one of the first journalists to report that Vermont's Sen. Jim Jeffords would leave the Republican Party in May 2001, giving control of the U.S. Senate to Democrats. In 2002, she broke the story of the government's secret intercepts of Al Qaeda translations on September 10, 2001, for which she received the prestigious Dirksen Award from the National Press Foundation.

Television is in Dana Bash's blood; she "grew up in control rooms"[3] as she watched her father, Stu Schwartz, a longtime ABC producer with *Good Morning America*, at work. She followed in her father's career footsteps after graduating cum laude with her BA in political communications from George Washington University. She tells of the difference in job opportunities her mother faced when she graduated from Northwestern University with the same degree in journalism that her father had. "The only job my mother could get was as a secretary, which in those days included picking up the drycleaning, while my father instantly found employment in broadcasting, even though they both had the same education—a degree from the best journalism school in the county."[4]

In 2003 Dana Bash switched from Capitol Hill reporting to become a White House correspondent for CNN. She commented, "The atmosphere could not be more different" at the other end of Pennsylvania Avenue. "On the Hill it's kind of open. You walk through the halls, you bump into people you cover constantly," which doesn't happen at the White House, making it tougher to do the kind of digging she's known for. "A lot of the issues are very similar—you're talking about a bill or a policy," she observes. "You just come at it from a different way."[5] In March, 2006, she went back to covering Congress and has been working as a congressional correspondent since. Though her career trajectory demonstrates her strong work ethic and persistence, she recognizes that several women in broadcasting who went before her have paved the way for her to be successful at the most difficult and prestigious levels of journalism. She recalls telling Judy Woodward one day as she prepared for a stand-up report from the White House, "I'm standing here on the North Lawn of the White House because you stood here before me."[6]

Adept at both stand-up live reporting and in-depth interviewing, in 2004 she interviewed First Lady Laura Bush in Sea Island, Georgia. She began the interview: "Before we get to issues about this summit here in Sea Island, first I wanted to talk about what's happening back in Washington. Today is the state funeral for President Reagan. Have you spoken with Nancy Reagan?" Mrs. Bush replied, "I haven't spoken to her. The President spoke to her on Saturday from France as soon as we found out about Ronald Reagan's death. But I haven't quit thinking about her—she just was an unbelievable role model for all of us. My father died of Alzheimer's and I know how very, very difficult the disease is and how difficult it is for the caregivers. And she was stalwart and so devoted to him. So we'll see her tomorrow night. As soon as we get back to Washington, we'll pay a call on her." Dana Bash continued: "And you had some special access, if you will, to President Reagan, since your father-in-law was his vice president. Tell us about a special moment, either the first time you met him or another memorable moment."

Mrs. Bush responded, "Well, he was so funny. I think that's what people really remember. He was a big man, he was a very attractive, big man. But he had this very modest and self-deprecating sort of sense of humor, so he really made you feel comfortable. I know what it's like to meet the President of the United States. And when we met him, we were very intimidated. We didn't know what to say. But he could immediately make us feel comfortable. And I think that's what the American people loved about him. That, and that he so obviously believed in the American people and he was so optimistic about our future."[7]

Invention

Dana Bash plans out questions to ask her subjects in advance; however, her often live interviews require her to be able to ask questions as her interviewees are responding. Her knowledge of politics is evident and her ability to both report live and interview subjects effectively makes her a versatile broadcast journalist with both editorial and on-air experience. She does not mince words or try to ease into difficult questions. Instead she is able to get to the most salient issue and ask a question of the interviewee immediately. For example, she tied in the death of Ronald Reagan to the stem cell issue and was able to ask First Lady Laura Bush about her position while also having her comment on the death of Ronald Reagan. She continued: "I want to ask you about something relating to Nancy Reagan. First of all, your mother-in-law, Barbara Bush, publicly disagreed with her husband, President Bush, on the issue of abortion. Nancy Reagan has come out recently and said that she supports stem cell research in order to try to find a cure for Alzheimer's. You mentioned that your father also had Alzheimer's. What is your personal view on stem cell research?" Mrs. Bush replied, "Well, everyone supports stem cell research, and so did the President. And there are lines, embryonic lines of stem cell for research. It's a very delicate balance between what we want to do for science and for research and for what is ethically and morally right to do. There's adult stem cell research that's available for people. There are lines of embryonic stem cells that are available for research. And we all want a cure for Alzheimer's. And I know there are many, many researchers who are working with stem cell but also with other medicines and other possibilities of prevention and vaccines for Alzheimer's." Dana Bash asked, "Do you think the federal funding for the existing lines should—it should stop there, the existing lines?" Mrs. Bush said, "Well, I think that's—we need to really be very delicate about it and figure out what's the best way to do it, because there is a moral and an ethical part of it as well."[8]

Disposition

Her planning is evident in how she is able to transition from one topic to the next, as she did in the Reagan interview. She organized her report about President Bush's speech from Fort Bragg by first offering the public's perception of the president and then what the White House hopes to change by strategizing with both the content of the speech and the place where the speech will be given:

> Well, six in ten Americans now do not think President Bush has a plan in Iraq, and the goal of tonight's speech is for Mr. Bush to explain to America that he actually does. And he will acknowledge the fact that Americans clearly are concerned, and make it personal, say that he, too, is concerned about the increasing violence, the suicide bombings that they see on their TV screens coming from Iraq. And the White House knows that is a trend that they're going to have to change. They're going to have to make Americans think and understand that Iraq is part of the global war on terrorism.

Style

Dana Bash has a very fast-paced, direct style. For example, she responded to Lou Dobb's pointing out the importance of the president's address by saying: "Look, they hear the criticism. They understand that not just Democrats, but Republicans say that the president has to be straight with the American people, and has to give an update. And they say that part of the reason why the president's numbers are so low is that it's been some months—six months since the president has had this kind of conversation, if you will, with the American people about what's going on in Iraq."

Delivery

Dana Bash speaks quickly and has a loud, clear voice that demonstrates her authority and confidence. She appears prepared and alert, often batting her eyes repeatedly as she delivers information, which appears to be a nervous gesture. Her voice is powerful and her enunciation is clear. She seems to fill every second of time and usually finishes her utterances with the anchor's name.

Conclusion

Dana Bash represents the younger broadcast journalist who grew up with role models, including her own father, who had long and productive careers. She notes, "Everything is random and dependent upon having people around you who will give you breaks."[9] She advises young people interested in a career in broadcasting that they have to be willing to work really hard in unglamorous ways. She notes, "I was working at CNN, taking the tapes, logging them in and writing on them what happened. I worked three years as an associate producer. That's the key—it is hard to juggle, and in the beginning you have to work and sometimes you aren't even paid for it, but it pays off. What's hard in the cable world is the schedule. For example, today I had a 7 a.m live shot regarding Alberto Gonzalez and Sununu coming out and saying he should be fired. Then I had . . . live shots nine, ten, eleven, then I had to completely change gears and report on Iraq at 6:00 on Lou Dobbs. A twelve-hour day like this is not unusual."[10] By the time Bash went to college, she had years of experience viewing female broadcasters who had come before her. She is one of the newer faces who will likely continue to build on the work previously started by other women in broadcasting. Though the door was open for her by broadcasters like the next subject of this analysis, Candy Crowley, who pointed out that "There are a lot more women now and a lot fewer 'weather girls,'"[11] Bash's long days on the job are proof that though there are more women in broadcasting, to be successful requires a work ethic uncharacteristic of most other careers.

CANDY CROWLEY

> I covered Capitol Hill for a long time and was always astounded by the nonpolitical motivation of a lot of people that are up there who really do want to make the world better, want to make the U.S. better. So don't come away believing that because there are political implications that there are always political motivations.[12]

Magda "Candy" Crowley has become a presence on CNN, reporting on Washington politics. A Missouri native, she has distinguished herself with witty, yet serious and intelligent coverage of the presidential campaigns of

Figure 4.2.   Candy Crowley

Ronald Reagan, Ted Kennedy, Jesse Jackson, George Bush, Pat Buchanan, Paul Tsongas, Bill Clinton, and George W. Bush. Since the nomination of Jimmy Carter, she has reported from all but one of the national political conventions. Her strong, confident voice and insightful questions and commentary make her a fixture on the political scene. She is a self-described "political junkie" who revels in participating in the campaigns and the other political rituals that she covers.

The 2000 presidential election was anything but routine, even for a veteran like Crowley. She notes, "There are only a few times when you know you are covering history, and that was one of them."[13] I've often likened this [covering the 2000 election] to childbirth in that while you are going through it, you keep telling yourself, 'I'm never going to do this again,' then afterwards, you think, 'Wow, let's do this again.' I love covering campaigns because it's almost like writing a novel. For a year and a half you cover the same story and the ups and downs of all the players. And I think what was interesting about this election is, obviously, that just as we thought we were writing the final chapter, we started another one. Surprise is always so interesting to me as a reporter because so many stories in Washington and politics can be so predictable."[14] It was also a long and difficult assignment for any journalist, she explains, and one that failed to produce that signature post–Election Day story of victory and loss. In such an environment, Crowley denies neither the pitfalls of her profession nor the frustrating complexity of her subject matter, but she affirms her affection for the job. "I despair over my industry, or politics in general, but in the end something saves me . . . I think, 'Look where I am! Look who I'm meeting! Look what I'm learning!'"[15] She recalls that moment when she realized that she was becoming a political reporter:

> The first convention I ever covered was the Democratic convention in 1980. Senator Ted Kennedy had challenged then President Jimmy Carter for the nomination. Kennedy lost and gave an intensely personal convention speech, "The Dream Shall Never Die." It drew the connection for me between the personal and the political. I love covering people, who they are, what they're about, where they came from, what they think, what they want you to know, what they don't want you to know. During that speech it was so clear to me that politics is less about policy than people. It was what I wanted to cover.[16]

After graduating in 1970 from Randolph-Macon Women's College in Lynchburg, Virginia, Candy Crowley began her broadcast journalism career as a newsroom assistant for WASH, a Washington, D.C., radio station. During the early 1980s, she worked as a general assignment and White House correspondent for the Associated Press before moving to NBC-TV's Washington Bureau. Crowley left NBC to join CNN in 1987.[17] Roderick P. Hart notes in *Modern Rhetorical Criticism* that verbal dimensions of credibility include power, competence, trustworthiness, goodwill, and similarity.[18] Candy Crowley exudes credibility and an unbridled ebullience for the stories she covers. Those viewers who watch her obviously share her interest in politics, and for viewers Crowley represents one of us—the interested many—who are compelled by the political stories as they unfold in front of us. Her love of politics—which appears as a sport when she reports—is palpable. She has been reporting on politics for more than a quarter of a century and her experience is evident in her quick responses and plethora of references to which she is quick to make. Listen to the enthusiasm and sense of reverence for historical tradition and ritual, with which she describes her attendance at the inauguration of George W. Bush in 2001:

> The podium was a spectacular place to be if you're a journalist and probably if you're an American. It was the most fascinating mix of politicos that I've ever seen collected in one place. It gave new meaning to the term "seat of power." Seated on the platform was the 39th president of the United States, Jimmy Carter; the forty-first president of the United States, George H.W. Bush; the forty-second president of the United States, William Jefferson Clinton; and the forty-third president of the United States, George W. Bush. Almost all fifty governors were there, along with Supreme Court justices, the House of Representatives and the Senate and political dignitaries. And I

couldn't tell you enough about the sight looking out over the Washington Mall, from the Capitol up to the Washington Monument, and seeing the people who came out despite the fact that it was so cold and so rainy.[19]

Her dogged pursuit of stories made her the subject of a CNN story in 2006 about reporters who are "road warriors" or people who spend more time on the road than at their homes. For example, during the extraordinary circumstances surrounding the 2000 election, when she covered the Bush campaign, she was in Texas for seven consecutive weeks. Reporter Elizabeth Yuan asked Candy Crowley: "What do you do to stay on top of your game?" Crowley advised, ""Being on the campaign trail could mean being away for several weeks and landing in several states on a single day. If I have to wake up at 6 a.m., I set out everything I need. I sometimes put the toothpaste on the toothbrush. I put the bathmat on the floor. I never scatter my stuff around the room," she said. "I even open the bar of soap" for the shower, adding that it's hard to open on little sleep. This way, "I can go into autopilot and not have to think" after waking up, she said. "Keep your head in the game."[20] This sort of pragmatic approach to traveling is the same kind of solid, straight-to-the-point type of reporting that Crowley offers CNN viewers.

Her expertise of politics frequently puts her into the role of teacher and she frequently gives her opinion on political issues. She expressed her opinion on the Democratic takeover of Congress on the CNN show *Reliable Sources* in November when Howard Kurtz asked: "Candy Crowley, let's face it, journalists were bored with one-party rule and they hope the Democrats conduct plenty of investigations in Congress and issue subpoenas so that they can feast on the conflict. True or false?"[21] Candy Crowley commented, "You know—I mean, you know, yes, in some ways. And here's why:

> because journalists love a story. So I don't think it's you know, that gives the implication that we're rooting for something one way or the other. I think what journalists root for is a good story. You know, something that gets the adrenaline pumping. And so, you know, yes, in the sense that we want a good story, no in the sense that we want to see somebody or other brought down." Kurtz asked, "Candy Crowley, How do you make decisions about how far you can go on election night?" Crowley responded, "Well, again, we had pollsters around going, "Listen, this is the first wave, the first wave of polls is notably skewed." But the margins were big enough that you knew no matter how skewed they were, that this was probably going to be a Democratic night.

Her authority on the subject of Congress became the focus of an interview that appeared in a book published by the Brookings Institute. Editors

Stephen Jess and Marvin Kalb sought out her opinion. Kalb asked, "Candy, you're up there on Capitol Hill every day. Is there any direction, does one have a sense of an organized effort to debate where we are in this war against terrorism?" In 2003 she said, "No, not at this moment. People were stunned, so that sort of set everybody back, including people on Capital Hill, who not only watched what went on in New York, but really sort of feared for their own lives. So everybody was sort of as in a stunned silence. After that you have the tendency to allow the administration to do something, simply because it can move faster than the Congress ever can and third, you have a nation that seems to be largely in favor of it."[22] In 2006, however, Candy Crowley had a more urgent message about the war: "I just get the sense that what the American people want and the only thing that's going to help those poll numbers is the end of those roadside bombs, the end of the watching the death toll go down instead of up."[23]

Candy Crowley's interviewing skills are apparent in this special program where she "turned the tables" on well-known interviewer Larry King, and asked him questions. Crowley asked Larry King, "Now, when you're on the story, and particularly when you're on the political story, how do you— you've interviewed John McCain probably a zillion times, more or less. How do you get something different? How do you prepare yourself for that and how do you get them to talk to you?"

Larry King responded, "Well I don't have an agenda. I've never had an agenda. And I don't presume. So I don't know what I'm going to hear. And so all I do is ask the best questions I can. I ask short questions. Most of my questions are one sentence. If I ask over two sentences, there's something the matter." Crowley seemed comfortable in the role of the interviewer, even with the legendary talk show host, Larry King, and she asked questions that gave Larry King an opportunity to disclose his communication strategies. Crowley is a likeable spokesperson and a interviewer who is both able to put her guests at ease with her casual and friendly style and still challenge them with pointed questions that make the interview interesting for viewers.

Invention

Often Candy Crowley is on the scene, reporting on political events as they happen. Her years of experience give her the ability to respond with meaning and insight. Notice how she responds to Wolf Blitzer's request for commentary regarding the end of the John Kerry presidential campaign as Kerry prepared to make his concession speech:

I'm thinking right now of a conversation that we had when we did a CNN special on John Kerry. Talked to his oldest friend, somebody he'd known from
grade school, who said, "You know, I sat down with John a year ago and I said,
'John, you've got this beautiful wife. She's rich. You've got all this money.
You're a U.S. Senator. Why would you want to run for president?'

"And John Kerry said, 'Well, because I have things I want to do. And you
know, the worst that can happen is that I'm a U.S. Senator with a beautiful
wife and a lot of money.' So, that's where he is right now."

I mean, this is a "Don't Cry for Him, Argentina." There's a lot that is still
ahead.

He has the rest of his term to serve out. They—I think the worst part of this,
for them, is they really believed in that last week—you know, the Bruce
Springsteen sort of rock tour that we did in Madison, having those 80,000,
they thought, in the streets of Madison. We went to Milwaukee in the final
days—pouring rain, very cold, big crowd, thousands standing there, waiting
for him. Same at the airport, people who stood for three and four and five
hours. And after a while, inside your bubble, you begin to believe that that's
what the world looks like. So, this was really tough for them, because as they
moved in—they're now saying, well, we knew Ohio was tough. We thought it
was even. But the fact is that the feel of this campaign, when they got off the
plane here in Boston yesterday, was we're going to win this. So, it was a very
rough night. And I'm sure this is a very rough moment for the senator.[24]

As a political reporter covering the Kerry campaign, it is apparent that
Crowley saw herself as part of the campaign in the respect that she notes,
"*We* went to Milwaukee . . ." She explains well to the audience, many of
whom may not have much political experience, how the opinion of a campaign may differ from poll numbers because of the emotion stirred when a
large crowd is addressed. The most notable aspect of her choice of words
and the excitement with which she reveals is part of the political campaign
process.

When interviewing, she tries to make the subject feel comfortable. She
says, "one of my techniques is that before the interview I'll talk about almost anything other than what I want to talk about when the camera's on. I
want them to know I'm a human being. I'm not out to get them. I'm there
to find out what they know. I'm not there to make them look bad or look
stupid."[25]

Disposition

"I don't write out questions. I'll put topics down. I find that writing out
questions gets in the way of listening. The best interviewer is the best listener.

The people you're interviewing will lead you places. I've heard way too many interviews where it's question one, question two, question three, thank you very much. I don't just like to go after the sound bite."[26] She says, "Relaxing the interviewee is key. I usually throw soft balls the first couple of questions (unless time is really limited). People come to interviews with something they want to say. I let them say it. Then I ask about what I want to know. I also am unfailingly polite (not to be confused with docile). A rude, snarl interview may be good TV, but it shuts down the interviewee and you get nothing of interest. Tough questions, good. Rudeness, bad."[27]

Candy Crowley was described by a *Hartford* (Connecticut) *Courant* staff writer as "rubbing her hands together several weeks ago in anticipation of her plum primary day assignment in Connecticut." In addition to offering commentary on politics, Candy Crowley has significant experience interviewing candidates and in August, 2006, Crowley interviewed Ned Lamont, who ran for senate in Connecticut and beat longtime Connecticut senator Joseph Lieberman in the primary, though lost in the general election to Senator Lieberman. Candy Crowley, maintaining direct eye contact, held a microphone up to candidate Lamont and asked, "What do you make of Senator Lieberman's decision or possibility that he may run as an independent?" Not showing any emotion to Lamont's response, Crowley followed up with "Are you saying that he hasn't been a good Democrat?"[28] She told the *Hartford Courant*: "As soon as the polls began showing Lieberman was in trouble, I knew Connecticut was going to be the place to be. It's the political story of the summer, no matter how it turns out. Give me a smack down any day."[29]

Style

Crowley's typical use of style in her reports—her rhetorical style—has an intellectual, yet casual characteristic. For example, when asked by Anderson Cooper after the midterm election in Connecticut, "How do Democrats try to bring more people into the tent and win more elections when many of them who are trying to be more moderate, can't get past the primaries?" Crowley responded, in reference to a popular movie, "It's sort of 'honey I shrunk the middle' period in politics. It is very hard for a centrist, as Joe Lieberman is, on the other side we have Lincoln Chafee who is Republican, who has often gone up against George W. Bush. He's in trouble in his home state. The middle is having a tough time. These are very sharp partisan times."[30] She rarely smiles at the end of her report and instead focuses into the camera with sustained eye contact and a straight face. Up and coming CNN journalist Zain Verjee notes that it is Candy Crowley whom she admires most among all active journalists. She says, "her writing is magical, lyrical and deliciously witty."[31] She sounds like a political wonk, with her extensive understanding of American politics. Her command of her material is evident whether she is interviewing a politician or offering commentary. She frequently begins her responses to hosts' questions with a colloquial "well."

Delivery

Candy Crowley has a distinctive broadcast voice that serves her well not only on television but on the radio when she hosts programs on XM Satellite Radio. Deep and strong, her voice has impact and her eye contact is sustained and direct. There is a sense of pride in her delivery. She has reverence for democracy that comes through in her earnest, thorough delivery of the stories. "I'm totally obsessed," she admits. "I really love politics. And the closer you get to the voters, the more you see what the founders of this country had in mind. There is nothing more pure to me than the people who show up on voting day. They're the ones who run this country."[32]

Conclusion

Candy Crowley is a recognizable presence in broadcast journalism mostly for her significant understanding and ability to teach the viewers about the political stories she covers. Her passion for her work is visible in the enthusiasm and energy she emits as she criss-crosses the country in pursuit of the stories about campaigns and politicians. The style and content of her broadcasting have remained consistent throughout her career and she has become a familiar figure on Election Night, reveling in the surprise and the wonder of democracy along with the viewers.

ANDREA MITCHELL

> Our job as journalists is to throw ourselves into this great game, celebrating moments of political courage while never hesitating to expose hypocrisy and corruption. Sometimes, that requires "talking back" to power, whether to presidents, dictators, or lesser scoundrels.[33]

Andrea Mitchell is a seasoned political reporter, often sought after for her explanation and opinion of political events. She commented on the power

Figure 4.3.   Andrea Mitchell

of the press and how it was used during the Kennedy presidency. She says, "I think that there was an aura about Jack Kennedy. He seduced the press . . . and he also orchestrated the image of the young, carefree vigorous athletic president with a devoted wife, and adorable children, and probably the only true fact in all of that was the adorable children."[34]

She covers burgeoning international issues for all NBC News broadcasts, including *NBC Nightly News with Brian Williams*, *Today*, and MSNBC. She is also often a guest on *Hardball with Chris Matthews*. She frequently anchors the 11 am. hour of *MSNBC Live*.

An accomplished musician, Mitchell graduated with a BA in English literature from the University of Pennsylvania in 1967, where she served as news director of student radio station WXPN. Richard Albert was a classmate of Andrea Mitchell's at the University of Pennsylvania and he commented about his recollection of his famous classmate: "It was unusual at the time for women to be active in the radio station and Andrea Mitchell worked 24/7 at the station and was the only woman, at the time, who had such a real passion for it."[35]

Andrea Mitchell joined Philadelphia NBC affiliate KYW radio and TV as a reporter that same year. At KYW, she spent much of her time covering the controversial mayor of Philadelphia, the colorful Frank Rizzo. *The* (Philadelphia) *Daily News* noticed that Andrea Mitchell took her work seriously and described her as "KYW's soft-voiced but hard-nosed city hall reporter, one of the best in the business, leads off the questioning. She asks the mayor about the issue that had the whole city talking, the police corruption report. Frank Rizzo, the man who pledged to run his administration in a fishbowl, passes. He'll only answer questions on parking at the airport, he tells reporters."[36]

Andrea Mitchell moved to CBS affiliate WTOP in Washington, D.C., in 1976. Two years later, she moved to NBC's network news operation, where she served as a general correspondent. In 1979, she was named NBC News' Energy correspondent and reported on the late 1970s energy crisis and the Three Mile Island nuclear incident. Mitchell also covered the White House from 1981 until becoming chief congressional correspondent in 1988.

She has been the chief foreign affairs correspondent for NBC News since November 1994. Previously, she had served as chief White House correspondent (1993–1994) and chief congressional correspondent (1988–1992) for NBC News. Mitchell married her second husband, Alan Greenspan, then the Federal Reserve Chairman, in 1997. Previously, she was married to Gil Jackson; that marriage ended in divorce in the mid 1970s. She is a frequent guest on Don Imus's radio program.

In July 2005, Mitchell was forcibly ejected from a room after asking Sudanese President Omar el-Bashir some pointed questions. "Can you tell us why the violence is continuing?" (referring to genocide in Sudan's Darfur province). "Can you tell us why the government is supporting the militias?" "Why should Americans believe your promises?" At this point two armed security guards grabbed her and shoved her out the door. "It is our job to ask," Mitchell said after the incident. "They can always say 'no comment' . . . but to drag a reporter out just for asking is inexcusable behavior."[37] She recounted the experience for then NBC *Today Show* host Katie Couric:

> I went in and asked a question. I asked the president of Sudan why Condoleezza Rice should trust his promises to stop the killing since his own government is supporting the militias that are doing the killing? And immediately two security guys grabbed me from behind, one grabbed my left arm and started dragging me out of the room. I kept asking questions, and they kept dragging me out, Katie, and they had guns. So I got the questions; I didn't get any answers.[38]

Prior to the incident, Sudanese officials expressed reservations about allowing American newspaper or television reporters to join the Sudanese press pool. Sean McCormack, the U.S. State Department's assistant secretary for public affairs, said to his Sudanese counterpart, "I'll convey your desires about not permitting reporters to ask questions, but that's all I'll do. We have a free press." McCormack's Sudanese counterpart replied, "There is no freedom of the press here." The incident prompted Secretary of State Condoleezza Rice to demand an apology from Sudanese government for the rough handling of aides ad reporters who were traveling with her. The secretary of state gave Sudan's foreign minister a ninety-minute deadline to make a personal apology, and he met it. "It makes me very angry to be sitting there with their president and have this happen," Rice told reporters afterward. "They have no right to push and shove."[39]

A similar incident happened during the Clinton administration when Andrea Mitchell asked President Assad why he still supported terrorism. She writes:

> The White House and Syrian presidential aides were flabbergasted. No reporter, and certainly not a woman, had ever dared ask Hafez al Assad a question at a photo opportunity. To my amazement, instead of ignoring me, he began to answer, vigorously challenging the premise of my question. As he did later in a joint news conference with Clinton, Assad denied that anyone could name one incident in which Syria had committed a terrorist act. But before he could finish, I suddenly felt myself being lifted off the ground. With the camera safely focused on the presidents, two burly Syrian security men had come up from behind, grabbed me under the elbows, and were carrying me out of the room.[40]

She has covered the political campaigns of many presidential candidates and also the senate race of Hillary Rodham Clinton. In the book *Postfeminist News*, she comments about the advantage Hillary Clinton had in featuring her daughter, Chelsea, in her senate campaign in 2000. She said, "It doesn't hurt to have Chelsea in front of the cameras, especially since Mrs. Clinton's Republican opponent, Rick Lazio, likes to remind voters about his young and photogenic family."[41] She notes that her toughest interview was with former prime minister of England, Margaret Thatcher, with Fidel Castro a close second. She said, "Thatcher is really tough because she's so smart and unwilling to take any grief from anyone. And Castro isn't easy. First of all, he likes to start interviews at midnight. He's very smart and very well read, and his answers are very long. It's hard to get him off his ideological speech."[42]

Invention

Andrea Mitchell's questions have been so pointed over the years that more than once she was literally removed from an interview. How does

Mitchell develop her questions? Her intellectual nature is part of her persona as an interviewer. Her deep knowledge of issues helps her develop
questions that get to the most germane element of the story. When Ronald
Reagan told his chief of staff, Mike Deaver, that he wanted to call on Andrea Mitchell from NBC at the next presidential news conference, Deaver
said, "No, you don't."[43] Her penchant for preparation is evident in this
statement when she describes her studies for President Reagan's trip to
China. She says, "I had prepared endlessly for this part of the trip. The idea
of Reagan, a fervent anti-Communist, negotiating with the leaders he still
called The Red Chinese, fascinated me. I read books by all the old China
hands and talked to State Department experts and intelligence officials."[44]
It was her keen grasp of the tension between the personal and public image of Hillary Clinton that resulted in the answer that Hillary Clinton gave
which sparked a media maelstrom and much discussion of the role of gender and political power among communication scholars. It was Andrea
Mitchell who asked and Hillary Clinton famously answered: "I suppose I
could have stayed home and baked cookies and had teas, [which is what
most of the press reported] but what I decided to do was to fulfill my profession, which I entered before my husband was in public life."[45]

As Campbell and other scholars[46] note, Clinton's response started a public
discourse about the place of women in politics and society. That Andrea
Mitchell knew just what question to ask is significant. It demonstrates her sophisticated journalistic instincts that gave her the idea to ask Clinton a question about a possible conflict of interest. Mitchell comments about how she
came to approach Clinton: "*The New York Times* raised questions about the
role of Hillary's law firm in an obscure Arkansas land deal. Then, *The Washington Post* added more detail about Hillary's law practice. By now, Hillary was
so protected by aides that there was no way to get to her." So Mitchell arrived
at the diner and drank cup after cup of coffee before even the Secret Service
arrived to block off any of the areas. Mitchell was waiting for the chance to talk
to Hillary Clinton and "inside the diner, Hillary was on her own. My pre-dawn
stakeout at the diner had provoked an incident that had become emblematic
of the Clinton campaign."[47] Instead of focusing on Bill Clinton, Mitchell ze-
roed in on Hillary and produced a much more significant story than any of the
journalists covering Bill Clinton. Mitchell tells of the importance of doing the
"gruntwork" of a journalist when she says: "It was an example of how important it is to cover an event yourself, no matter how routine, rather than relying
on a producer or a surrogate. I'd learned that lesson covering Frank Rizzo in
Philadelphia, and then again during the Reagan years. Unfortunately, it gave
me a reputation for being very aggressive, for getting in people's faces—not a

popular quality with candidates or their aides."[48] Though the scholarship on Clinton's response is impressive, the question whether there was a way [for Mrs. Clinton] to avoid the appearance of conflict that prompted her response came from Andrea Mitchell, and it exemplifies the invention strategies of Mitchell that have produced the responses to which the public has responded.

Disposition

The correspondent type of reporting that Andrea Mitchell has done most often has required her to often have just one or two substantial questions ready, if—that is an important distinction—she gets the chance to ask any questions at all. This is an important distinction in the organization that Mitchell has had to have in her career compared to women profiled who were conducting longer interviews. Mitchell's reporting has required her to consider her questions carefully and to strategically place herself where she was most likely to get an interview. It also requires her to cultivate relationships with the players that she interviews so that they are likely to respond to her if she has the opportunity to ask her question. These are all aspects of her communication strategy that Mitchell has developed throughout her long career. Her ease communicating with famous politicians is evident in this exchange with former New York mayor Rudy Giuliani: "I'm here with the mayor, who do you have any second thoughts? You know, Hillary Clinton is going to be as Senator Clinton sitting up there?" Mayor Giuliani answered: "No, I'm very content with the decision that I made. I get another year as mayor of New York City. I had the last six months to go through my treatment for prostate cancer, which will be over with in about two months, and I'll be back to normal. I'm pretty much back to normal already. I hope."

Andrea Mitchell noted: "You'll be leaving after your two terms and you can relate to the way Bill Clinton is probably feeling giving up power today." Mayor Giuliani said, "Yeah, I was thinking about him last night when I—I came in about 11:00 at night. We walked past the White House, took a look at it and I was thinking, well, it has to be a sad night, no matter what, as you come to the end of your term. But, in a certain way, it's actually easier for him, as it will be for me. You weren't voted out of office, all right. You're leaving on your own power and as—by operation of law—so I think, actually, that's a little bit easier then if he'd been voted out of office." Mitchell closed, "Rudy Giuliani, thanks very much." Mayor Giuliani said: "Thank you, Andrea. Wonderful to see you." Mitchell wished him well: "Lots of luck to you."[49]

Asked whether she thinks that journalists have backed away from asking tough questions in order to get a big interview, she says, "I think there are cases of that. I don't think it really characterizes the profession. The problem I would have in answering that is, you know, it is very hard to define who and what is a journalist these days. I think in that sense we have confused our listeners, viewers and readers. We have blurred too many lines."[50]

Style

Andrea Mitchell's use of language in her reporting—her rhetorical style—has several notable characteristics. Andrea Mitchell has an ease with her subjects, borne of her own intellectualism and years of experience in the broadcasting field. Though petite, she has taken on some of the most formidable public officials with grace and a humanity that makes her subjects comfortable with her. She offers a well-considered question that prompts the subject to respect her preparation and persistence, as she described with her first encounters with President Reagan, when she covered the Reagan presidency. Her persistence paid off time and time again as presidents and other politicians singled her out of a crowd and answered her well-considered question.

Delivery

Andrea Mitchell enunciates her words carefully. Her impressive vocabulary bolsters her ethos and she clearly and confidently reports her stories. As a real Washington insider, she often blended in with the dignitaries she covered and spoke to them at a level they could respect and respond to in kind. Her enthusiasm and reverence for the political process and her role as a journalist is apparent in the interest she holds in the topics she discusses. A warm and human quality is apparent in her commentary, for example, as she commented on the funeral of former president Gerald R. Ford. She said, "At Ford's direction, his casket is being borne by a simple hearse, not a horse-drawn caisson as was used for other former presidents. Jimmy Carter, who defeated Gerald Ford in 1976, became his closest friend among the former presidents, and fittingly, it will be Carter, the one former president who will speak at Gerald Ford's final burial tomorrow in Grand Rapids, Michigan."[51] Andrea Mitchell has a dignified presence and a distinctive, strong, and confident broadcast voice.

Conclusion

Whether she was covering a legendary mayor of a big city, corrupt state politics, the White House, or globe-trotting in search of the latest international story of significance, the persona of Andrea Mitchell that has come through is her "enthusiasm for the story."[52] Though half a century has passed since she stood in front of the microphone in her elementary school and earnestly announced, "Good morning, boys and girls. This is Andrea Mitchell reporting from the principal's office,"[53] Mitchell has retained the wide-eyed schoolgirl wonder that her career—a living history lesson—has offered her. She says, "I've often thought about why I so love daily journalism. Fundamentally, it's the sheer joy of storytelling, the spinning of the narrative itself. It's like reading a good novel, or watching a movie. How will the story end? What will be the outcome of that close Senate vote? On the most exciting stories, honest reporters will tell you that we have no idea either.[54] Her youthful enthusiasm for the sport of journalism remains.

JUDY WOODRUFF

Figure 4.4. Judy Woodruff

In fact, there often emerged a Greshem's Law[55] of journalism, where if the bad doesn't drive out the good, it at least sets the agenda for the public dialogue. Now this is frequently exacerbated, I believe, by the television pundits, the ubiquitous pundits, who parade as journalists but never have covered a police beat and never covered a state legislature. They've never paid their dues; the concept of accountability is alien. All that matter to them are attention and ratings.[56]

Judy Woodruff has focused her career in broadcasting on in-depth, substantial reports that delve into issues that are sociologically and politically

significant. While working at PBS, she engaged in longer, educational features and at CNN she became well known for her political acumen and
hosting the popular *Inside Politics* program. Her ability to moderate a vice
presidential debate and to converse with government leaders on topics
ranging from budget issues to relations between Israelis and Palestinians
immediately separates her from lesser broadcast journalists. In her 2007
PBS interview with former president Carter, who was the Nobel Peace
Laureate in 2002 and who fathered the Camp David Accords and peace
treaty between Egypt and Israel in 1978 during his presidency, Woodruff
pointedly remarked to the former president about his controversial book,
Palestine: Peace Not Apartheid. Woodruff said at the start of the interview,
"that title has brought some sharp critiques from Americans sympathetic
to Israel, and its publication comes amid both renewed tensions and some
peaceful gestures between Israelis and Palestinians."[57] The interview continues on a deep, intellectual level. Woodruff continues to question the title of the book: "The title, you chose, *Palestine: Peace Not Apartheid.* Did
you mean to be provocative, because this immediately calls to mind South
Africa, the repression of blacks by whites?" The former president explains:
"Yes. But I don't consider the word 'provocative' to be negative. I wanted
to provoke . . . " Woodruff interrupts: "The word 'apartheid.'" President
Carter clarifies:

> The whole title, I wanted to provoke discussion, debate, inquisitive analysis of
> the situation there, which is almost completely absent throughout the United
> States, but it's prevalent every day in Israel and in Europe. This is needed, I
> think, for our country to understand what's going on in the West Bank. And I
> chose this title very carefully. It's Palestine, first of all. This is the Palestinians'
> territory, not Israel. Secondly, the emphasis is on peace. And the third thing is
> not apartheid. I don't want to see apartheid. And since now the entire peace
> process is completely dormant, there hasn't been one day for good faith sub-
> stantive negotiations in the last six years to bring peace to Israel, I wanted to
> rejuvenate this process.

Woodruff continues, "And you say it's dormant, and yet today Secretary of
State Condoleezza Rice announcing she's going to meet with the leader of
the Palestinians, Mr. Abbas, later this week. Isn't that a sign of progress, potential progress?"[58] Uflappable, Judy Woodruff continues with the interview and with an exchange that clearly shows she is at least equal to her
guest in intellectual rigor and an understanding of the issues. This type of
highly developed conversation is illustrative of Judy Woodruff's career in
journalism and demonstrates her keen intelligence and her dedication to

the more traditional tenants of journalism rather than the more contemporary journalistic tendency to increase ratings with stories that have ques-
tionable journalistic value. In many ways Woodruff's career path and presentation style suggest that she is a journalist's journalist, tackling topics of
import and preferring the cerebral over the superlative. Woodruff says:

> To what extent do you abandon the principles of journalism to satisfy the pub-
> lic's need to be entertained? Hopefully not at all. I think we've gotten to be
> captives of this notion that the public has a short attention span and you don't
> get it on and off in thirty to sixty seconds, they're not going to watch it. I'd like
> to see us start moving back in the other direction.[59]

Born in Tulsa, Oklahoma, Woodruff grew up as an "Army brat," a fact
that she says taught her "how to cope."[60] She writes, "Whether it was the
first day in a new school—and there were seven new schools between the
first and seventh grades—or how to explain to my Taiwanese pedicab driver
that I had lost the way, I learned how to handle unfamiliar situations."[61] After two years on scholarship at a small Baptist college, North Carolina's
Meredith College, she transferred to her first choice—Duke University—
and earned a degree in political science. She takes great pride in her alma
mater, serving as a trustee emerita, and in 2006 she took time away from her
broadcasting career to teach a course in media at Duke. A self-described
wonk and news junkie even as a student in the late 1960s at Duke,
Woodruff had her eye on Washington. She spent two summers in D.C. before her junior and senior years. What she noticed, though, is that men had
a stranglehold on national political journalism. More than once she was
told, with a straight face, "We're not looking for a woman, we're looking for
a reporter," she wrote in her memoir, *This Is Judy Woodruff at the White
House*.[62] So Woodruff paid her dues. After graduation, she worked in Atlanta for the CBS and NBC affiliates, as a news secretary and later as a reporter. She says that she "entered the news business through the back door,
when I was hired as a ninety-dollars-a-week news secretary. Television news
fascinated me, and it was a logical choice for someone with a political science degree who didn't want to teach or attend graduate school."[63] She
knew that she would have to start small since, she writes, "Nancy Dickerson was among the very few women reporters covering politics at the network level, which was my ultimate goal."[64] Eventually she also anchored the
noon and evening news, and later joined NBC News as a general assignment reporter in Atlanta. She served as the chief White House correspondent for NBC from 1977 to 1982, as well as covering Washington for *The*

Today Show. She moved from NBC to PBS, and from 1984 to 1990 was the host of *Frontline*. During her time at PBS she also reported for *The MacNeil/Lehrer News Hour*. From 1993 to June 2005, she was the host of the acclaimed *Inside Politics* on CNN. In August 2005, Woodruff was named a visiting fellow for the fall semester at Harvard University's Joan Shorenstein Center on the Press, Politics and Public Policy. Judy Woodruff has covered every presidential election since Jimmy Carter—as White House correspondent for NBC, chief Washington correspondent for *The MacNeil/Lehrer NewsHour*, and finally at CNN since 1993. By her own admission, she positively adores politics:

> It's corny, but I'm one of those people who get goose bumps on election night when they count the votes. It never ceases to amaze me that we decide whose hands will be on the levers of power in the richest, most powerful country without spilling a drop of blood. Sure, nasty things are done in the process, but we don't shoot each other to decide who's going to be in charge.[65]

In 2006 Woodruff returned to PBS to work on a documentary about young people and their thoughts on world events, produced in conjunction with MacNeil/Lehrer Productions. In addition to her work on the documentary *Generation Next: Speak Up. Be Heard,* Woodruff serves as a Special Correspondent on the *News Hour,* typically as a moderator for discussions on politics and economics. She also fills in occasionally as anchor of the *News Hour.* Additionally, in 2006, as a guest correspondent, Woodruff also contributed to the National Public Radio (NPR) Morning Edition week-long series "Muslims in America" as part of NPR's fifth-year observance of the September 11, 2001, terrorist attacks. In addition, she anchors the monthly *Conversations with Judy Woodruff*, which airs on Bloomberg Television.

Her husband is Al Hunt, formerly of CNN and *The Wall Street Journal*, now managing editor of the Bloomberg News Washington, D.C, bureau. They are the parents of three children: two biological children—Jeffrey and Ben—and an adopted Korean daughter, Lauren. "Family really is the most important thing to her," says NBC News correspondent Andrea Mitchell, who is godmother to Lauren. This maternal devotion was sorely tested after their eldest son, Jeff, was diagnosed with spina bifida, a defect of the spinal cord. When Jeff was 16, surgery left him paralyzed on one side, with limited sight and speech and loss of short-term memory. Judy Woodruff has become a spokeswoman and advocate for spina bifida. In 2006 she appeared on CNN when a news story about another baby born with spina bifida was in the news.

CNN's Betty Nguyen interviewed Woodruff: "Former CNN anchor Judy Woodruff's twenty-four-year-old son has spina bifida. And Judy knows first-hand what life may be like for Baby Noor and her family. She joins us now from Washington. So good to see you again, Judy. Judy responded: "Thank you, it's great to see you too, Betty. Thank you for having me on." Betty Nguyen said: "Well, we appreciate you sharing your story so we can under-stand what the Baby Noor's parents are getting ready to endure and what's ahead in this road to recovery. First of all, talk to us about your son, Jeffrey. When did you find out that he had spina bifida?" Judy answered, "Betty, we—Jeffrey was diagnosed about a month before he was born. I had a sono-gram, which as you know, is when they do sound waves of the mother's uterus, and it was determined that he might have spina bifida at that point and he may have what's called hydrocephalus. This is when you have addi-tional cerebral spinal fluid, this is the fluid that washes the brain and spinal column. They knew before he was born that he might have this. When he was born in September of 1981 that's when we knew for sure. It is crucial that when a baby is born with spina bifida that there be surgery as soon as possible to close up the opening in the back because, Betty, what it is, spina bifida essentially means that the spinal column did not form properly and that part of the spine—the spinal cord is literally outside the body."

She continued with more information, "Well, there's an organization, Betty, called the Spina Bifida Association of America which does everything in its power to educate Americans about spina bifida and I just want to get in a quick word here about folic acid. This is something that research has identified over the last ten or twenty years if women take enough of this, all women of child bearing age should get at least 400 micrograms of folic acid every day and if there's a history of spina bifida in the family, even much more than that. But they know if you take folic acid you can reduce the in-cidents of spina bifida by as much as 70 percent, so that's crucial. We want to get that word out above all." Judy Woodruff and her husband have ded-icated their time to the association, hosting the annual Spina Bifida Associ-ation Annual Celebrity Roast. Because she sees herself as a mother first, she has dedicated herself to the spina bifida cause, while at the same time con-tributing to the world of broadcast journalism with her distinctive grace and considerable knowledge of issues and events.

In 2005 Judy Woodruff and Al Hunt gave husband-and-wife commence-ment speeches at Montgomery Community College in Maryland. Woodruff is a founding cochair of the International Women's Media Foundation, an organization dedicated to promoting and encouraging women in communi-cation industries worldwide. She serves on the board of trustee of the Freedom Forum and Global Rights: Partners for Justice, and in 2005 became a member of The Knight Foundation Commission on Intercollegiate Athletics and the Board of the National Museum of American History. "She's always a little insecure," Washington bureau chief David Bohrman says. "Even on camera. She's the smartest kid in the class, knows more about politics than anybody, but still. . . ."

Invention

A hallmark of the type of reporting Judy Woodruff does is that it is longer and more narrative than the work of many correspondents. Her ability to write clearly is important for her stories to be understood by the viewer. For example, here is how Woodruff relates government spending to her viewers, "Pick up any consumer's guide and you'll find buying tips to help you decide which product gives you the most for your money. Unfortunately, we cannot normally do that with the items the federal government buys with our tax dollars. But because defense takes up such a large part of the budget and the President is asking some experts to try to answer the question anyway: have we been getting our dollar's worth out of defense?"[66] Woodruff discusses this style of reporting, which is more investigative than simply interviewing the president about his defense spending. She says, "I don't think we should put him [the president] on as often. I think that one network should have the guts—and we are able to do it here [at MacNeil/Lehrer] because we have more of an accordion-style newscast—if it doesn't make any news, we don't run it."[67] The "accordion style" that Judy Woodruff refers to means its "unfolding" nature. The tendency of PBS and in her position at CNN is to let stories get big, instead of having to cram them into a specific, usually very short, time segment.

Disposition

Judy Woodruff's questions for 2004 Democratic candidate Howard Dean were direct. She began: "Let me ask you about the south. As you said you were just there. And among some of the other things you said yesterday was southerners shouldn't vote on issues of guns, God and gays. My question to you is, are you at all concerned that's going to turn off some people of faith in the South, who wants to know what you have to think about God?" Howard Dean responded: "They're going to find out what I think. And I'm pretty outspoken about what I think about all areas. I actually spoke in an African-American church yesterday. And I was very open about talking about Jesus and God's will and so forth and so on, but the truth is that the way to win elections is not to play them on the Republicans' ground. We cannot be talking about divisive social issues. What we've got to be talking about is the things we all have in common. That is health care, jobs and education." Judy Woodruff, "At the same time, Governor, I'm sure you know the Republicans are already starting to talk about the fact that you—I think by your own acknowledgment, left the Episcopal Church in some dispute over a bike path, and you switched to another denomination, the Congregationalist denomination. They're asking what does this say about the depth of your commitment to your own faith?"

Howard Dean: "You know what it really says? It says the Republicans are talking like they're out of the Pharisees. Because if you're a Christian, you're a Christian. I don't believe it ought to matter what kind of a denomination you are. As a matter of fact, if you're a religious person, you're a religious person. I don't think it ought to matter what religion you are. So people who talk like that are what Jesus would call the Pharisees. And I think that's enough of that kind of stuff in the Republican Party. We are all in this together, whether you are a Christian, or a Jew or a Muslim or a Hindu. And there's plenty of all to go around in this country." Judy Woodruff pressed on: "Was it just over a bike path that you left the Episcopal Church?" Howard Dean said, "Yes, as a matter of fact it was. I was fighting to have public access to the waterfront, and we were fighting very hard in the citizens group to allow the public to use it. And this particular diocese decided to join a property rights suit to close it down. I didn't think that was very public spirited. One thing I feel about religion, you have to be very careful not to be a hypocrite if you're a religious person. It is really tough to preach one thing and do something else. And I don't think you can do that." Judy Woodruff: "And you don't believe, Governor, the Republicans are going to have a field day with comments like these?"

Howard Dean: "The Republicans always have a field day with things like this. That's the reason Democrats lose, is because they're so afraid of the Republicans having a field day with comments like this or like that, that they never make any comments. I agree this campaign's colorful. This campaign has motivated Democrats like no campaign in a long time, probably since Bill Clinton in 1992. And before that I can't tell you. John F. Kennedy maybe. And it's not because of me; it's because of us together. This is a campaign about us, not me." Judy Woodruff:

"But you criticized President Bush as recently as yesterday for not having—not providing more leadership, for example, in the war on Iraq. How are the American people going to know what your moral values are, what your moral compass is unless you talk more about those values?" Howard Dean said: "I talk about them every day. Jobs, health care and education is a set of values that I think we embrace in this Democratic Party, including everybody has a set of values that we embrace but the Republicans only talk about."

Judy Woodruff's long career in political reporting is evident in the calm, thorough, and informed way she questions Howard Dean.

Style

Judy Woodruff's characteristic use of language in her broadcasting career—her rhetorical style—has several distinct characteristics. She is very direct with her questions; for example, asking a young woman featured in a story about the lives of "Generation Y," "How much do you owe on credit cards and for your college education?" After the young girl responded, "About $16,000," Judy Woodruff asked her, "And that doesn't bother you?"[68] She sustains direct eye contact with her guests, she engages them in a conversational style that makes them open up. One of the ways she does that is by staying respectful, yet getting to the most important part of the story. Her quick thinking and experience give her the ability to fashion follow-up questions that elicit responses from her guests that help to give her reporting a starting quality to it.

For example, she very colloquially asks Howard Dean, "And you don't believe, Governor, the Republicans are going to have a field day with comments like these?"[69] She often uses the phrase, "I want to understand this better," in order to get her guests to explain their answers more fully. She injects her personal relationship to her story about the "Generation Y, which she dubs "Generation Next': "As a mother of three between the ages of sixteen and twenty-five, I thought I knew something about Generation Next when I started this project. But—no surprise—I've found out that there was much more to discover than I ever dreamed. I have come away mainly heartened by what I've learned. Sure there are bumps along the way. But I'm optimistic that like every generation before them, they have the capacity for greatness that the times call for. I'm Judy Woodruff. Thank you for joining us."[70]

Delivery

Judy Woodruff has a smooth, sophisticated delivery. Though she once took speech classes to eliminate her southern drawl, there is little to distract the viewer from her clear and concise presentation. Authoritative in her tone, she is well known for her relentless research of her stories. She embodies a lady-like southern charm with a no-nonsense persona that has given her access to the most coveted interviewees.

Conclusion

Judy Woodruff has had a long and impressive broadcasting career, and was one of the pioneering women broadcast journalist who gained access to political reporting at a time when only men were visible. Her sophistication, intelligence, and warm, rich tone made her a successful journalist. Similar to the work that Katie Couric has done to build awareness for colon cancer, Judy Woodruff used her "electronic hearth" as a tool to educate the public about her child's illness, spina bifida. Her ability to connect her own experiences, as she did with her lengthy documentary work on "Generation Y," to her stories and become an advocate for several causes has earned her respect among her colleagues and admiration with her long-viewing public.

NOTES

1. Dana Milbank, "In the House, Suddenly Righteous Republicans," *The Washington Post*, January 4, 2001, A2.

2. transcripts.cnn.com/TRANSCRIPTS/0701/26/cnr.02.html (accessed March 25, 2007).

3. Nina J. Easton, "Unsung Heroes II," *American Journalism Review*, July/August, 2002, http://www.ajr.org/Article.asp?id=2564 (accessed February 28, 2007).

4. Dana Bash, interview with Nichola D. Gutgold, March 15, 2007.

5. Kathryn S. Wenner, "She's Not Bashful: CNN producer Dana Bash Moves to the Other Side of the Camera to Become a White House Correspondent," *American Journalism Review*, January, 2003, http://www.ajr.org/Article.asp?id=2738 (accessed February 28, 2007).

6. Dana Bash, interview with Nichola D. Gutgold, March 15, 2007.

7. http://www.whitehouse.gov/news/releases/2004/06/20040609-10.html

8. Ibid.

9. Dana Bash, interview with Nichola D. Gutgold, March 15, 2007.

10. Ibid.

11. Candy Crowley, e-mail correspondence with Nichola D. Gutgold, March 2, 2007.

12. Stephen Hess and Marvin Kalb, eds., *The Media and the War on Terrorism* (Washington, D.C: Brookings Institute Press, 2003), 249.

13. http://www.rmwc.edu/admissions/alumprofiles/ccrowley.asp.

14. "Election Reflections: Candy Crowley," Monday, December 18, 2000, 1 p.m. EST, http://www.cnn.com/chat/transcripts/2000/12/18/crowley.html (accessed January 2, 2007)

15. Ibid.

16. Candy Crowley, e-mail correspondence with Nichola D. Gutgold, March 2, 2007.

17. Ibid.

18. Roderick P. Hart, *Modern Rhetorical Criticism* (Needham Heights: Allyn and Bacon, 1997), 222–23.

19. "Candy Crowley's spectacular view of the inauguration," January 20, 2001, http://cnnstudentnews.cnn.com/2001/ALLPOLITICS/stories/01/20/crowley.debrief/ (accessed January 2, 2006). Web posted at: 9:11 p.m. EST.

20. Elizabeth Yuan, "Staying on Top of Your Game," CNN, July 28, 2006, 3:48 PM EST.

21. Howard Kurtz, Candy Crowley, "Are Journalists Quietly Rejoicing Over Democratic Takeover of Congress?; Did Media Scapegoat Rumsfeld?" *Reliable Sources*, CNN, November 12, 2006, 10:00 a.m. EST.

22. Stephen Hess and Marvin Kalb, editors, *The Media and the War on Terrorism* (Washington, D.C.: Brookings Institute, 2003).

23. Ali Velshi, Candy Crowley, "Stories Behind the Stories," CNN, May 28, 2006.

24. CNN Breaking News "Sen. John Kerry Arrives at Boston's Faneuil Hall Deliver His Concession Speech," November 3, 2004, http://edition.cnn.com/TRANSCRIPTS/0411/03/bn.03.html (accessed January 2, 2006).

25. Rob Armstrong, *Covering Politics: A Handbook for Journalists* (Ames, Iowa: Blackwell Publishing, 2004), 224.

26. Ibid., 223.

27. Candy Crowley, e-mail correspondence with Nichola D. Gutgold, March 2, 2007.

28. www://cnn.com/chat/transcripts/2006/6/8/lamont.html (accessed January 2, 2006).

29. Maryellen Fillo, "Senate Race 'Like Christmas Morning' for Media; National Press Converges on State to Cover the Political Story of the Summer That Is Seen as a Referendum on War," *Hartford Courant* (Connecticut), August 8, 2006, A2.

30. Anderson Cooper, "Judgment Day Arrives for Senator Joe Lieberman," 360 DEGREES 10:00 p.m. EST, August 8, 2006, 10 p.m. EST.

31. Media Bistro, the DC Fishbowl Interview, September, 14, 2006, http://www.mediabistro.com/fishbowlDC/television/zain_verjee_the_fishbowldc_interview_43144.asp (accessed January 2, 2007).

32. Norman Sklarewitz, "Political Journalism," September 1, 2006, http://airtran magazine.com/contents/2006/09/candy-crowley/ (accessed January 2, 2007).

33. Andrea Mitchell, *Talking Back . . . to Presidents, Dictators, and Assorted Scoundrels* (New York: Viking Press, 2005), xvii.

34. Colleen Toomey, producer, The President and the Press, Films for the Humanties and Sciences, 1998.

35. Richard Albert, interview with Nichola D. Gutgold, October 20, 2007.

36. Ibid., 17.

37. Andrea Mitchell, "There Is No Freedom of the Press Here," MSNBC.com, July 21, 2005, http://www.msnbc.msn.com/id/8616820/ (accessed January 11, 2007).

38. NBC news transcripts, *The Today Show*, "Secretary of State Condoleezza Rice Demands and Gets Apology from Sudanese Government for Rough Handling of Aides and Reporters Traveling with Her," July 21, 2005, Thursday, 7 a.m. EST.

39. "Rice Gets Apology for Incident in the Sudan," *USA Today*, July 21, 2005, http://www.usatoday.com/news/world/2005-07-21-rice-sudan_x.htm (accessed January 4, 2006).

40. Andrea Mitchell, *Talking Back . . . to Presidents, Dictators, and Assorted Scoundrels* (New York: Viking Press, 2005), 250.

41. Mary Douglass Vavrus, *Postfeminist News: Political Women in the Media* (New York: State University of New York Press), 2002, 158.

42. Barbara Kiviat, "10 Questions for Andrea Mitchell," *Time*, September 14, 2005, http://www.time.com/time/magazine/article/0,9171,1093739-1,00.html (accessed January 3, 2006).

43. Ibid., 64.

44. Ibid., 72.

45. Karlyn Kohrs Campbell, "The Discursive Performance of Femininity: Hating Hillary," *Rhetoric & Public Affairs* (1998): 1–20.

46. Karrin Vasby Anderson, "From Spouses to Candidates: Hillary Rodham Clinton, Elizabeth Dole, and the Gendered Office of U.S. President," *Rhetoric & Public Affairs* 5, no. 1 (Spring 2002): 105–32.

47. Andrea Mitchell, *Talking Back . . . to Presidents, Dictators, and Assorted Scoundrels* (New York: Viking Press, 2005), 185.

48. Ibid., 186.

49. NBC News transcripts, NBC News Special Report: Inauguration of George W. Bush (11:10 a.m. on ET) January 20, 2001, Saturday, Rudy Giuliani Talks About Senator Clinton and His Cancer Reporters: Andrea Mitchell.

50. Patricia Sheridan, "Breakfast with Andrea Mitchell," *Pittsburgh Post-Gazette*, October 9, 2006, http://www.post-gazette.com/pg/06282/728480-129.stm (accessed January 19, 2007).

51. NBC news transcripts, *Today*, 7:00 a.m. EST, NBC, January 2, 2007, Tuesday. "Former President Gerald Ford's Funeral Today," reporters: Andrea Mitchell.

52. Ibid., 25.

53. Ibid., xv.

54. Ibid., xv.

55. D. D. Guttenplan, "Britain: Dumb and Dumber? A transatlantic Spat Over the Quality of 'Quality Press,'" *Columbia Journalism Review* (July/August 1997), http://archives.cjr.org/year/97 (accessed January 24, 2006).

56. The Theodore H. White Lecture with Judy Woodruff, Joan Shorenstein Center for Press, Politics and Public Policy, Harvard University John F. Kennedy School of Government, 2001.

57. http://www.pbs.org/newshour/bb/middle_east/july-dec06/carter_11-28.html (accessed January 29, 2007).

58. Ibid.

59. Shirley Biagi, *Newstalk II State of the Art Conversation with Today's Broadcast Jornalists* (Belmost: Wadsworth Publishing Company, 1987), 52.

60. Judy Woodruff with Kathleen Maxa, *This Is Judy Woodruff at the White House* (Menlo Park, CA and London: Addison-Wesley Publishing, 1982), 75.

61. Ibid.

62. Ibid., 84.

63. Ibid.

64. Ibid., 82

65. Mark Matousek, "Gritty Woman CNN's Judy Woodruff Balances Hard News and Hard Knocks," *AARP Magazine*, September & October 2004, http://www.aarpmagazine.org/people/Articles/a2004-09-13-mag-woodruff.html (accessed January 29, 2007).

66. Shirley Biagi, *Newstalk II, State of the Art Conversation with Today's Broadcast Jornalists* (Belmost: Wadsworth Publishing Company, 1987), 58.

67. Ibid., 50.

68. Judy Woodruff, "Generation Next Changes the Face of the Workforce," PBS, December 14, 2006, http://www.pbs.org/newshour/bb/business/july-dec06/geny_12-14.html.

69. *Judy's Woodruff's Inside Politics*, "The Dean Machine: Is Dean Unstoppable?"; "Bush Signs Medicare Reform Bill"; "GOP Heading for Big Apple," aired December 8, 2003, 3:26 p.m. EST http://transcripts.cnn.com/TRANSCRIPTS/0312/08/ip.00.html (accessed February 3, 2007).

70. Judy Woodruff, "Generation Next Changes the Face of the Workforce," PBS, December 14, 2006, http://www.pbs.org/newshour/bb/business/july-dec06/geny_12-14.html.

6

VETERAN AND VARIED

Diane Sawyer, Lesley Stahl, and Paula Zahn

DIANE SAWYER

Figure 5.1.   Diane Sawyer

I really love what you learn every day in the business. I love the breath-taking way we walk into people's lives and ask them anything we want and then leave. For a moment you have available to you the whole universe of a person's life—the pain and the suffering and the joy and the struggle. You can learn from it and take it with you, and then come back the next day with somebody else. That's what I like to do.[1]

Considered the "John Madden of network news"[2] because she has so often been brought in to save the ratings of a program, Diane Sawyer is one of the most versatile and well-known women in broadcasting. A Wellesley College graduate and former Junior Miss America, she has a dignified and sophisticated on-air personality that *Time* described as "wholesome, more high school prom queen than Hollywood glamour puss; with the rich, honeyed voice: husky and authoritative, but free of the severe tone affected by some females in television news."[3] Sawyer's career embodies the trajectory of many women who began in broadcasting before 1972. Her first job was as a weather girl and a part-time reporter at her hometown television station, Louisville, Kentucky's WLKY-TV. She describes the experience: "I was so bad at it." Besides her lack of meteorology background (her college degree is in English), Diane Sawyer's other problem was her eyesight. She didn't wear glasses on camera, and couldn't tell if she was pointing to the East or the West coast.[4] Despite that she didn't really want to be a weather reporter, she learned a lot about her craft during her time in Louisville and she was calm and self-assured on camera. Even more than that, few people in broadcasting—male or female—worked harder trying to be better than she did. While in Louisville, Diane Sawyer's beloved father died unexpectedly in an auto accident. A respected judge, his death "ignited further interest in government and politics."[5] She left her weather girl assignment and from 1970 to 1974, she served in the Nixon White House as an assistant deputy press secretary, where she was often referred to by Nixon as "the smart girl." After President Nixon resigned, she stayed on as his personal assistant, helping him pen his Watergate memoirs. Once Nixon's book was complete, Diane Sawyer accepted a job offer as a reporter with CBS News. Though she had little reporting experience, she quickly gained the respect of her initially skeptical colleagues with her impressive reports from Three Mile Island in Harrisburg, Pennsylvania, where a nuclear meltdown in 1979 became the subject of intense media coverage. The same impressive reporting of the Iran hostage crisis gave Sawyer experience and proved she had the right qualities to have a long career as a television broadcaster. When Sawyer accepted the job of State Department correspondent for *CBS News* (1978–1981) she began her ascent as a popular figure in television journalism. Diane Sawyer was the coanchor of *CBS Morning News* (from 1981), the coanchor of *Early Morning News* (1982–1984), and the first woman on the network's flagship public affairs program, *60 Minutes*, CBS (1984–1989). Occasionally, she substituted for Dan Rather on *CBS Evening News*, though her anchor stints were sparse, reportedly because Dan Rather was jealous of her.[6]

In 1989 Diane Sawyer left her successful position at CBS to sign a multi-year contract to coanchor *PrimeTime Live* on ABC News with Sam Donaldson. In 1999 she was named coanchor with Charlie Gibson on *Good Morning America.*

Diane Sawyer is willing to move between two styles, that of a tabloid journalist and the "legitimate" journalist. Diligent reporting pieces coexist with celebrity interviews, such as her coverage of the events of September 11, 2001, and the interview with Michael Jackson and Lisa Marie Presley. Her low-key questions to Tonya Harding during the 1992 Olympics, her audacity to ask Marla Maples, the second wife of Donald Trump, whether or not he was "really the best sex" she ever had, and her soft news focused *Good Morning America* cohosting contrast sharply with her groundbreaking interviews with heads of state, such as the exclusive interview with Syrian president Assand. Her versatility as an interviewer is similar to that of another Roone Arledge protégé, Barbara Walters. Diane Sawyer's experience working in the White House and her cerebral persona make it easy to imagine her interviewing political figures, but note the ease with which she converses with image-challenged pop stars Britney Spears and Michael Jackson.

The questions that Diane Sawyer asked of Britney Spears suggest that Sawyer took on the role of the big sister or motherly figure, asking the singer why she would allow herself to be photographed so scantily clad to promote her music. Sawyer asked: "Is it about shocking people?" To which Spears responded, "About shocking . . ." Sawyer said, "Yeah" and Spears defended her photos with, "You know what? When I was younger, I used to run around my house naked when I was thirteen and people, my dad would be like, I was just very like, free, but . . ." Diane Sawyer challenged Spears' explanation by saying, "This is not just about that, though. This is, as you know, this is . . ." Spears said, "I feel comfortable in my skin. I think it's an okay thing to express yourself and be the way you want to be. I mean, I wouldn't walk into a club or a party like that. But I think you know, I think it's fine."[7] Sawyer's interview with the another pop star, Michael Jackson, prompted a law suit over the mention of Jackson's alleged abuse of children. She began the 1995 interview, which included Michael Jackson's then wife, Lisa Marie Presley, by saying: "Glad you're here. It occurs to me, looking at the two of you, I have got to start by asking how this marriage took place, how it began. Let me guess, it wasn't over miniature golf and a . . . a hot dog or something. When did it start? What was the dating?" Michael Jackson explained: "Well, we first met, she was seven years old and I was seventeen. This was in Las Vegas. She used to come and see my show.

We had the only family show on the strip—the Jackson 5. And um, she used to come as a little girl and sit right up front. She came quite often. She came with a lot of bodyguards and . . ." Diane Sawyer asked: "Had you stayed in touch with her?" Michael Jackson responded: "Sure, sure. And then she'd come backstage and then I'd, you know, talk and say 'hi' and then she'd come again. And I thought she was sweet and loving and I hoped I . . . I always hoped I'd see her again." Michael Jackson said, "Well, well at first this is what happened. When she was eighteen I used to tell my lawyer John Branca, do you know Lisa Marie Presley 'cause I think she's really cute. And he'd laugh every time. He goes, 'I'll try my best,' that's what he'd say. Then he'd come back and I'd say 'well did you find out?' He'd say 'no, there's nothing. . . .' So I would worry him about this all the time. The next thing I noticed, there was a picture on a magazine cover where she's married, which really tore me to pieces because I felt that was supposed to be me, I really did." Diane Sawyer pressed: "And what, what was the countdown to your marriage? Tell me, who said the word marriage first?" Michael Jackson said: "I did."

Diane Sawyer noted: "As you know, the reaction to this marriage—and I know you feel strongly about it—but the reaction to this marriage has been across the spectrum. Everything from astonishment, to delight, to suspicion. That it was somehow too convenient. Lisa, did you ask Michael about the charges? Did the two of you think about the impact, of the marriage on the allegations?" Lisa Marie Presley: "Absolutely not. He called . . . I was in touch with him through the whole process of this—charges going on. I was talking to him when he disappeared. I was actually supposed to go to San Juan Puerto Rico when he left and disappeared, and I got a call that he wasn't going to be there and I was actually a part of the whole thing with him, by talking to him on the phone." Diane Sawyer asked: "Did you say to him, are they true?" Lisa said, "No I didn't. No . . . I actually did not." Diane Sawyer asked: "I want to take a minute here, and I'm gonna come back to the marriage . . ." Lisa Marie Presley insisted that they discuss the situation: "Could I just . . . sorry. He, he went on and on and on about it, so I didn't really have to say 'Are the allegations true?' It was 'Aaaarrrgh!' on the phone, you know, and. . . ."

Diane Sawyer said: "Over and over." And Lisa said: "Just constant . . . yeah." Diane Sawyer, turning to Michael said, "Well, because I know that you've wanted to express similar sentiments for a long time, I want to ask you a few things about the charges. But first I want to establish for the viewers here that there are no ground rules. You have said to me that you are not afraid of any questions. So, I wanted that to be understood by everyone before we proceed. I think I want to begin by making sure that the terms are clear. You have said that you would never harm a child. I want to be as specific as I can. Did you ever, as this boy said you did, did you ever sexually engage, fondle, have sexual contact with this child, or any other child?" Michael Jackson said: "Never ever. I could never harm a child, or anyone. It's not in my heart, it's not who I am, and it's not what I'm . . . I'm not even interested in that." Diane Sawyer transitioned to: "You said you don't sleep in separate bedrooms and I'm gonna confess, okay . . . this is live TV and I'm copping out right here, because I didn't spend my life . . . as a serious journalist to ask these kinds of questions. But I'm not oblivious to the fact, that, your fans had one question they most wanted to ask . . . of you." Lisa asked: "Do we have sex?"

Then Diane played a video of fans asking: Person 1: We wanna know, if you've done "the thing"? Person 2: Michael, I know this is an intimate question, but are you having sex, together, with Lisa Marie? Person 3: Do you guys really love each other or are you just doing this to satisfy the media? Person 4: Are you guys intimate? (end clip).[8] Obviously ill at ease asking Jackson and Presley about the sexual nature of their relationship, Sawyer reverts to a video clip of others asking. While Sawyer says, "I did not spend my life as a serious journalist to ask these kinds of questions," she had no qualms asking Marla Maples about the quality of the sex she had with Donald Trump! In 2007 she interviewed celebrity Nicole Richie, known mostly for her thinness and her friendship with Paris Hilton. Though Sawyer describes herself as a "serious journalist," she also avails herself to the tabloid reporting that gets ratings rather than a place in history books.

Although Diane Sawyer no doubts improves ABC's ratings when she concedes to an interview with a pop star or the wife of an infamous real estate magnate, she seems more comfortable in her interviews with high-ranking government figures. In an interview with then secretary of state Colin Powell, Sawyer begins, "There you were, national security advisor to Ronald Reagan, a very young Colin Powell, those years ago." Obviously it is her political reporting that she believes adds ethos to her reputation as a serious journalist. With ease she converses with Secretary Powell: "You have now worked for Ronald Reagan, for President Bush senior, and for the current President Bush. Tell us the biggest difference in Ronald Reagan's style." Her credibility to the viewers is on par with her interviewee, and Diane Sawyer continues the interview with Powell effortlessly moving from topic to topic. Though she interviews pop culture figures and political figures with the same sense of control and authority, the viewer gets the sense that at her core she is a political reporter—even a political wonk when she lets it come out— and she is most at home with political leaders who hearken her back to her early career days in the Nixon White House.

In 2007, she interviewed Syrian President Bashar al-Assad, a forty-one-year old doctor who contended that he could help broker peace in the Middle East. She begins, "There are a chorus of voices in the United States saying that talking to Syria is the way to end the war in Iraq. Can you stop the violence in Iraq? Are you waiting to hear from the Americans? Why not begin it now?" President Assad says, "We are hearing, but we don't expect that much. We don't expect that they're going to. After nearly four years of occupation they haven't learned their lesson, they haven't stopped the dialogue. I think it's too late for them to move toward that life." Diane Sawyer transitions, "Describe the current President Bush to me in your view." Assad replies: "I'd rather give objective view. . . . I've never met him personally to describe him, but what I know about this issue that this administration, in general, are not interested in peace at all. This administration is not willing to achieve peace. They don't have the will, and they don't have the vision. This is, in brief, what I know about this administration not about the president in particular." Sawyer then broadens her questioning: "Who do you admire the most in the world?" When Assad demurs by listing biblical figures, Diane Sawyer gets more specific: "And is there anyone operating on the world stage today that you admire? Any leader, any diplomat?" And then Assad concedes, "Maybe Bush, the father, because of his will to achieve the peace in the region. Of course, President Clinton, he has the same will, and he is admired in our region and respected." Then Diane Sawyer brings it to an upcoming presidential election by asking, "And, Mrs. Clinton?" [9] The ease with which she moves from one question to another, obviously on the same intellectul plane as the interviewees, demonstrates her agility as a reporter and her value as a seasoned interviewer and broadcast heavyweight. When Sawyer finished interviewing Iranian President Mahmoud Ahmadinejad about his country's role in Iraq, he said: "Those were combative questions. Women should not be asking tough questions about war, but about love and family and culture."[10]

Invention

Diane Sawyer asks questions that the viewer is thinking about. Her ability to converse with guests in a colloquial, yet authoritative, way is reminiscent of Barbara Walters's style. Her celebrity is also on par with some of the most well-known women in broadcasting also featured in this book, including Walters, Christiane Amanpour, and Katie Couric. Having *Good Morning America* as a forum has given Sawyer's formerly standoffish persona a softer feel and this has translated into her becoming more well known and more liked than ever. In 2006 she ranked number 78 in Forbes "100 Most Notable Celebrities" and was noted as "frequently spotted on the New York City social scene."[11] She is able to warm up to guests in the guise of being a girlfriend, as she did with Marla Maples, and then can talk political talk with grace with heads of state.

Disposition

Diane Sawyer organizes her questions very logically for her interviews. She is able to keep her questions extemporaneous by responding to answers with revised questions in order to get her desired response. For example, when Assad demurred from her question about whom he admires most with the response of biblical figures, Sawyer was quick to follow up with a question that ensured an answer from contemporary politics. Her experience gives her the confidence not to demure from asking a revised question and challenging even the most stately guest.

Style

Diane Sawyer's typical use of language in her interviews—her rhetorical style—has notable characteristics. *The Washington Post* notes that Sawyer "can deflect questions as smoothly as she asks them," noting that when Sawyer is asked about when she might leave *Good Morning America*, she says, "Honest to goodness, I've been working flat out and I am so happy, and that's all I've been thinking about and doing right now."[12] She is quick-witted and disarming, often looking her interviewee directly in the eye and smiling.

Delivery

Diane Sawyer's smooth and serious tone work to boost her ethos as a news anchor. Her delivery is authoritative and she modulates her voice to help sustain interest in her stories. Her passion for her investigative stories is conveyed through her facial expressions of curiosity and concern about her wide-ranging topics—from pop stars to heads of state—and she conveys a sense of urgency and intrigue to her audiences.

Conclusion

Diane Sawyer has grown to prominence in broadcasting and is, most significantly, the first woman to serve as host of the coveted CBS *60 Minutes* program. Her intelligence, versatility, and star power have given stability to *Good Morning America* and have demonstrated her value to the network and her authoritative yet friendly appeal to viewers.

When she renewed her contract with ABC, *The New York Times* noted, "Diane Sawyer agreed to a new contract with ABC News yesterday, ending as ardent a courting as television news has ever seen, one that involved every network and extravagant offers of both money and programs. The new ABC deal, for an estimated $5 million a year, will make Ms. Sawyer a presence on two more prime-time news magazines, in addition to maintaining her anchor position on *Primetime Live*."[13] All four major networks have sought her services, and she has become a "brand name," a person the viewers remember, and a television personality who can deliver ratings. She remains one of the most visible news figures in television.

LESLEY STAHL

Figure 5.2.   Lesley Stahl

From the beginning of my life at the network [CBS] there was a sisterhood. At first it was a tiny little group, but ever since there's been a sense of family among the women reporters. Our circle was a refuge, a place where we didn't have to discuss sports, a place where we could be ourselves. This was far more true years ago, when there was a sense of hunkering down together. People tell me today that I work in a men's club, but it isn't true. Just about half the producers at *60 Minutes* are women.[14]

"Brenda Starr" is the nickname Lesley Stahl was given by her CBS colleagues who admired her aggressiveness. Assigned to cover the Watergate break-in because most of the other Washington bureau reporters were out of town and the story was considered minor, she couldn't be removed later because she had become so expert. Yet it was Daniel Schorr who handled the story for the *CBS Evening News*; Lesley Stahl's main outlet at the time was radio and the CBS Morning News.[15]

In her autobiography, *Reporting Live*, Lesley Stahl declares that "I was born on my thirtieth birthday. Everything up to that was prenatal."[16] Actually, Lesley Stahl was born in Swampscott, Massachusetts, in 1941. Her father was an executive with an oil company and her mother was a homemaker. Both parents continually reminded her that she could "have it all": marriage, children, career. [17] She graduated cum laude from Wheaton College, a woman's college in Norton, Massachusetts, and wanted to go to medical school. Her plans changed, however, when she realized "I couldn't touch anything in class, the smell disgusted me."[18] After a short stint as a speechwriter she decided that journalism was for her and landed a job as a field reporter for NBC in London with Chet Huntley and David Brinkley. In a few years she went to Boston to be a producer for the local CBS affiliate and in 1971 "wangled her way on camera."[19] When the station in Boston lost its broadcast license, Lesley Stahl went to work for CBS as a reporter in the Washington Bureau. She writes, "I was hired in the affirmative action sweep of 1972, and so I shared 'office space' (a corridor in the back) with Connie Chung and Bernie Shaw."[20] In her long and varied career with CBS, she has held several positions. Her reputation as a hard-hitting, no-nonsense reporter began in earnest when she covered hard news during Watergate. To get an interview with John Dean, then counsel to President Nixon, she followed him into the men's room! She served as an anchor/moderator on *CBS Morning News* and as the only woman ever to moderate *Face the Nation*, and then took a position as coeditor at *60 Minutes*, a job she describes as "reporter's paradise."[21]

Lesley Stahl reported on a four-and-a-half minute story that ran during the 1984 presidential campaign. Its subject was how the White House staged events for Ronald Reagan and manipulated the press, especially television. Stahl later said that a White House official called her soon after the piece aired and said he'd loved it. She asked, "How could you?" He said, "Haven't you figured it out yet? The public doesn't pay attention to what you say. They just look at the pictures." All she had done was to assemble, free of charge, a Republican campaign film, a wonderful montage of Reagan appearing in upbeat scenes.[22] This experience underscored for Stahl the importance of controlling interviews and making sure that she got the result she wanted by the end of the interview. Her communication style is forceful and unflinching, and she rarely lets a subject leave the interview until she has gotten the result she is seeking.

In 2002 she began hosting *48 Hours Investigates*, the popular CBS murder mystery investigative show. She continues as host and coeditor of the venerable newsmagazine program *60 Minutes*. Though well into her sixties, she is considerably younger than Morley Safer, Mike Wallace, and Andy Rooney, who continue to appear on the program. Her longevity in the business is demonstrated by her original reports that aired when Walter Cronkite was anchor at *CBS Evening News*.

"A tough reporter, she is also an engaging conversationalist, equally at ease discussing career or family, high heels or Watergate's historic subversion of the government"[23] noted TV critic Joanne Ostrow. Stahl says, "I know my reputation. I ask the hard questions. I'm tenacious, unrelenting."[24] Bob Schieffer, longtime CBS colleague of Stahl's, notes that "of all the moderators who have headed *Face the Nation*, none asked more pointed questions than Stahl. Her interviewing style was as subtle as a runaway bus coming at you head-on, and because of it she sometimes got answers that others didn't."

Several important interviews demonstrate Stahl's ability to get the answers that can be difficult, if not impossible, to get. In 1986 Secretary of State George Schultz appeared on *Face the Nation* during the most controversial time in the Reagan administration. The Iran-Contra Affair was a political scandal during the Reagan administration in which members of the executive branch sold weapons to Iran, an avowed enemy, and illegally used the profits to continue funding rebels, the Contras, in Nicaragua. "We need to respond to terrorism," Shultz told Stahl, "and among our responses is our denial of arms shipments to Iran. That policy remains our policy. It is in effect, and there it is." Stahl said, "I don't want to badger you, but you are not answering my question." Surprisingly, Shultz said, "Well, no, you can badger me." To which Stahl said, "Why did you—okay, good. Why did you not tell the Arabs the truth?" Shultz said, "It is clearly wrong to trade arms for hostages. So that is our policy . . . It isn't the right thing for governments to trade arms or anything else for hostages, just because it encourages taking more." Stahl asked if there would be more arms shipments. "It is certainly against our policy," Shultz responded. "That's not an answer," bold

Stahl said. She pressed further: "Why don't you answer the question directly? I'll ask it again: Will there be any more arms shipments to Iran, either directly by the United States or through any third parties?" Shultz said, "Under the circumstances of Iran's war with Iraq, in pursuit of terrorism, its association with those holding our hostages, I would certainly say, as far as I'm concerned, no." Stahl then asked a question that demonstrates her keen sense of understanding of the situation and timing: "Do you have the authority to speak for the administration?" "No," said Shultz and with that the interview ended.[25]

After the 2000 election, in which the largest electoral crisis in American history took place, and after thirty-six days of legal and political wrangling, Al Gore conceded the presidency to George W. Bush. In November, 2002, Gore began to emerge publicly, advancing speculation that he may run again for the White House. Though on a national book tour and interviewed repeatedly, Gore refused to comment about whether or not he planned to run again, until interviewed by Lesley Stahl on *60 Minutes*. In Lesley Stahl's 2002 interview with Al Gore he revealed that he would not run for president, something that the American public was on the edge of its seat to learn.

Stahl began the interview by getting right to the most pertinent question: "You know, you've been all over television, all over the newspapers for this last week. You've given back-to-back interviews, you've answered virtually every question except one, and that is, are you or are you not going to run in 2004? Are you going to run?" Al Gore responded, "Well, I've decided not to run and I . . ." Stahl interrupted him: "You've decided not to run."

Al Gore confirmed: "I've decided that I will not be a candidate for president in 2004. My family all gathered here in New York City over the last few days and I found that I've come to closure on this. I don't think it's the right thing for me to be a candidate in 2004." Lesley Stahl said, "Well, I think a lot of people are just going to be bowled over. You're not a candidate. You've been looking like a candidate. Tell us how you have arrived at what I think is going to be a stunningly surprising decision." Al Gore said, "Well, I've run for president twice, and there are many other exciting ways to serve. I intend to remain actively involved in politics. I want to help whoever the Democratic Party's nominee is in 2004 to—to win the election. I'm going to explore a lot of other opportunities." Somewhat skeptical of Gore's explanation, Stahl followed up: "The ambition to be the commander in chief, the ambition to sit in the Oval Office, that's gone." Al Gore further explained: "Well, I personally have the energy and the drive and the ambition to make another campaign, but I don't think it's the right thing for me to do. I—I think that a campaign that would be a rematch between myself and President Bush would inevitably involve a focus on the past that would in some measure distract from the focus on the future that I think all campaigns have to be about." Lesley Stahl then went on to ask Al Gore if he thought that he could beat President Bush and what Democrat in his opinion could.

Lesley Stahl's hard-hitting interview with Bush administration officials Paul O'Neill and Richard Clarke remain one of the most significant news stories of 2004. In her voiceover, Lesley Stahl oriented the viewer to the situation. She began, "Right now a special presidential commission is investigating whether the attacks on the World Trade Center and the Pentagon on 9/11 were preventable. The questions they're in effect asking are what did the president know, and when did he know it about al-Qaeda. There are few people in a better position to answer those questions than Richard Clarke, the administration's former top advisor on counter-terrorism."

Richard Clark began: "Rumsfeld was saying that we needed to bomb Iraq, and—and we all said, 'But no, no. Al-Qaeda is in Afghanistan. We need to bomb Afghanistan.' And Rumsfeld said, 'There aren't any good targets in Afghanistan, and there are lots of good targets in Iraq.'" Lesley Stahl plainly inquired: "But didn't they think that there was a connection?" Mr. Clarke responded: "No. I—I think they wanted to believe that there was a connection, but the CIA was sitting there, the FBI was sitting there, I was sitting there saying, 'We've looked at this issue for years. For years we've looked for a connection, and there's just no connection.'" Lesley Stahl asked the question many viewers wanted answered: "Was Iraq supporting Al-Qaeda?" Mr.Clarke said, "No. There's absolutely no evidence that Iraq was supporting Al-Qaeda."

Invention

Lesley Stahl doesn't take time to ask nuanced questions at the beginning of her interviews. She goes for the jugular and asks the questions that are most important. She isn't afraid to accuse an interviewee of lying and she is determined to get whatever she wants answered by simply following up with the same question if it hasn't been answered.

Disposition

Lesley Stahl is expert at following up with a question that requires the interviewee to give her a simple, clear response. She also challenges interviewees who are being, in her opinion, less than forthright. For example, with

Shultz she challenges him with: "Why don't you answer the question directly? I'll ask it again: Will there be any more arms shipments to Iran, either directly by the United States or through any third parties?" Shultz said, "Under the circumstances of Iran's war with Iraq, in pursuit of terrorism, its association with those holding our hostages, I would certainly say, as far as I'm concerned, no."[26]

Style

Lesley Stahl has been described as the most hard-hitting reporter on *60 Minutes*. She is confident and direct in her ability to ask pointed questions and pursue tough interviews. She was clearly overjoyed to move away from covering Washington to working as a host on *60 Minutes*, mostly because her own style was able to come out as a *60 Minutes* host. She has a no-nonsense, straightforward persona.

Delivery

Lesley Stahl has a commanding, yet open and casual delivery. Often the corners of her mouth turn up to suggest a smile, and sometimes she will smile or laugh as if to soften her approach when she clearly disagrees with an interview subject. For example, in her interview with Nancy Pelosi, she actually laughed in response to Pelosi's remarks. Stahl sets the stage with her voiceover: "Pelosi has called her Republican colleagues 'immoral' and 'corrupt,' and has said they're running a criminal enterprise."

Pointedly, she says to Pelosi: "I mean, you're one of the reasons we have to restore civility in the first place." Pelosi clarifies: "Well actually, when I called them those names, I was being gentle," Pelosi says. "There are much worse things I could've said about them." Stahl counters: "Oh really? It's hard to imagine. But if you're Speaker, I'm wondering—how you'll work with him. I mean, here are some of the things—only some of the things you have called him, 'an incompetent leader,'" Stahl says. "You said, 'In fact, he's not a leader. He's a person who has no judgment.'" "That's right," Pelosi says.

Lesley Stahl explains to Pelosi: "It even stings to hear it now. I mean, obviously, the two of you are bound to get along just great," Stahl replies, laughing. Pelosi explains: "You know, we're professionals. You could go through a long list of things his surrogates have said about me. I know they have to do what they have to do, and they know I have to do what I have to do. And what I have to do is make a distinction in the public that's between the Democrats and the Republicans in order to win," Pelosi says. "This isn't personal." "It sounds personal," Stahl remarks. "This isn't personal," Pelosi says. "He's 'incompetent,' he's. . . ," Stahl continues. "Well, I think he is," Pelosi states. "Well, that's personal," Stahl points out. "Well, I'm sorry, that's his problem," Pelosi replies. "How does this raise the level of civility?"[27] Stahl asks. Her ability to follow up with her guests shows her comfort and agile style as a communicator.

She maintains eye contact with her subjects and her voice is resonate and infectious. She has an authoritative, yet approachable, air and she delivers her voice-over and questions with precision and eloquence.

Conclusion

Lesley Stahl says she wants to "stay in the game as long as Mike Wallace."[28] Her enthusiasm for journalism and for working on 60 Minutes comes through in her on-air reports. Working with "the very best in the business" as she says in her autobiography, has put her in those ranks. If there is parity for females in journalism, then she will no doubt stay in the game, if she chooses to, as long as Mike Wallace.

PAULA ZAHN

> I think there is an expectation on the American public's part that we re-main in control. [But] everything has changed with this story [the cover-age of 9/11]. This is a story that happened in our backyard. This is the place where I'm raising my children, where they go to school. It's im-possible not to feel something. For God's sake, we're human beings.[29]

Most recently Paula Zahn was seen nightly after *Larry King Live* as anchor for CNN's weeknight prime-time evening program, *Paula Zahn Now*, an issues-driven program offering live newsmaker interviews and meaningful discussion and analysis from an exclusive roster of contributors. In August, 2007, she left the network, replaced by NBC broadcaster Campbell Brown. Paula Zahn began her work at CNN on the now historic morning of September 11, 2001, joining then anchor Aaron Brown, in the coverage of world-changing events of that day. After leaving the Fox network, she was planning on a six-month break to spend time with her husband and three children before starting at CNN, but the September 11 attacks brought her to CNN earlier than she anticipated, and, she noted, "within minutes of get-

Figure 5.3.   Paula Zahn

ting to the bureau I was on the air and I was being treated like I had been at CNN for years."[30] She described how she had learned about September 11 on that day: "I had just walked into my apartment, having dropped off my three children at school."[31] And instead of the six-month break she anticipated after she left the Fox Network, Paula Zahn reported to work September 11, 2001, for her first day at CNN.

Although all the broadcasters who covered September 11 as the day unfolded were speaking impromptu, because of her willingness, like a soldier reporting for duty at the onset of a war, Paula Zahn's coverage of the September 11 events demonstrated Paula Zahn's experience and dedication as a broadcast journalist. This type of news event, completely unannouced and unprecedented, like the death of a president, required Zahn to respond quickly and appropriately. It required her to report to a new job and a new station, and at that a national, twenty-four-hour news station, and not miss a beat. Here is an example of her impromptu reporting of the day's historical events:

> You can see behind me the remnants of the fire still coming from that area where two commercial hijacked jets rammed into tower one and tower two of the World Trade Center. Within the past hour, building number seven, which is also attached to that area, collapsed; the south and north tower. We are now being told by officials that the Marriott Hotel, which is in the vicinity of this area is also in this position of being so degraded it might collapse as well. Just

to bring you up to date, we are facing, in New York City right now, a lot of folks got trapped here this morning when a lot of public transportation shut down. We are now told that some of the outbound bridges are now opened up for people to leave the city. We can confirm now that the nation's airports have been completely shut down at least until noon tomorrow. Some conflicting information on that. Another report suggests that those flights might be postponed indefinitely."[32]

Her voice was strong, direct, unwavering. Her appearance is regal and elegant. A tall woman who wears clothing well, she looks younger than her age. Her approach is friendly and warm, yet sophisticated and intelligent.

By January, 2002, she launched her CNN morning news program titled *American Morning with Paula Zahn.* Before joining CNN in September 2001, Zahn most recently was host of *The Edge with Paula Zahn,* a daily news program on Fox News Channel. She joined Fox in 1999 as anchor of its evening news, *The Fox Report.* Previously she spent ten years at CBS News, where she cohosted *CBS This Morning* and anchored the *CBS Evening News Saturday Edition.*

She also coanchored the 1994 Olympic Winter Games in Lillehammer, Norway and served as prime-time cohost of the 1992 Olympic Winter Games in Albertville, France. Earlier, Zahn served as coanchor of *World News This Morning* and anchored news segments of *Good Morning America* on ABC. She joined ABC in November 1987 as anchor of *The Health Show.*

Her journalistic path started with a cello scholarship from Stephens College in Missouri, where she began to hone her skills working for the campus television station. She noted, "I always loved to write and I was blessed with an insatiable curiosity."[33] Her impressive career began at WFAA-TV in Dallas, and in 1979 she moved to San Diego to work for KFMB-TV. She also worked at KPRC-TV in Houston, WNEV-TV (now WHDH-TV) in Boston and KCBS-TV in Los Angeles before joining ABC News. She reflected back on her earlier days and said that "I have some not-so-fond memories of probably one of the best news directors I ever worked with, who would, when dissatisfied by one of my scripts, rip it into forty little pieces in front of everybody else in the newsroom. I'd take another stab at it and rarely would he rip up the scripts in as many pieces the second time."[34]

One of the most controversial moments in Paula Zahn's career came over that first weekend of January, 2002. CNN aired an advertisement for *American Morning* which called Zahn "sexy" and paired the adjective with a "needle pulled off record" sound effect some interpreted to be a zipper opening. The ad was quickly pulled after the network received significant criticism for what was considered an undignified and sexist portrayal of a serious journalist. CNN attributed the ad's content to a lack of oversight. MSNBC parodied the ad, hyping host Chris Matthews with the words: "Looking for someone who's tough, smart, oh, yeah, and just a little sexy? Forget it! He's not looking for compliments. He's out to cut through the spin and show you every side of the story."[35] "A promotion like that [the ad with Paula Zahn being described as "sexy"] is unrelated to her professional abilities and you can't help but think it's a promotion we would be unlikely to hear about a male anchor," said Barbara Cochran, president of the Radio and Television News Directors Association.[36]

In 2003, during the war in Iraq, Paula Zahn moved back to prime time, hosting a two-hour program called *Live from the Headlines* which offered continuing coverage of the war and other events. A hip and heavily promoted newsman, Anderson Cooper, replaced Aaron Brown the first of the two hours by early summer, and by September, her show *Paula Zahn Now* premiered. In 2003, Zahn anchored and provided the latest news on Operation Iraqi Freedom, interviewing multiple guests, including family members of troops, diplomats, Iraqi-Americans, and politicians. In 2004 Paula Zahn interviewed Joe Lieberman and Elizabeth Edwards as the race for the White House intensified.

Paula Zahn opened the program with her rich alto voice and her urgent tone:

> Good evening. Welcome. I'm Paula Zahn. The world, the news, the names, the faces, and where we go from here on this Monday, January 26, 2004. The homestretch in New Hampshire, less than twenty-four hours left. Is there a clear front-runner in the nation's first primary? And which Democrats won't survive? We're behind the scene at crunch time. Well, we've got a full plate of politics for you, with just four hours to go until the first ballots are cast in the Granite State. I'll be talking with Joe Lieberman, hoping to finish in the top four. I'll also be chatting with Elizabeth Edwards, the outspoken wife of the presidential candidate John Edwards.

Paula Zahn's straightforward interview style is evident is the opening question of her interview with Senator Lieberman. She said:

> Senator Lieberman joins us now from Manchester. Good to see you, sir. Welcome. Senator, you said you have to do better than expected. What does that mean? How do you have to do?

After the senator finished with a long-winded, rather evasive response, Zahn attempted to clarify his response with the question: "All right, you say you'll know it or we'll know it when you see it. Would you be satisfied with a fourth-place finish in New Hampshire?"

Lieberman conceded, "Yes, I mean—look, I think, last week, most people were saying I was fifth and falling." Paula Zahn said, "But, Senator, if you don't do, in your own words, better than expected?" Joe Lieberman said, "I'm just not thinking that way. And I know those are the kinds of questions that people in the media have to ask on the eve of the primary." Paula Zahn did what she could to try to get an admission from Lieberman that he would drop out of the race, which, indeed he did. She is expert at the follow-up question, based on what the interviewee has said in the answer, and she is careful to use the interviewee's own words to attempt to have more clarification on the questions.

Paula Zahn interviewed Elizabeth Edwards, the wife of presidential candidate John Edwards. She began the segment: "Among the candidates' wives, none have seemed as active and enthusiastic about hitting the campaign trail as Elizabeth Edwards. She has helped her husband shape his campaign themes. And she's always ready to tell anyone who asks where her husband stands on specific issues. Elizabeth Edwards joins us now from Manchester, New Hampshire. "Good to see you again. Welcome. How important is New Hampshire to your husband's campaign?" Elizabeth Edwards answered, "It's important. I mean, he's had over 100 town halls in New Hampshire. He's been visiting here for a long time, given out over 50,000 copies of his "Real Solutions" plan."[37]

Invention

Paula Zahn asks simple, straightforward questions. For example, she asked Elizabeth Edwards, wife of presidential candidate John Edwards: "I'm just curious about the management of candidates' wives. Has anybody in your husband's campaign ever come to you and counseled you on what to say, what not to say, or how to say it?" Notice the colloquial, "I'm just curious" which offers an intimate setup for her exchange with Edwards.

Disposition

Her simple, straightforward, midwestern approach is apparent in the simple organization of her questions. Her style is extemporaneous and she is able to use information from answers to fashion follow-up questions that often bring the interview to the conclusion she is seeking. For example, in her interview with Lieberman, she was trying to get him to explain just what would make him drop out of the presidential race, and her follow-up questions narrowed the exchange to the point where he has to simply say, "I'm not thinking that way" in order to avoid the admission of when he would leave the race.[38]

Style

Paula Zahn rose to prominence in broadcasting that gave her an ethos on par with her interviewees. Her rhetorical style reflects the ease with which she conversed with her famous guests. Authoritative, she is able to ask questions that include detail that demonstrates her knowledge and research of the situation. For example, in her interview with Elizabeth Edwards she asks a pointed and potentially damaging question without being off-putting or confrontational. She asked: "Kerry has made an issue of your husband's age, your husband, of course, being fifty, saying that he has no international experience, no military experience, and very little experience in political life, except for the four years he served in the Senate. Why is age not a handicap in your husband's case?"[39]

Delivery

Paula Zahn has a rich, alto voice and a commanding presence as an interviewer. Statuesque and poised, she is as impressive a figure as her guests. Her delivery, however, is not as formal as her appearance. She smiles readily and frequently adds a casual "So" or "I'm curious" to her questions. To Elizabeth Edwards she said, "So how do you view New Hampshire within the arc of what he faces next, as he heads South? Is it as important as what happens in the South? And what does he really got to do Tuesday night?"[40]

Conclusion

Roderick P. Hart notes in *Modern Rhetorical Criticism* that verbal dimensions of credibility include power, competence, trustworthiness, goodwill, and similarity.[41] Paula Zahn exudes these qualities, though she is also an example of a broadcast journalist who had to confront several important obstacles commonly faced by women in broadcasting. A beautiful woman, she had to deflect the embarrassing promotion of her CNN work as "sexy" and she transitioned from network news to cable broadcasting when it still wasn't established that the cable news broadcasting would have as equal, and now greater, a ratings hold on the market.

NOTES

1. Richard Zoglin, "Star Power: Diane Sawyer, with a New Prime-time Show and a $1.6 Million Contract, is Hot. But Are Celebrity Anchors Like Her Upstaging the News?" *Time*, August 7, 1989, 46–51.

2. Ken Auletta, "Promise Her the Moon," *The New Yorker* (New York), February 14, 1994.

3. Zoglin, "Star Power," 46–51.

4. Rose Blue and Joanne E. Bernstein, *Diane Sawyer: Superwoman* (Hillside, New Jersey: Enslow Publishing, 1990), 32.

5. Ibid., 37.

6. Zoglin, "Star Power," 46–51.

7. ABC News, *Good Morning America*, November 12, 2003, "Britney Spears, Exclusive Interview with Pop Star," Diane Sawyer, 7 a.m. EST.

8. ABC News, *Primetime Live* (ABC 10:00 p.m. EST) June 14, 1995, transcript # 406 accessed from: http://web.lexis-nexis.com.

9. "Syrian President Says He Can Help Broker Peace—ABC News' Diane Sawyer Talks Exclusively to President Bashar al-Assad About Iraq and Mideast Peace," ABC News, Feb. 5, 2007, http://abcnews.go.com/GMA/print?id=2849435.

10. Howard Kurtz, "Diane Sawyer, On the Ground and in High Gear," *The Washington Post*, February 19, 2007, C01.

11. www.forbes.com/lists/2006/53/AU0O.html (accessed March 30, 2007).

12. Kurtz, "Diane Sawyer, On the Ground And in High Gear," C01.

13. Bill Carter, "Sawyer Makes New Deal with ABC," *The New York Times*, February 17, 1994, A-4.

14. Jacci Duncan, *Making Waves: The 50 Greatest Women in Radio and Television* (Kansas City, Andrews McMeel Publishing, 2001), 245.

15. Barbara Matusow, *The Evening Stars* (Boston: Houghton Mifflin Company, 1983), 181–82.

16. Lesley Stahl, *Reporting Live* (New York: Simon and Schuster, 1990), 11.

17. Duncan, *Making Waves*, 241.

18. Ibid.

19. Ibid., 242.

20. Ibid., 244.

21. Ibid., 245.

22. Michael Schudson, *The Power of News* (Cambridge: Harvard University Press), 1995, 115.

23. Joanne Ostrow, "Stahl Upbeat on News CBS Pro in Denver for Lecture Series," *Denver Post*, March 28, 1999, J01.

24. Duncan, *Making Waves*, 241.

25. Bob Schieffer, *Face the Nation: My Favorite Stories from the First 50 Years of Award-Winning News Broadcasts* (Simon and Schuster, 2004), 102.

26. Ibid., 102.

27. *60 Minutes*, "Nancy Pelosi: Two Heartbeats Away: Lesley Stahl Profiles the Woman Who Could Become the Next Speaker of the House," October 20, 2006, accessed online: http://www.cbsnews.com/stories/2006/10/20/60minutes/main2111089.shtml.

28. Ibid., 245.

29. Suzanne C. Ryan, "Zahn's Job Starts with 'The Most Challenging Story of Our Careers,'" *The Boston Globe*, October 6, 2001, F3.

30. Barbara Turnbull, "Primetime Diva Has Paid Her Dues," *Toronto Star*, May 15, 2006, E-7.

31. CNN tribute, "America Remembers: The Events of September 11 and America's Response," DVD, 2003, CNN.

32. CNN Breaking News, September 11, 2001, 7:05 p.m., CNN.com transcripts.

33. Ibid.

34. Ibid.

35. Richard Huff, "CNN: Out, Darn Spot," *Daily News* (New York), January 8, 2002, 74.

36. David Bauder, "CNN Yanks Zahn 'Sexy' Promotion," Associated Press Online, January 8, 2002.

37. CNN, *Paula Zahn Now*, January 26, 2004.

38. Ibid.

39. Ibid.

40. CNN, *Paula Zahn Now*, January 26, 2004.

41. Roderick P. Hart, *Modern Rhetorical Criticism* (Needham Heights: Allyn and Bacon, 1997), 222–23.

7

FROM MORNING TO EVENING

Katie Couric

Figure 6.1. Katie Couric

I hope I am a woman with the kind of values everyone has—a person who can be the viewers' eyewitness and ask the questions they would want to ask and feel the way they might feel.[1]

"Tough. Fair. A Straight Shooter." With these words, Bob Schieffer, veteran news broadcaster and interim anchor of *The CBS Evening News*, described Katie Couric and urged *CBS* viewers to tune in to *The CBS Evening News* when "his friend" Katie Couric takes over as anchor.[2] Dan Rather retired from the anchor chair after twenty-four years, and the appointment of Ms. Couric as his successor makes broadcasting history, since Katie Couric is the first sole woman anchor of a network evening news broadcast.

For fifteen years, Katie Couric's infectious smile, intelligence, warmth, and friendliness made her a comfortable presence with which to start the day as cohost of *NBC*'s highly rated morning news and variety show, *The To-day Show*. She became the equivalent of a next-door neighbor for millions of Americans just waking up and thinking about what to wear, what to eat, and how to get where they were going for the day. Katie Couric knows that as a morning anchor, her relationship with viewers is key. "Morning show anchors take a very interesting role in people's families. People feel very familial with them, and get very comfortable with them. People don't want too much cynicism. I hope people want intelligent questioning. I hope people want to get to the bottom of issues. I hope people want us to be appropriately challenging. But some people say to me, 'I turn you on in the morning and you always seem like you have a smile on your face and you're happy.' And I'm, like, 'Well, O.K.' Some days, I'm really tired or whatever. But there's a certain reassuring quality about morning television; it reminds people that the world is still in one piece and turning, and here's what people need to know about."[3] Indeed, communication scholar Roderick P. Hart notes that "television achieves intimacy by fitting in neatly with our everyday worlds. It becomes our unassuming friend from morning until night."[4] Although the same friendliness expected of a morning show anchor seems at odds with the qualities some critics contend that viewers require in an evening news anchor. Jonathan Last of *The Philadelphia Inquirer* notes, "Reading the news night in and night out may not take much, but anchoring an event—an election night, or the crash of a space shuttle—requires an enormous reserve of charm, stamina, quick thinking and, above all, gravitas. This last quality is the most essential. It's the one trait shared by every successful anchor from the grandfatherly Walter Cronkite to the aloof Ted Koppel."[5] According to Last, gravitas gives an anchor ethos. Roderick P. Hart contends that credibility can be measured in a speaker's verbal dimensions. He describes the credibility dilemma faced by John F. Kennedy in 1960. "Although his campaign for presidency was moving apace, he could not shake the charge that his Roman Catholicism would curtail his political independence as a chief executive."[6] The schism in the public's acceptance of Kennedy as president is akin to the negative perceptions that Katie Couric has had from those who contend that her morning show host "perkiness" persona would not allow Americans to accept her in the historically gravitas heavy position as network news anchor. As Hart explains, a speech by Kennedy to the Greater Houston Ministerial Association may have helped him win the presidency and that it wasn't anything the speech had in it, per se, but the speech-act that won over the voters.[7] Katie Couric will be ultimately successful as a CBS anchor because by just *being* in the anchor chair she has changed the perception of what an anchor is in American broadcasting. Her presence paves the way for future female anchors, much like John F. Kennedy's Catholicism unlocked the keys to the White House for future Catholics or other "firsts" vying for the presidency. Of course, ratings are the ultimate measure of success in television, but in terms of changing public perception, Katie Couric has already moved history forward.

MEMORABLE MORNINGS

For one notable *Today Show* broadcast, Katie Couric flew through the air dressed as Peter Pan to celebrate Halloween, and for another broadcast she dressed like, and impersonated, infamous real estate tycoon Donald Trump, who was a guest on the show. Media expert Ken Auletta notes that, "on morning television, breaking news is usually less about Iraq and judicial nominations than about the tabloid narrative of the moment: the Michael Jackson trial, the disappearance of Jennifer Wilbanks (the "runaway bride"), the [Tom] Cruise–[Katie] Holmes courtship, a severed finger found in a bowl of chili, or a high-school senior missing in Aruba."[8] The "variety show" nature of morning news programs have led some critics to wonder if Katie Couric would effectively make the transition to the serious evening news. It didn't hurt Tom Brokaw, who was a coanchor of *The Today Show* from 1976 until 1982 when he was replaced by Bryant Gumbel. Tom Brokaw went on to a distinguished career as the anchor for *NBC Nightly News*. Another newsman, Harry Smith, became coanchor of *The CBS Morning Show*, demonstrating that there is flexibility to move from evening news to a morning show. John Chancellor and Barbara Walters were both *Today Show* hosts before they moved to anchor network news. Diane Sawyer vacillates between her *Good Morning America* cohosting and her *Primetime Live* position, perhaps adding to the argument that whether morning or night, a competent broadcasting professional is able to execute the job successfully. In a poll conducted by *TV Guide* and the *Associated Press*, 49 percent say they prefer Katie Couric as a morning show cohost, versus 29 percent who say they prefer her in the evening. But she has the vote of no less than venerable news veteran Walter Cronkite, who told the *New York Post*, "I think she's highly capable and I'm absolutely delighted that she's come over to *CBS*."[9]

Katie Couric admits that *The Today Show* includes less serious news now than it once did. "It was a little more serious in tone [when Couric started on the show in 1991]. It was a lot of pretty serious newsmakers, at least for the first hour and a half, with less of a premium on lifestyle pieces."[10] In addition to the more "tabloid" type news stories regularly featured on *The Today Show* and other morning programs, Katie Couric has reported some of the most important news stories of the past two decades. For example, she reported on Election Night 2000 the evening of the election, and when election night turned into the next day with no new president, Katie Couric appeared refreshed and full of authority when she continued reporting as co-anchor of *The Today Show*. During the terrorist attacks on September 11, 2001, Katie Couric reported with sensitivity and intelligence both the tragedy and the miracles associated with the story. Similar to the multi-dimensional career of Barbara Walters, Katie Couric's career illustrates her versatility as a broadcaster, whether she was cooking up a dish with a famous chef or interviewing a head of state.

This chapter will examine the communication strategies employed by Katie Couric throughout her career, and focus on the ethos associated with the television anchor position.

Katherine Anne Couric is the youngest of four children born in Arlington, Virginia, to Elinor Hene, a homemaker, and John Martin Couric Jr., a journalist at *The Atlanta Journal-Constitution* and *United Press International* in Washington. Her sister Emily Couric, a popular state senator, died of pancreatic cancer at the age of fifty-four on October 18, 2001, after a battle with the disease. Two other siblings include Clara Couric Batchelor and John M. Couric Jr. Katie Couric graduated from Yorktown High School and then enrolled in the University of Virginia in 1975, graduating in 1979 with a degree in American Studies. She was a sister in the Delta Delta Delta sorority. At the University of Virgina, she served in several positions at the school's award-winning daily newspaper, *The Cavalier Daily*. During her fourth year at the University, Katie was chosen to live as Head Resident of The Lawn, the heart of Thomas Jefferson's academic village.

Ms. Couric entered the world of journalism in 1979 when she was hired as a desk assistant for *ABC News*. She quickly climbed the news ladder at the then-fledgling *CNN*, starting as an assignment editor and eventually becoming a political correspondent for the 1984 presidential election race. Her tenure at CNN was short, partly because then, CNN president Reese

Schonfeld, upon seeing her on camera, remarked that he "never wants to see her on the air again." He thought that Katie Couric looked and sounded like a sixteen-year-old.[11] For the next four years, she was a producer in Atlanta, but CNN wouldn't give her a regular reporting slot. Katie Couric did, however, get on the air at WTVJ in Miami, then moved to WRC-TV, NBC's Washington affiliate station, where she won Emmy and Associated Press awards for her piece about a dating service for the handicapped. Katie Couric caught the attention of Tim Russert, chief of NBC's Washington bureau, who invited her to join NBC's national news team as a Pentagon correspondent in 1989.

After just a year of network broadcasting, she became the national correspondent for *The Today Show* before she moved up to the position of co-anchor for the show since the ratings collapsed when Jane Pauley was replaced with Deborah Norville. *The Today Show* viewers, who had grown accustomed to Jane Pauley, felt as though the younger, beautiful Deborah Norville had pushed the almost forty-year-old Pauley out. Ken Auletta explains that *NBC* thought "Young professionals who found thirty-nine-year-old Pauley a bit frumpy would identify with Norville's natty clothes and brisk manner. Men would look at her and swoon."[12] Instead, the ratings took a nosedive and Deborah Norville left, saying that she wanted to spend more time with her infant son. Katie Couric was named as the replacement, but before she accepted the job, she insisted that she get an equal share of the newsmaker interviews with cohost Bryant Gumbel. She explained, "Not to sound too 'Helen Reddy-ish,' but I felt like I had an obligation as a woman, and for the women who were watching, to have an equal role on the show, and not a subservient role."[13] Immediately, Katie Couric's quick wit, warmth, and down-to-earth sensibility made her a good fit with the rest of the team. The addition of the wholesome, petite brunette, Katherine Couric, who after one week on *The Today Show* was called "Katie" by everyone, helped bring the morning program back to number one in the ratings, and viewers responded to the new host with enthusiasm. Katie's arrival at the anchor desk in April 1991, at thirty-four, had a transformative effect. "We knew immediately that she was going to stick," says Phil Griffin, a senior vice president of *NBC News*.[14] By 1994, *The Today Show* was ahead in the ratings and maintained a lead for the next decade.[15] *Time* noted that since Katie Couric became a cohost on *The Today Show*, "the morning is now not just a TV news moneymaker but also an agenda setter: it is where newsmakers come first to state their cases and address their scandals."[16] Her ability to get interviews with some of the most important newsmakers of the time reveals that Katie Couric is able to attract not only viewers, but fans among the newsmakers. Katie Couric rapidly became one of the rising stars of *NBC News*. She was tapped for such entertainment-oriented jobs as hosting the annual telecast of the Macy's Thanksgiving Parade, and she was also given heftier responsibilities, such as cohosting *Now with Tom Brokaw and Katie Couric* from 1993–1994, in which she was matched with the network's top anchor in a prime-time news magazine. The show was cancelled because of low ratings, but Katie Couric subsequently became a contributing editor to *Dateline NBC*, another primetime news-magazine. Katie Couric's career was strengthened when she hosted the hard-hitting 1995 documentary *Everybody's Business: America's Children*. She moved effortlessly between programs such as The Macy's Thanksgiving Day Parade and interviewing heads of state. Her celebrity was confirmed by a cameo appearance on the hit television show *Murphy Brown* and as the nation watched as she went through her pregnancy on air in 1995. She was appealing to a wide range of audiences, and she exhibited the traits that Roderick P. Hart lists as necessary for a speaker to demonstrate the verbal dimensions of credibility.[17] She was able to ask tough questions, demonstrating her competence, and she had a lot in common with the audience: a young mother, wife, and career woman with a penchant for revealing the personal dimensions of the news.

In 1997, news anchor Matt Lauer joined *The Today Show*, forming what became the show's most successful morning team, as he and Katie Couric and company spent the next nine years atop the ratings heap. But as her fame was on the rise, personal tragedy struck. Her husband, lawyer and *NBC* legal analyst Jay Monahan, died in 1998 after battling colon cancer for eight months. Katie Couric spent a month off the air in private mourning with her two young daughters Ellie and Carrie, then returned in professional and graceful fashion while wearing her late husband's wedding ring on a chain around her neck. After a heartfelt thanks to all who supported her during her traumatic time, she proceeded to grill Monica Lewinsky's lawyer, William Ginsburg, in a surprisingly tough interview. One positive result of the tragedy was her effort to raise awareness for colon cancer, which is the number-two cancer killer in the United States. In March 2000, she launched the National Colorectal Cancer Research Alliance (NCCRA) to fund new medical research and to form educational programs that encourage prevention and early detection through proper screening. Also that year, Katie Couric had an on-air colonoscopy, which prompted a 20-percent increase in the number of procedures in what became known as "The Couric Effect." *The Journal of Internal Medicine* determined that because of her impact on increasing colonoscopies, celebrity spokespeople can have a substantial impact on public participation in preventive care programs.[18] Katie Couric raised five million dollars to establish The Jay Monahan Center for Gastrointestinal Health, a clinical center of the New York-Presbyterian Hospital and the Weill Medical College of Cornell University named in honor of her late husband, Jay Monahan.[19]

Over the years, Katie Couric has been on the cusp of many newsworthy events. In April 1999, she covered the shooting rampage at Columbine High School, in Colorado, and, like most people that day, felt shocked and helpless. She saw a need to reach out to children who were loners and outsiders, so she wrote *The Brand New Kid*, a rhyming book for young children about a foreign boy who's teased and ostracized for being the new kid at school. As Katie Couric continued to raise money and awareness for colon cancer, personal tragedy struck once again. Her sister, Emily Couric, Virginia state senator, lost her fifteen-month-long fight with pancreatic cancer. Katie Couric gave a moving eulogy at her funeral, saying that she was "the personification of excellence." It was a painful blow for her—the sisters were close—especially four years after the death of her husband. Meanwhile, Katie Couric continued her work on *Today* including her marathon reporting on the terrorist attacks of September 11, 2001, which occurred during *The Today Show* broadcast.

SEPTEMBER 11, 2001 BROADCAST

On September 11, 2001, *Today Show* cohosts Katie Couric and Matt Lauer and the other *Today Show* broadcasters experienced the news of the terrorist attacks on the World Trade Center, the Pentagon, and the plane crash in Shanksville, Pennsylvania, along with the rest of America since "the trauma of September 11th events began unfolding for many on the morning news programs."[20] The local affiliate stations turned the broadcast over to the network on September 11th, when it was clear that what was happening at the World Trade Center was more urgent than the news at the local level. The video showed the twin towers and Katie Couric said, "The World Trade Center is one of the busiest office buildings in New York." Weatherman Al Roker commented: "The New York State governor has his office in there." Katie Couric, Al Roker, Matt Lauer, and Ann Curry began the commentary on September 11 as the news filtered in to the network. Katie Couric's attention turned to the human dimension of the tragedy: "Obviously, horrified commuters were absolutely devastated when they heard this explosion. We talked with somebody a moment ago about that,

Jennifer Oberstein, and also another eyewitness, Elliott Walker, who is actually a producer here on *The Today Show*. Elliott, can you hear me? Tell me where you are and what you saw." Elliott Walker responded: "Well, I live in this area. I returned to my apartment. But I was walking down the sidewalk delivering my young daughter to school. And we heard a very loud sound that you hear when a plane is, you know, going fast past you 'Nnnn,' followed by an enormous crash and an immediate explosion. . . . We're very sensitive to this kind of thing in this neighborhood." Katie Couric continued: "Elliott, have you—of course—because of the incident that occurred in the early 1990s. Have you seen any—any evidence, Elliott, of people being taken out of the building? You say that emergency vehicles are there. Understandably so, but of course, the major concern is human loss." Notice how Katie Couric is able to remind the viewers to what the interviewee was referring (1993 World Trade Center attack) and move the interview further with a question about loss of life. Then, Ms. Walker shouted, "Oh my goodness there's been another collision. Can you see it?" Katie Couric responded, "Yes." And then obviously taken aback by what she was seeing [a plane crashing into the second tower], responded, "Oh my." Ms. Walker noted, "I think there may have been another impact. Can you tell? I just heard another very loud bang and a very large plane that might have been a DC-9 or a 747 just flew past my window, and I think it may have hit the Trade Center again. I think it may have been the other tower." Katie Couric interjected: "It's the second." Ms. Walker continued, "The first one was World Trade Center One, and it looks, from what I'm seeing on television, like it may have been the second building that was hit." Trying to figure out what just happened, Matt Lauer explained, "We're going to see—this is a piece of tape and we may actually see another plane enter the picture here in a second." Katie Couric and Matt Lauer were relying on eyewitnesses to explain what had happened, since they were in the studio. Another eyewitness, Jennifer Oberstein, expressed her emotions after just witnessing the attacks. Stuttering from shock, she managed, "I—I—I've never seen anything—it looks like a movie. I saw a large plane, like a jet, go immediately headed directly into the World Trade Center. It just flew into it, into the other tower coming from south to north. I watched the plane fly into the World Trade Center. It was a jet. It was a very large plane. It was going south. It went past the Ritz-Carlton Hotel that's being built in Battery Park. It went—flew right past, almost hit it, and then went into it." Katie Couric expressed what many were thinking: "This is so shocking, of course, to everybody watching." Again, in an excited, exasperated tone, Jennifer Oberstein continued, "I—I've never seen anything like it. It literally flew itself into World Trade Center." A few minutes later, Katie Couric updated the situation for new viewers just tuning in: "Well, of course, this is, as we've said, completely shocking video and a shocking turn of events. And we've been talking here that the first incident, one might surmise that it was some kind of accident. And then to have a second, what appeared to be 727 jet. Of course, the question of terrorist activity has to surface, and the question of whether this was an intentional terrorist act of some kind. We've got another eyewitness that we would like to speak with. Dan Dietrich is on the phone. Dan, tell me where you are and what you're seeing, or what you saw." Dan Dietrich offered his eyewitness account: "OK. What I saw was one plane coming in low from—from the north down—down over Seventh Avenue. It crashed into the top or the middle of one of the towers. Ten minutes later, I saw another plane crash into the other side of the tower at a lower level. It looked to be a small, you know, commercial plane, the first plane that I saw. It crashed into the top of the tower. And there was a huge fireball and there was a gaping hole in the side of the tower. As we were waiting outside and looking at it, another plane came in low—I believe from the other side—and hit the—sort of the—the middle of the other tower. Now, I—I saw both—both planes, two separate planes, crash into each tower." Katie Couric pressed for more detail, "And, Dan—and, again, the size of the planes, tell me about that." He replied, "I would say that the plane was a—a—a midsize, looked to be a commercial airliner. I don't know. I thought perhaps, you know, a commercial airline, a midsize, not— you know, not a jumbo jet." Then Katie Couric updated the viewers again, "This, of course, is unconfirmed, but we are getting information from an employee of United Airlines—and again we want to emphasize this is unconfirmed—but there is speculation that an American Airlines plane was hijacked and crashed purposefully—on purpose into the World Trade Center and that the second plane was another plane—perhaps hijacked—was then flown in to the second tower." Some banter between the hosts occurred and then Katie Couric introduced Bob Kur at the White House: "Bob, where are you and what can you tell us?" Kur notes that the president is in Florida and the people in the White House "are just standing around television monitors looking at this. And when I say people, I don't mean just the reporters, I mean the people who are actually in the office who work here at the White House." She then introduced David Gregory, on the phones from Longboat Key, Florida, where he was reporting on the president's activities. David Gregory noted that the president was about to speak at an education event, which was going to be cancelled. Katie Couric noted, "We should mention, David, that New York City Airport, or New York area airports have all been closed. The Lincoln Tunnel has been closed here in New York. While we're getting ready to listen to the president, let's go back to J—J—Jim Miklaszewski at the Pentagon. Jim, you talk about counterterrorist measures that are in place. Can you shed any light for us on—on what kind of things are in place in the event of an attack of this nature?" Jim Miklaszewski replied, "Katie, it's very difficult to—for the U.S. military to respond to this kind of thing at—you know, right now, because it is unclear exactly who is behind it and if there are any other potential attacks or incidents like this, because this has obviously not been officially declared a terrorist attack. But all the experts who are looking at these pictures say there is no doubt about it. This was a coordinated terrorist attack. But who and why is—is very much unclear right now. And the problem with trying to, then, put planes in the air to try to prevent any further attacks is, these are, after all, open air spaces for the most part. And it—and it's difficult for the U.S. military to simply scramble jets and—and put them in the air and—and then, according to officials here, then do what? This area, of course, according to officials here, is—is obviously going to be declared off limits in terms of any air traffic. But right now, officials here at the Pentagon are simply scrambling to find out first, what happened." Katie Couric noted that getting information was difficult, "Yeah, we're scrambling for information here. I just want to read this Reuters [news] wire that says, 'Two planes crashed into the towers of the World Trade Center on Tuesday morning causing huge explosions and killing at least six people." CNBC said there were at least a thousand injured. Both towers of the lower Manhattan landmark, where thousands of people worked, were the scenes of a bombing in 1993. The FBI told the Associated Press that it was, quote, 'foul play and not an accident.' A person who answered the phone on the trading floor at broker Cantor Fitzgerald, located near the top of the World Trade Center said, 'We're blanking dying' when asked what was happening and hung up. There was screaming and yelling in the background and a follow-up call was not answered." Jamie Gangel, a reporter, gave this update: "Katie, I've just spoken to top U.S. officials with the access to latest intelligence. And they said, quote, that 'This was clearly terrorist-related, no question about it.' They said that they couldn't give any further details now, not because they didn't want to share it, but because they just don't know yet. They're at the earliest stages." Katie Couric clarified, "So do they know, Jamie—a plane was, in fact, hijacked? Some kind of airbus. That was what the United worker told us, that apparently, that had been—that it was an American Airlines plane that had been . . ." Ann Curry interjected, "Hijacked." Katie Couric clarified, "hijacked from Boston to Los Angeles. But we're just getting initial reports of that. And again, we must tell you that we're trying to get as much information. But it is trickling in at a very slow pace. So all of this is unconfirmed. And, of course, speculation of a terrorist attack is unconfirmed, although that is what some Pentagon official—officials are saying."

Throughout the broadcast the video showed the buildings, not the hosts. The morning of September 11, Katie Couric's shift did not end at 9 a.m.; instead, she hosted for hours, as the network launched its twenty-four-hour coverage of the tragedy, as did every other major network.

In December 2001, she signed a new five-year contract worth $65 million, making her the highest-paid television news personality at the time. Her re-upping with *The Today Show* ensured that the yearly $300 million profits NBC grew accustomed to would continue unabated. In 2003, Katie Couric switched hosting responsibilities with *The Tonight Show* host Jay Leno and appeared for a night in a ratings stunt that proved successful for the network.

SIGNIFICANT INTERVIEWS AS *THE TODAY SHOW* COHOST

In October, 1992, Katie Couric received a tour of the White House from first lady Barbara Bush when the president, George H. W. Bush, stopped by for a surprise hello. Still a relative newcomer as *The Today Show* co-anchor, Katie Couric, speaking impromptu, kept the president talking for nearly twenty minutes with small talk and tough questions on the upcoming election. Jeff Zucker, who was the producer of *The Today Show* at the time, says, "I was in the control room trying to help, but mostly just watching in amazement. It was one of the most remarkable moments of broadcast journalism I've ever seen."[21] Katie Couric was able to switch gears quickly from admiring the décor of the White House, to asking some hard-hitting questions of the president, "Did you have any knowledge of the Iran-contra arms-for-hostages deal while you were vice president?" President Bush responded: "I've testified 450 times under oath, some of them, and our staff 3,500, that yes, but nobody's accused me of not doing it. In terms of the contra part of it, absolutely not. And no one has suggested that I did. Diversion of arms for support for the contras, no. And no one's challenged that. What was challenged, I think—I'll help you with the question—what was challenged . . . " Katie Couric pressed on: "I want you to go ahead. Clarify what you think was . . . " Bush responded: "What was asked was whether I knew that (Reagan's defense secretary) Caspar Weinberger and (Secretary of State George) Shultz, how strongly they opposed it. And I said to that there were two key meetings where they almost got into a shouting match, I'm told, that I did not attend. But I said all along that I knew about the arms going and I supported the president." Katie Couric clarified further: "You knew about the arms for hostages?" President Bush replied, "Yes, I've said so all along, given speeches on it."[22] This impromptu interview by Katie Couric demonstrates her ability to adapt her skills from one type of event to another without any difficulty. The interview was so unprecedented, that NBC adjusted its programming to air it. Katie Couric, known for her effervescent personality and her perennially sunny personality showed that she could handle more serious news than was often the fare of *The Today Show*. Her experience as Pentagon correspondent may have strengthened her skills as a political reporter, but her ease at interviewing a president—in his home—impromptu—also demonstrates what Richard Sennett, in his insightful book about social bonds, referred to as "transcendent position."[23] Katie Couric's ability to transcend the agenda of learning about the White House from First Lady Barbara Bush and instead grilling the president on important world issues, gave Katie Couric an illusion of independence and power over the president. What could he do? To refuse to answer Katie Couric's questions would be a negative for the program, which was clearly designed to be a public relations tool for the Bush presidency.

In another interview with political powerhouses Bob and Elizabeth Dole, again Katie Couric demonstrated that although she may be a comfortable presence to wake up to in the morning, she has the ability to make her interviewees uncomfortable at times. In July, 1996, Katie Couric interviewed presidential candidate Bob Dole and his wife, Elizabeth Dole, on *The Today Show*. She didn't waste any time getting to one of the most controversial issues of the campaign when she asked: "What would you say to people who say he's in tobacco's pocket, he's in the pocket of the tobacco industry?" Senator Bob Dole replied, "I don't—I don't know if anybody's in the tobacco pocket." Couric said, "He's an apologist."

Then Dole responded, "Obviously when the Republicans control, we get more contributions from companies, as we have since 1994. I haven't any idea whether I've had any money directed to my campaign by tobacco companies. I'm not in their pocket. And my view is, as I've said time and time again, again, the liberal media crosses that out, goes right back to the Democratic line, I mean, you should—you know, you may be violating the FCC regulations by always, you know, sticking up for the Democrats, advertising their . . ." Senator Dole blamed the media by saying, "You can't respond because the media has already made up their mind. I've said, I don't know whether it's addictive. I'm not a doctor. I'm not a scientist. People shouldn't smoke, young or old. Now what else do you do?" Katie Couric pointed out that, "C. Everett Koop is, is pretty non-partisan, wouldn't you say?" And Dole said, "Oh, he's a Dole supporter, a Dole contributor." Couric pointed out, " Well, he criticized you quite severely for your comments." Even Elizabeth Dole felt she had to get into the conversation to try to defend her husband, when she added, "You saw the answer, my husband's letter." Katie said, "Yes, I did. I saw the letter. I did. But I'm saying, you know, you're saying it's the liberal media. But even Dr. Koop had a real problem with your comments." Bob Dole said, "Dr. Koop, you know, he watches the liberal media, and he . . ." Couric replied, "He's brainwashed?" Bob Dole said, "probably got carried away. Probably a little bit."[24] *The Washington Post* described the interview by saying, "He got into a spat with the personification of perkiness, the nation's favorite niece, *The Today Show*'s Katie Couric."[25] Other media sources described Dole as "snarling" at Katie Couric. Dole's interview with Couric did not improve Dole's standing in the polls and it did nothing to erase his public image during the 1996 campaign for president, as a dour man. Communication scholars Clayman and Heritage note that "Bob Dole's 1996 campaign suffered an important setback when, in an interview on *The Today Show*, he expressed a seemingly cavalier attitude about the addictiveness of tobacco.[26] Similar to the way Katie Couric took President Bush by surprise by asking hard-hitting questions during the White House tour with Mrs. Bush, she asked very tough questions of the Doles when the interview appeared to be more of a personality interview, since it included the candidate's wife, Mrs. Dole.

Soon after President Clinton won reelection in 1996, Katie Couric interviewed him in the Cabinet Room in the White House. She asked the president, the only Democrat to win reelection since Franklin Delano Roosevelt, "What kind of assurances can you offer the American public that it's not going to be four more years of politics as usual . . . that you will roll up your sleeves and work with the Republican Congress?" President Clinton thoroughly responded: "Well, first of all, it hasn't been—first of all, I asked you to look at what happened, and it hasn't been—it hasn't been four years of politics as usual. Compare where we are today with where we were four years ago. We changed the economic policy of the country, the one oriented on— toward balancing the budget, investing in our future, growing the economy, expanding trade. Our country never produced 11 million jobs in four years before. We changed the social policy of the country in a way that emphasized cooperation across party lines in things like crime and welfare. We had the biggest drop in welfare in history. We had the biggest drop in crime in twenty years. So I think if you look at what we're doing, I—it's the—the enormous amount of consistent labor toward a goal which has produced the progress and the difference in now and four years ago. And now we have some other big challenges we still have to face that I believe we—we can get the same results on. And I think that the—the message of the voters in the election is that they want the Congress and—and me to work together. We had a year of very partisan discord—or three years, really. And then about three months before the last Congress ended, we all started working together. And virtually my entire program was passed and people found favor with it. And I think it redounded to the credit of everyone who was here. And that's what the American people want us to do. They want us to lay down our partisan sniping. Nothing was ever built on petty political and personal hatreds and division. You know, you build a—you build a future with labor and with—with dreams. And I—whenever it starts to get small around here, I just tell everybody to think big. Don't be small, be big. And you just have so many days here."27 Katie Couric didn't refrain from asking the president a pointed question about his agenda, even though the occasion—the upcoming inauguration— was jubilant. In October, 1997, Katie Couric interviewed First Lady Hillary Clinton to discuss the child-care conference that the first lady directed. Before the interview ended, Couric asked her about her plans for her life after she leaves the White House. "Do you think about what you all will do after you leave the White House?" Mrs. Clinton hedged, "No, I don't spend much time thinking about that. I—I really," and Katie Couric challenged her: "Oh, come on, I don't believe you."28

Although Hillary Clinton insisted that she had no immediate plans for the future, that Katie Couric would follow up, never letting her smile dim, with the incredulous statement "I don't believe you" is characteristic of the anchorwoman's confidence when interviewing political figures. She simply doesn't take the first answer, and follows up with casual, yet confrontational, language.

Another significant news event, the Columbine High School massacre, occurred on Tuesday, April 20, 1999, at Columbine High School in Jefferson County, Colorado, near Littleton. Two teenage students, Eric Harris and Dylan Klebold, carried out a shooting rampage, killing twelve fellow students and a teacher, as well as wounding twenty-four others, before committing suicide. It is considered to be the deadliest school shooting in America. Two days after the shooting, Katie Couric went to Columbine High School and spoke with some of the victims' families. She began, in a hushed and sad tone: "Well, eighteen-year-old Isaiah Shoels was to have graduated from Columbine next month. Instead, he was killed Tuesday, shot in the face while crouched under a table in the school library. Michael Shoels is Isaiah's father. Mr. Shoels, thank you so much for being here. We are so terribly sorry about your son."

Mr. Michael Shoels: OK.

Katie Couric: I understand from everyone at the school that Isaiah was extremely well-loved by the students, a very popular young man. Can you tell me a little about him?

Mr. Shoels: Well, Isaiah was very outgoing. He was a—you know, he was—he had a lot, you know, he had a lot to live for, you know what I'm saying? And I really do feel that he was taken out a little bit too early. I mean, behind a, you know—this situation is getting bad. It's getting bad.

Katie Couric had just lost her husband the previous year to colon cancer. Her sensitivity to suffering must have been heightened by her own loss and she showed empathy, while at the same time, probing for the news story. She said, "Eyewitnesses say your son was singled out because he was an African-American?"

Mr. Shoels replied, "Yes. That's what happened. I mean, that's not a way to go. It's—it's bad you have to go in a situation like that." Katie Couric replied, "What have people told you, Mr. Shoels, about what happened to Isaiah?" Mr. Shoels: "They—some of his friends are saying that he was supposed to have been going to lunch. And he decided to go to the, you know, the library, instead, you know, because he had a paper to do. And they said when—when they came in, they was—they was actually hunting him, you know. They was looking for him especially, and that's wrong." Katie Couric: "You think he had two strikes against him?" Mr. Shoels: "That was most definitely it. I mean, it's no ifs, ands or buts about it. That's what happened." Katie Couric: "Because he was not only black . . ." Mr. Shoels: "Yes." Katie Couric: ". . . but he was an athlete." Mr. Shoels quietly responded, "Yes."[29]

Still reeling from her own personal grief, and not at all prying and inappropriate, the way some news reporters can be when interviewing people who have experienced tragedy, the tenderness and sympathy expressed by Katie Couric as she interviewed this man about the loss of his son, was evident in her tone of voice, her facial expressions, and her choice of words. Obviously, the father's emotions were still very raw, having lost his son in a violent school shooting just two days earlier.

Another news story that stirred the emotions of Americans was the death of dashing John F. Kennedy, Jr., and his beautiful wife, Carolyn Bessette, who were traveling in a plane piloted by Kennedy, along with his wife's sister Lauren, in July of 1999. The plane plummeted into the ocean, killing the three on board.

John F. Kennedy, Jr., the son of the slain president and a popular public figure, was interviewed by Katie Couric just two months before his death. It was the last television interview that Kennedy gave. In the interview, Katie Couric and John Kennedy, Jr., discussed his late mother's parenting style. Katie Couric complimented the former first lady, John Kennedy's mother, on how she raised John and his sister, by saying, "Because, I mean, if you look at a lot of political families and a lot of families who grow up with the incredible glare of the spotlight that you all have, and you see you and your sister, you think, 'God, they're remarkably well-adjusted—or seem to be.'" John F. Kennedy's self-deprecating humor was evident in his response, "*Seem* to be, right. Exactly." Then Katie Couric followed up her original statement by saying, "But you know I think it's a real tribute to your mom that you all turned to be really nice, productive people." John Kennedy accepted the compliment, "Well, thank you. She would—she would be glad to hear you say that. She took a lot of pride in being a good mother and I'm glad it—people think it worked." Katie Couric then introduced a film clip of John F. Kennedy, Jr.'s, late father stating that if he had a son or a daughter, they would get involved in politics, and she asked if the magazine Kennedy, Jr., founded, *George*, is his unique kind of political contribution. Mr. Kennedy responded, "Exactly. And I think that everyone has to find their way into politics or any other profession on their own. Do—do it on their own speed and in their own—in their own way." Katie Couric then said, "And in their own time table. That sure sounds like you haven't given up the notion of maybe going into politics." Coyly, John Kennedy Jr., said, "Maybe, maybe not." As though speaking to a friend, Katie Couric responded, "Oh, come on, John." John Kennedy, Jr. replied, "I hate—no one's ever asked me that question before, and . . . " Katie Couric followed up, and then summed up the interview with this question: "Really? I know, I'm so original, aren't I?"[30]

Katie Couric had been well acquainted with John F. Kennedy, Jr. They had met several times over the course of the years previous to his final interview with her on *The Today Show*, and two years earlier, in May, 1997, Katie Couric had posed, in man-styled clothing, reminiscent of a character from the classic film starring Rosalind Russell, *His Girl Friday*, for the cover of *George* magazine.

In 2003, Katie Couric interviewed Hillary Clinton again. She had become New York Senator Hillary Clinton and Katie Couric asked her about the Bush administration, the Democratic primary candidates, and her political future. Clinton's new book, *Living History*, had recently been published, and on the first day the book was released it sold 200,000 copies. Katie Couric asked Senator Clinton: "As you know, Senator Clinton, there's been lots of criticism that the Democrats are feckless, clumsy, too slow to articulate an alternative vision to President Bush's. And if they are articulating it, it's not being heard. Why can't the Democrats seemingly get their act together?" Hillary Clinton responded, "You know, Katie, I have a great deal of appreciation for how hard it is, you know, when you have someone in the White House who commands the bully pulpit, it's hard. When you don't have the leadership in either house of Congress, it's hard. I think last year when we had the majority in the Senate we did quite a good job on many issues of drawing the contrast with the president and with the Republicans. And, of course, I think it's now understood by everyone that there is a real echo chamber for the Republican philosophy and policies on radio, television, in much of the press that the Democrats don't have. Now, having said that, we have to do a better job. We're not doing as good a job as we should." Then Katie Couric tried a fast-paced word game to try to get Mrs. Clinton to answer without much thought. She explained, "Let me mention some names quickly and you just give me your quick response with a couple of words."

Katie Couric: "It's kind of a name game. Ken Starr."

Mrs. Clinton: "Oh! Prosecutor."

Katie Couric: "Surely you have some better adjectives than that."

Mrs. Clinton: "Read my book. I have some good adjectives."

Katie Couric: "Al Gore."

Mrs. Clinton: "Good man."

Katie Couric: "George W. Bush."

Mrs. Clinton: "President."

Katie Couric: "Oh, come on! Come on!"

Mrs. Clinton: "Well, you know, there was some debate about that initially, so yeah."

Katie Couric: "Martha Stewart."

Mrs. Clinton: "Friend. She's a friend of mine, and I feel very sorry about what she's going through now."

Katie Couric: "Do you think it's unfair?"

Mrs. Clinton: "Well, I—as I say, I've been through a lot of things that I considered unfair and I'm pulling for her."

Katie Couric: "Monica Lewinsky."

Mrs. Clinton: "Ken Starr."

Katie Couric: "Any other adjectives?"

Mrs. Clinton: "No. You know, I think that what Ken Starr did, invading hers and other people's privacy, was wrong and really unfortunate for our country."

Katie Couric: "Bill Clinton."

Mrs. Clinton: "My husband and a good president."

Katie Couric: "Hillary Clinton."

Mrs. Clinton: "Oh, a work in progress. And I hope that maybe after people read the book they will come up with some of their own adjectives and maybe some new ones that they haven't thought of before."[31]

Katie Couric's send-off after fifteen years at *The Today Show* offers a glimpse of the vivacious journalist's personality and impact on the show and the public. Crooner Tony Bennett serenaded her with "The Way You Look Tonight" and country singer Martina McBride sang "This One's For the Girls." As part of the sendoff show, *Today* talked to six people that Katie Couric had interviewed throughout her years as *Today Show* cohost. They included an inspiring school principal, a woman brutally raped in Central Park, survivors of the Columbine school shooting and the World Trade Center bombing, and parents of a boy who had died of brain cancer. "In meeting her and talking to her, I felt that it helped heal me as well," said Lauren Manning, who was burned during the terrorist attack. Couric's parents and two daughters were also in the audience for what Katie Couric jokingly called the "celebration of moi."[32]

KATIE COURIC JOINS CBS

As Katie Couric readied herself for her new job as evening anchor on CBS, the media was filled with speculation on how effective she would be in the job and, mostly, what she would wear and how she would style her hair. A story appeared on NBC News about how a publicity photo for *CBS Evening News*, featuring Katie Couric, had been airbrushed to make the new anchor appear slimmer. The caption on the screen, while the anchor told the story, read "Can CBS News Be Trusted?"[33] The controversy spurred the debate about the standards of appearance for women in television and how they differ from the standards for men. One talk show pundit commented that

"No one ever mentioned that a photo of Charlie Gibson has been re-touched to make him appear more buff to anchor the news." Katie Couric said that she hadn't known about the digitally reworked version until she saw the issue of *Watch!*, the CBS magazine that is distributed to CBS stations and on American Airlines flights. Katie Couric told the New York Daily News, "I liked the first picture better because there's more of me to love."[34] Gil Schwartz, executive vice president of communications for CBS Corporation, said that the photo alteration was done by someone in the photo department who "got a little zealous."[35]

When Harry Smith, cohost of *CBS This Morning*, interviewed Katie Couric about her new position and pointed to the fact that so much hype was about her appearance and qualifications, Katie Couric commented, "I think there is some residual sexism, and I think women are sort of judged by different standards. But I try not to get too preoccupied by that. I think that I feel very confident in who I am as a person and as a professional."[36]

Katie Listens Before Talking

Before she made her September 5, 2006, debut as anchor of the "CBS Evening News," Katie Couric went on a "listening tour" of six cities in which 100 so-called regular folks would be able to talk to her—no press coverage allowed—about what they were interested in seeing on the re-vamped newscast. Ms. Couric also headlined a charity event in each city, CBS News says the tour was Ms. Couric's idea. (It's perhaps worth noting that the news star's outside publicist Matthew Hiltzik helped coordinate a 1999 "listening tour" that helped transform Hillary Clinton from a former first lady into New York's junior senator.) Asked how much a twenty-two-minute broadcast truly could be impacted by feedback gathered on such a tour, "Evening News" executive producer Rome Hartman said: "We are not going to furiously scribble down everything that everybody says and then turn around and remake the newscast in the image of this. But it is a genuine effort to hear people out, and I think we're going to come to the end of it and be able to compare notes and say, 'You know what struck me? There were some really interesting, consistent threads.' Nor does Mr. Hartman have a problem with the no-press-allowed rule, because the idea is, "What can we do to make sure that these are as comfortable and as natural as possible? Where people will really feel they're not performing, they're not on stage, they're not being asked to make sound bites? If you have cameras and lights, it changes the conversation. . . . We're not banning anybody. I don't think there's any issue about freedom of the press." Of the listening tour, Katie Couric noted "I think face-to-face conversations with people and really getting a sense of where they are and their likes and dislike, their frustrations, is invaluable."[37] In addition to meeting her CBS audience in person, Katie Couric also spent her time on the road raising money for cancer awareness.[38]

The day of Katie Couric's debut as the anchor on *CBS Evening News*, local news affiliates around the country let viewers know about her debut. Philadelphia's Eyewitness News reported during the 4:00 a.m. broadcast about Katie Couric's historic broadcast that was just an hour-and-a-half away. Cohosts Larry Mendte and Alicia Lane interviewed Katie Couric about her new assignment. Katie Couric said that she would have regretted not taking advantage of the opportunity to be anchor more than she would regret taking it. By e-mail on September 5, 2006, Katie Couric sent a note to subscribers describing her anticipation of the evening and the stories being presented. The note began in casual and enthusiastic Katie Couric style:

> Hi, everyone, Well, the big day is finally here! Tonight will be the first time I'll be anchoring The *CBS Evening News*, and I am very excited and humbled. I really hope we can make this broadcast useful and meaningful for you. That's really our goal, and we're going to work hard to get there—starting with tonight's broadcast.[39]

After the description of the evening's news stories, she concluded with:

> Also today we launched our blog, *Couric & Co*. We'll be swapping stories, sharing opinions—and, we hope, reading about your views. Please check it out and let us know what you think. Thanks so much!
> Katie Couric
> CouricandCo@cbs.com[40]

In addition to the above e-mail and blog, *CBS Evening News With Katie Couric* is simulcast live on the Internet every evening, which makes *CBS News* the first of the network newscasts to use the Internet for simultaneous transmission of the news.[41] She told Larry King that CBS is, like all broadcasting companies, trying to incorporate the new technologies, such as the Internet, into the presentation of the news. Also offered to viewers is *Eye to Eye*, a daily, five-minute, afternoon on-demand Web/iTunes program with extended interviews hosted by Couric; *CBS News First Look With Katie Couric*, a weekday, early-afternoon, on-demand Web program previewing the nightly newscast; and *Katie Couric's Notebook*, a minute-long Web/iTunes podcast in which Couric reports on a top issue. James Horner, the Oscar-winning composer of the film score for *Titanic* and other popular soundtracks, was even commissioned to compose new theme music for *CBS Evening News with Katie Couric.*

When Katie Couric began her first broadcast as the anchor, she opened by saying, "Hi, everyone. I'm very happy to be with you tonight." She then introduced the broadcast's lead story, a piece on the resurgence of the Taliban in Afghanistan. Her introduction normally would have been read by an announcer, but in this case, viewers heard the voice of *CBS News* legend Walter Cronkite make the introduction. The 30-minute broadcast ran smoothly and ended with an appeal from Couric for suggestions from viewers on how she might sign off at the end of each show. For now, Couric chose this ending: "I'm Katie Couric. Thank you so much for watching. I really hope to see you tomorrow night."[42]

The New York Times noted, "Ms. Couric was subdued thoughout the broadcast, perhaps a little spooked by all the fuss over her appointment. The network's readiness campaign—the focus groups, the listening tour of America, the wardrobe questions—have prompted ample attention and some snickering. CBS executives have complained that Ms. Couric is being held to a cattier standard."[43]

CBS is hoping that the new approach to the news, and Katie Couric, can boost ratings, lure additional advertising dollars and reenergize a news division demoralized by a flawed story on President Bush's National Guard service that prompted the departure of four *CBS News* employees. Indeed, on her first night as anchor, CBS drew an audience estimated at 13.6 million viewers, which was the largest for the network's evening news in eight years.[44] But the audience that tuned in for Katie Couric's first week on the CBS Evening News shrunk substantially by the end of her first week, when the broadcast averaged 7.4 million viewers, 45 percent fewer than watched her Tuesday debut, according to Nielsen Media Research.[45] The first four nights of Katie Couric's broadcast included a total of nineteen minutes of hard news, with the rest features, interviews, and commentary, according to the Tyndall Report, which studies broadcast news content. By contrast, ABC's *World News Tonight* had forty-six minutes of hard news and *NBC Nightly News* had forty-four minutes.[46]

As part of Katie Couric's employment with CBS, she occasionally contributes pieces to the newsmagazine program *60 Minutes*. On September 24 she interviewed Secretary of State Condoleezza Rice. Katie Couric noted that Rice sees the struggle against the enemies of the United States as a fight of good vs. evil, a lot like the struggle she experienced as a child growing up in segregated Birmingham, Alabama. Katie Couric questioned the motives for the war in Iraq: "Is it really priority number one, in terms of philosophically and pragmatically, for the United States to be spreading democracy around the world?" Dr. Rice corrected Couric: "Well, first of all, the United States is not spreading democracy. The United States is standing with those who want a democratic future. What's wrong with assistance so that people can have their full and complete right to the very liberties and freedoms that we enjoy?" Katie Couric brings her daughter's assessment into the interview: "To quote my daughter, 'Who made us the boss of them?'" Dr. Rice again, corrected the wording used by Katie Couric, "Well, it's not a matter of being the boss of them. It's speaking for people who are voiceless." Katie Couric asked her again about the motives for the war: "You have said that your goal was, quote, 'to leave the world not just safer, but better.' Right now, Iraq doesn't seem safer. Iran and North Korea have not fallen into line. Do you honestly believe that the world is safer now?" Dr. Rice noted: "The world is safer because we're finally confronting these terrorists. We're finally confronting this challenge. And so I think we are safer. We're not yet safe. And I know that I'm not going to see the final outcome of the Middle East that we describe as democratic and prosperous and, in that way, truly stable. But all that I can do on my watch is to try to lay a foundation so that that will become the Middle East of the future. And I think we've done a great deal to begin to lay that foundation."[47]

Invention

Katie Couric has one of the most useful skills for a journalist: the ability to challenge, however diplomatically or casually, even the most elite of interviewees. She will ask for a more thorough answer by using casual phrases, such as "I don't believe you" (said in a friendly, not confrontational, way) and "Oh, come on," while all the while grinning her trademark wide grin. This disarming way of challenging her subjects is effective in making them follow up with more thorough and revealing answers. *Time* described this way of asking probing questions, "personable but persistent."[48] Regardless of the news event, often Katie Couric focuses on the human dimension. This is a hallmark of her speech. For example, when her husband died of colon cancer she became an activist, using her celebrity to encourage viewers to get tested. She often referred to her role as a mother when interviewing guests as a way to relate to the subject matter and to make sense of what the implications of the interview information could be for mothers who are watching. During the September 11 broadcast Katie Couric continually brought her reporting to the human element, instead of focusing on the terrorist attack. She kept reminding the audience about the loss of life and whether or not there was more information to report regarding the condition of those involved in the attack.

Disposition

Katie Couric routinely begins an interview in a courteous and genuinely welcoming way. But as *Time* noted, [Katie] Couric has a gymnast's flexibility and a sometimes deceptive amiability: more than one interviewee has fallen into the Venus flytrap of her neighborly charm.[49] She quickly switches gears from warm and welcoming to getting down to the business of having her most urgent questions answered. Note the warm, even gushing welcome for Secretary of State Condoleezza Rice, and then the quick turn to very direct questions about the nation at war: "Condoleezza Rice, Madam Secretary, good morning. So nice to have you here. We're—we're really honored to have you in our studio. So let's talk about the situation in Iraq. As you know, Madam Secretary, every morning it seems we're reporting bad news from that part of the world. Over 1,700 U.S. military forces have been killed so far, 484 car bombings in the last year alone. Public support for this war is declining, there's no question about it. Almost every poll indicates that's the case. What must President Bush do tonight to convince Americans that this war will not go on indefinitely?"[50] Early in her career, Katie Couric would stick very carefully to a script of questions, but as her career grew, and her repertoire of interviews increased, she became more comfortable with an extemporaneous interviewing approach. According to a *Today Show* producer, "She wasn't a very good interviewer at the beginning. At first, she would stick to the list of ten questions (the list the producer developed).[51] Katie described her approach: "I try to make people feel like there's no glass between us. I used to be terrified that I would draw a blank in the middle of an interview, so I'd write out every question and memorize them. Now I just trust my instincts, which makes it much more spontaneous."[52]

Style

One of the qualities that has likely worked to endear her to her *Today Show* audiences over the years is her informal and almost girlish quality. For example, often, Katie Couric begins a response to a question with the word "gosh" or the phrase "oh my gosh." In answer to the question, "What do you wish for yourself in the new millennium?" Katie Couric replied, as if caught off-guard: "Oh my gosh, such a heavy, deep and real question.

That I continue to be fulfilled in my job; that I continue to make women and men proud of the job I'm doing—and that my daughters don't become juvenile delinquents."[53] In another interview, she responds to growing older in front of a camera, and says, "It's not like I'm going to be on the air until I'm seventy-five and I think, 'Gosh, how am I going to look like I'm forty for twenty more years?'"[54] Another girlish or casual quality to Couric's speech is her likelihood to address guests, especially celebrities or others, in this instance historian Doris Kearns Goodwin, with a colloquial "hey." In an interview with author and historian Goodwin, Katie Couric begins the exchange with a very casual "Hey, Doris. . . ."[55] On September 11, her use of language was immediately relatable to the audience. She described what she saw as "completely shocking" and those who witnessed the event as "obviously horrified commuters."

Delivery

Early in her career, as an assignment editor for CNN's Washington bureau, her occasional on-air assignments prompted the president of CNN to order that producers "never let her appear before another camera" mainly because her voice was described as have a "tin-whistle quality" that was grating to the ear.[56] Determined not to allow this criticism to deter her, Katie Couric took voice and diction lessons.[57] Her delivery now is clear and strong, though not remarkably distinctive. Her personality punctuated her delivery and made it successful, especially on *The Today Show* where she had the opportunity to reveal her personality and the emotion behind the stories she was telling. As anchor on CBS, she has commented that she purposely has refrained from delivering the news in a more formal, dramatic way than her natural speaking style. She commented, "That's a little too performance-art."[58]

Despite the tradition of evening news anchors to present the news in a formal style, Katie Couric continues to offer a more casual, contemporary delivery style. Occasionally she is perched atop the anchor desk to delivery a story, which is antithetical to the more stilted, conservative talking head that has been traditional in the role of the anchor.

Conclusion

Her history-making debut as the first solo female anchor of the evening news has been the result of Katie Couric's long and varied career in television. She came into our homes as the perennially smiling morning coanchor of *The Today Show*, but she proved her mettle in reporting on some of the world's most riveting events. She is a most modern television professional—well educated, hard working, with a tendency to focus most on the personal, human side of the news. The nation shared with her the birth of her children, and the death of her husband—which she turned into a personal crusade against colon cancer—and the death of her young, politician sister. She sits in the chair once occupied by the most venerable of anchor figures—Walter Cronkite—and she inspires a new generation of women anchors, perhaps still in high school, to aim high. Her persistence in the face of rejection and human tragedy offers insight into what it takes to be successful in broadcasting and beyond. Her colloquial style is in sync with the times. Less formal than the anchors of yesteryear, she has adopted a style when delivering the evening news that seems natural and is comfortable to watch. She summed up her choice to move to CBS: "It's new, exciting and exhilarating. I'm loving it and I'm loving the people at CBS. I have no second thoughts about it at all."[59] She added: "I'm hopefully a good communicator and people relate to me and they can understand the news, since we are at a critically important time in history."[60] One year into her tenure as the new anchor, and after a heady start, the ratings for the *CBS Evening News* are at historic lows. The network put plans in motion to go back to the more traditional style of the broadcast, and sent Katie Couric to Iraq, where she got an exclusive interview with President Bush during his September, 2007 surprise visit. Regardless of how the new approach goes for Ms. Couric and CBS, Couric has made history as the first female solo anchor of a major network broadcast and by doing so she has given women in broadcasting one more reason to feel their progress.

NOTES

1. Jacci Duncan, *Making Waves: The 50 Greatest Women in Radio and Television* (Kansas City: Andrews McMeel Publishing, 2001), 87.

2. Transcribed from a CBS commercial airing on CBS June 25, 2006.

3. Ken Auletta, "The Dawn Patrol: The Curious Rise of Morning Television, and the Future of Network News," *The New Yorker*, August 8, 2005, http://www.newyorker.com/printables/fact/050808fa_fact1 (accessed August 22, 2006)

4. Roderick P. Hart, *Modern Rhetorical Criticism* (Needham Heights: Allyn and Bacon, 1997), 187.

5. Johnathan Last, "New Anchors Lack Stamina and Gravitas," *The Philadelphia Inquirer*, September 24, 2006, C3.

6. Hart, *Modern Rhetorical Criticism*, 221.

7. Ibid.

8. Auletta, "The Dawn Patrol," http://www.newyorker.com/printables/fact/050808fa_fact1 (accessed August 22, 2006).

9. TV Guide, April 6, 2006, http://www.newsmax.com/archives/articles/2006/4/6/112752.shtml (accessed August 26, 2006).

10. Howard Kurtz, "Katie Couric, Thinking About Tomorrow; After 15 Years at 'Today,' CBS-Bound Host Is Ready to Begin Her Next Chapter," *The Washington Post*, May 30, 2006, C-1.

11. Auletta, "The Dawn Patrol," http://www.newyorker.com/printables/fact/050808fa_fact1 (accessed August 22, 2006).

12. Ken Auletta, *Three Blind Mice: How the TV Networks Lost Their Way* (New York: Vintage Books, 1992), 548.

13. Auletta, "The Dawn Patrol," http://www.newyorker.com/printables/fact/050808fa_fact1 (accessed August 22, 2006).

14. Cable Neuhaus, "Whatever Katie Wants," *AARP*, November–December, 2006, http://www.aarpmagazine.org/people/couric.html (accessed September 28, 2006).

15. James Poniewozik, "Katie Couric: The New Anchor Is Shaking Up the News" *Time*, April 30, 2006, http://www.time.com/time/magazine/article/0,9171,1187398,00.html (accessed August 30, 2006).

16. Auletta, "The Dawn Patrol," http://www.newyorker.com/printables/fact/050808fa_fact1 (accessed August 22, 2006).

17. Roderick P. Hart, *Modern Rhetorical Criticism*, 221.

18. http://www.monahancenter.org/about/index.html (accessed August 22, 2006).

19. Peter Cram, MD, MBA; A. Mark Fendrick, MD; John Inadomi, MD; Mark E. Cowen, MD, SM; Daniel Carpenter, PhD; Sandeep Vijan, MD, MS, "The Impact of a Celebrity Promotional Campaign on the Use of Colon Cancer Screening: The Katie Couric Effect," *Journal of Internal Medicine* 163, no. 13 (July 14, 2003): 1601–5.

20. Lori Robertson, "We Have a Breaking Story," *American Journalism Review*, October, 2001, 1.

21. NBC News, *The Today Show*, September 11, 2001, DVD on loan from the Television News Archives, Vanderbilt University.

22. Bill Carter, "Bush's Iran-Contra Response," *The New York Times*, October 14, 1992, A-22.

23. Richard Sennett, *Authority* (New York: Knopf, 1993), 88.

24. http://www.pbs.org/search/search_programsaz.html (accessed August 23, 2006).

25. George F. Will, "Dole's Tobacco Debacle," *The Washington Post*, July 7, 1996, C07.

26. Steven Clayman and John Heritage, *The News Interview: Journalists and Public Figures on the Air* (Cambridge: Cambridge University Press, 2002), 3.

27. NBC News transcripts, *Today Show* (7:00 a.m. EST) January 20, 1997.

28. NBC News transcripts, *Today Show* (7:00 a.m. EST) October 23, 1997.

29. NBC News transcripts, *Today Show* (7:00 a.m. EST) April 22, 1999.

30. NBC News transcripts, *Today Show* (7:00 a.m. EST) July 19, 1999.

31. NBC News transcripts, *Today Show* (7:00 a.m. EST) June 11, 2003 .

32. NBC News transcripts, *Today Show*, May 31, 2006.

33. "CBS Alters Photo to Slim Couric Down," http://msnbc.msn.com/id/14584870/from/ET/ (accessed August 30, 2006).

34. "Promotional Photo of Slimmer Couric Was Altered by CBS," *The Morning Call* (Allentown, PA), August 31, 2006, A11.

35. Ibid.

36. *CBS This Morning*, September 5, 2006 (transcribed from broadcast).

37. "Katie Ready to Hit the Ground Running," www.tmz.com/2006/08/29katie-ready-to-hit-the-ground-running/ (accessed 9/5/06).

38. Ibid.

39. "CBS News Evening News," cbsnews_evening_news_newsletter-dgn2=psu.edu@cbsig.com (e-mail received September 5, 2006)

40. Ibid.

41. Anne Becker and P. J. Bednarski, "CBS Evening News to Be Shown Live on Internet," *Broadcasting & Cable*, August 17, 2006, http://www.broadcastingcable.com/article/CA6363379.html (accessed September 5, 2006)

42. "Katie Couric Weighs Anchor," http://www.cbsnews.com/stories/2006/09/05/eveningnews/main1966506.shtml (accessed September 5, 2006).

43. Alessandra Stanley, "For the New Face of CBS News, a Subdued Beginning," *The New York Times*, September 6, 2006, A15.

44. "New Kids on the Block," *The New York Times*, September 10, 2006, B2.

45. "Couric's Audience Shrinks," LATimes.com, September 11, 2006, http://www.latimes.com/entertainment/news/la-et-qtcbs12sep12,1,632636.story?coll=la-headlines-entnews&track=crosspromo (accessed September 11, 2006).

46. David Bauder, "CBS Is Taking 'Evening News' in a New Direction," *The Morning Call* (Allentown, PA), September 19, 2006, E5.

47. *60 Minutes* 7:00 p.m. EST, CBS, September 24, 2006, lexisnexis@prod.lexisnexis.com (accessed October 1, 2006).

48. Poniewozik, "Katie Couric," http://www.time.com/time/magazine/article/0,9171,1187398,00.html. (accessed August 30, 2006).

49. Ibid.

50. NBC News transcripts, *Today Show* 7:00 a.m. EST, NBC, June 28, 2005 Tuesday.

51. Edward Klein, *Katie Couric: The Real Story* (New York: Crown Publishers, 2007), 72.

52. Ibid., 73.

53. Judith Marlane, *Women in Television News Revisited* (Austin: University of Texas Press, 1999), 225.

54. Jacquelyn Mitchard, "Katie Unplugged," *Parade*, August 12, 2006, 6.

55. www.presidentialfest.com/about.html (accessed August 27, 2006).

56. Louis Baldwin, *Women of Strength: Biographies of 106 Women Who Have Excelled in Traditionally Male Fields, AD 61 to the Present* (Jefferson, North Carolina: McFarland and Company, 1996), 222.

57. Ibid.

58. *CBS This Morning*, September 5, 2006 (transcribed from broadcast).

59. CNN, *Larry King Live*, November 1, 2006, recorded from television.

60. Ibid.

8

TURNING UP THE VOLUME

The Future of Women in Television Broadcasting

Maurine H. Beasley in her book *First Ladies and The Press: The Unfinished Partnership of the Media Age* argues that "the first lady is the single most visible symbol of American womanhood."[1] Women in broadcasting represent another powerful and visible symbol of American womanhood with direct implications of how far women have come in the workplace. To be visible and vocal, as all television broadcasters must be, is to be powerful in the media-obsessed American culture. To trace the trajectory of women in television broadcasting is to get a sense of the progress of all career women. And for many young women who came of age as television gained prominence in American homes, the women of broadcasting news represented all that they could do and become.

Katie Couric made history when she became the first sole female anchor of an evening news broadcast—CBS—in 2006. Halfway into her first year on the job *Time* noted that "Old Is In. The hottest anchor is the most traditional" when it reported that Charles Gibson, anchor of *ABC News*, was ahead in the ratings war. "Gibson's success has been seen as a vindication of old fashioned gravitas over flash." The article goes on to describe Gibson as the "anti-Couric: avuncular, male, older."[2] Worth noting, however, is that even before Couric gained prominence on the *CBS Evening News* as anchor, a profound shift in how Americans received their news was under way. More and more Americans go online to get news updates, whether on computers or handheld devices such as the Apple iPhone. No longer must

Americans wait for "Uncle Walter," "Aunt Katie," or for that matter, any other broadcasting figure to deliver the news. Authors Mark Halperin and John F. Harris keenly point out that "Today one strains to recall that not that long ago there really was a 'small group of men'—and at that time they were all men—who served as gatekeepers for what the public learned about national politics."[3]

In this book, the compelling rhetorical biographies of a dozen of perhaps the most tenacious and talented women in broadcasting demonstrate that they not only were able to break into and ultimately thrive in the formerly male-dominated arena of broadcasting, they were able to change as much as the media did in order to stay vital in the constantly morphing world of television news. Some of the women were even able to promote their own causes, such as Katie Couric's colon cancer awareness mission and Judy Woodruff's generous interviews to attempt to educate the American public on the illness that struck her son, spina bifida. Many of the women are deeply patriotic, such as Candy Crowley, who, like Christiane Amanpour, has a missionary zeal for her work as a journalist.

THE RISE OF SEVERAL IMPORTANT WOMEN IN TELEVISION BROADCASTING

No better example, perhaps, of the elasticity to stay and grow in the news business that has radically changed from when she entered it is Barbara Walters, who is as famous as the people she interviews. Having entered the business as a writer, her ambition and hard work and longevity have given her respect from her colleagues and the public. Many celebrities request to be interviewed by "Barbara," which to many signifies that they must have "made it big" if they are being interviewed by her. She moves from interviewing heads of states—she has interviewed every American president and first lady since Richard and Pat Nixon. And many of the most controversial world leaders have sat down to tell their stories to Barbara Walters including Menachen Begin, Margaret Thatcher, Fidel Castro, Anwar Sadat, Vladimir Putin, Boris Yeltsin, King Hussein of Jordan, and Premier Jiang Zemin. With equal intensity and preparation she has interviewed pop stars and movie stars. She is credited as being the woman who has made the prevalence of more women on television more likely. Bob Schieffer, longtime CBS broadcaster, notes, "Until Barbara Walters came along, there had not been many female interviewers, and viewers were unaccustomed to women who posed pointed questions.[4] Because of this, Walters had to adopt a style that was both professionally excellent and appealing to viewers who initially rejected the idea of having a female interviewer interrogate guests. Known for her meticulous preparation and for achieving fame that is on par with her guests, she has been able to achieve at the highest levels in broadcasting, while keeping her career thriving over five decades. Most recently, her embrace of the more colloquial and conversational style of television that emerged in recent decades could be seen in her daytime female talk show *The View*, which she created and often cohosts. The communication style she has perfected is one of genuine interest in her guests, impeccable preparation, and a familiarity with her guests that has developed over the years from repeated interviews. That she is as well known as her guests makes her as much a fascination to viewers as the interviewees themselves.

Two other notable women broadcasters are Connie Chung and Elizabeth Vargas. Notable for several reasons, but perhaps the most pertinent to this study, is that they were each cohosts of major network broadcasts. Connie Chung cohosted the *CBS Evening News* with Dan Rather and Elizabeth Vargas and Bob Woodruff cohosted *ABC World News Tonight*, albeit briefly. Connie Chung is a significant female figure in the history of broadcast news. The early trajectory of her career was on a steady rise and she was determined to make a name for herself. She was as aggressive as could be, following one Watergate figure into church to get an interview, which is reminiscent of Lesley Stahl's aggressive means of following a Watergate figure into the men's bathroom to secure her interview. As she continued to conduct more and increasingly important interviews, Connie Chung gained notoriety as a tenacious and hard worker, and she became one of the most recognizable faces on television, rising to the position of coanchor of the *CBS Evening News with Dan Rather*. She moved from network to network, however, and in the past few years, Chung has faded from television and is no longer a popular broadcast figure. The style of ambush-oriented interviewing that characterized Connie Chung's early career transitioned into more in-depth interviews, and it was that style—the long and in-depth interview—that was not as successful for Chung as the initial "get" type of story that characterized her early career.

Elizabeth Vargas rose to prominence when she was named coanchor with Bob Woodruff of *ABC World News Tonight*. Her style of questioning is pointed and direct, yet her delivery, which is calm and measured, suggests an earnest curiosity that solicits an earnest reply. Her forceful and robust use of questioning assists in the development of the thesis that she puts forward in her stories. Elizabeth Vargas became one of the few women to hold the coveted position of network news anchor in the United States. Her intelligence, drive, and experience served her well. The "insatiable curiosity" fostered by her travels as a young girl were requisite for her career in broadcasting and aided her rise to the top of the field.

Christiane Amanpour is one of the most extraordinary women ever to rise to the top of broadcast journalism. The topics she chooses demand a serious and urgent delivery and a more comprehensive treatment than a mere segment on the evening news. In 2007 she went face to face with religious zealots for her special "CNN Presents: God's Warriors." In the provocative special, Amanpour examines the intersection between religion and politics and the effects of Christianity, Islam, and Judaism on politics, culture, and public life. Her stories demand a vast knowledge of very complex issues, an ability to communicate in multiple cultures, and the ability to make understandable to the audience complex, intellectual topics. For instance, in the special "God's Warriors" Amanpour interviews Noa Rothman, the granddaughter of Israeli Prime Minister Yitzhak Rabin, whose 1993 peace treaty with the Palestine Liberation Organization upset many in the proreligious settlement movement. A militant Jewish fundamentalist assassinated Rabin in 1995. Because of her extensive experience in international affairs, Amanpour is able to orient the viewer to this intellectual topic with the connection of the role of religion in American politics. Well prepared, she takes no shortcuts in getting the story as fully to the audience as possible. Traveling to ten countries to get the best picture of Osama bin Laden for the "In the Footsteps of bin Laden" special is typical of her preparation. When her voluminous research is finally edited down to the script, her delivery is dramatic and exclamatory, zeroing in on the most salient features of the story.

Dana Bash represents the younger pack of broadcast journalists who grew up with role models, including her own father, who had long and productive careers. By the time Bash went to college, she had years of experience viewing female broadcasters who had come before her. She advises young people interested in a career in broadcasting that they have to be willing to work really hard in unglamorous ways. Now a CNN congressional correspondent, she covers both the U.S. House and the Senate with her extensive knowledge of the political process and her plucky, up-from-the-bootstraps style that has propelled her career forward at a time when more women are vying for coveted broadcasting positions.

Candy Crowley is one of the most recognized political reporters on television. Unfailingly polite and politically astute, she has garnered interviews with the most compelling political figures in contemporary times. Her witty, yet serious and intelligent, coverage of every political convention since the nomination of Jimmy Carter, has given her a following on national television that is especially fervent in election years. Her enthusiasm for her work is evident in her reflection of why she is a reporter. Her recollection of the coverage of the first political convention of her career demonstrates her patriotism and devotion to the craft of political broadcasting. Candy Crowley exudes credibility and an unbridled ebullience for the history-making political stories that she covers. Her love of politics is palpable as she reports— as she has for more than a quarter of a century—on the political process in America.

Andrea Mitchell is a well respected, veteran broadcast journalist who is often sought after for her punditry on political events. Whether she was covering a local, state, or national story, Mitchell gained a reputation for her pointed questions and her enthusiasm for the story. Her intense love of storytelling, and the wonderment of how the story ends, has kept her devoted to her career for decades.

Judy Woodruff has dedicated her career to in-depth, substantial reports that delve into issues of sociological and political importance for both PBS and CNN. Judy Woodruff gained a following for her popular CNN show *Inside Politics*, which illuminated her political acumen. Her longer, documentary-style programs have allowed her to investigate issues and advocate for causes that have been important to her and to viewers.

Diane Sawyer has grown to prominence in broadcasting and most significantly, is the first woman to host the hugely respected *60 Minutes* program on CBS. Often called in to rescue sagging ratings, Diane Sawyer has demonstrated a longevity in broadcasting that is rivaled by few and no doubt has been propelled by the ease with which she switches from hard-news journalist to tabloid journalist. Her celebrity is on par with many of her guests and the most well-known women in broadcasting featured in this book. Sawyer is an excellent example of a woman in broadcasting who literally went from "weather girl" to anchor, and her ability to move forward in an industry constantly in flux is a testament to her talent.

Lesley Stahl never lost her lust for the hard-news, edgy stories that have been a tradition at CBS. Known for her tough, pointed questions and her ability to follow up and ask exactly the question needed to get the answer she wanted, Stahl is a good example of a journalist who came up in the 1972 hiring sweep and never came down. She gained a reputation for her intrepid investigating and she has demonstrated a love of politics and television, as so many women in this book have. She noted, "So what had I learned in twenty years in Washington? I learned that it's not only 'the economy, stupid,' It's also television, stupid. Television has become the center not only of campaigning and governing but also of diplomacy and decision making."[5]

Paula Zahn's career is representative of a woman in broadcasting who worked hard to rise through the local ranks to national prominence. She is also an example of a broadcast journalist who had to confront several important obstacles commonly faced by women in broadcasting. A beautiful woman, she had to deflect the embarrassing promotion of her CNN work as "sexy" and she transitioned from network news to cable broadcasting when it still wasn't established that cable news broadcasting would have as equal, and now greater, a ratings hold on the market.

Katie Couric's rise to sole female anchor gave impetus to this project. She is a contemporary broadcasting figure who represents many of the changes that have occurred in television news broadcasting from its inception. Her history-making debut as the first solo female anchor of the evening news has been the result of Katie Couric's long and varied career in television. She came into our homes as the perennially smiling morning coanchor of *The Today Show*, but she proved her mettle in reporting on some of the world's most riveting events. She is a most modern television professional— well educated, hard working, with a tendency to focus most on the personal, human side of the news. The nation shared with her the birth of her children, and the death of her husband, which she turned into a personal crusade against colon cancer and the death of her young, politician sister. She sits in the chair once occupied by the most venerable of anchor figures— Walter Cronkite—and she inspires a new generation of women anchors, perhaps still in high school, to aim high. Her persistence in the face of rejection and human tragedy offers insight into what it takes to be successful in broadcasting and beyond.

In September, 2007, *The New York Times* noted that, "As the first woman to be a solo anchor, Ms. Couric was promoted by CBS News like a movie star, and received extraordinary attention and scrutiny. But after a heady start at the top, the CBS news report quickly fell behind the broadcasts of NBC and ABC, and now holds a distant third place—in some weeks with even fewer viewers than Bob Schieffer had as his interim anchor.[6]

OVERCOMING THE OBSTACLES FOR WOMEN TELEVISION BROADCASTERS

The tradition of "Murrow's Boys" and the perception both by network power holders responsible for hiring, and the viewing public, that anchoring is a "man's job" has made the rise of women in broadcasting slow. Dutch communication scholar Geert Hofstede's observation of feminine and masculine cultures is especially important to the history of women in broadcasting. Hofstede notes that "femininity stands for a society in which social gender roles overlap: both men and women are supposed to be modest, tender, and concerned with the quality of life." Masculinity, on the other hand, "stands for a society in which social gender roles are clearly distinct: men are supposed to be assertive, tough and focused on material success."[7] The United States ranks relatively high on the measures of masculinity, ranking fifteenth out of fifty-three countries.[8] It took thirty years for a woman, Katie Couric, to become the sole anchor of a network news broadcast, CBS, and her ratings and press coverage have been low and critical. Less important to this study is whether or not the first woman anchor is successful. The more penetrating question is: what took her so long to get there?

RHETORICAL TRAITS OF WOMEN BROADCASTERS

Roderick P. Hart's seminal research on credibility examined the verbal dimensions of credibility, which include power, competence, trustworthiness, goodwill, and similarity, and it is the last one—similarity—that has made the rise of women as network anchors slow to become realized in America. That women were not as visible in the workforce at the beginning of the rise of television news is one reason that there were fewer women in broadcasting. Still, once women became hired in increasing numbers, after 1972, there was a protracted rise of women of prominence in television broadcasting. Two women who became coanchors of evening newscasts, Barbara Walters and Connie Chung, were quickly assigned other responsibilities when the coanchoring did not prove successful. That the male would have to "share" the anchor chair with a woman was not well received by either viewers or the male anchors.

One issue that has remained a double standard for women in broadcasting is that of appearance. While women are able to enjoy success on television as broadcasters, they are held to what may be described as a "television beauty qualification" (TBQ). There seems to be an increased pressure for women of all ages to be youthful and attractive and television anchorwomen, who may be the most visual image of a working woman to many girls and women, seem to be held to an especially high standard of appearance. In 1987 Christine Craft, who at age thirty-six, was told she was "too old, too ugly, and not deferential enough to men" broke wide open the issue of the double standards in appearance for men and women in broadcasting when she sued her employer for discrimination. Now in her sixties, Craft works as a radio announcer in Sacramento, California, and says that although things have changed for women in broadcasting, in that they are able to work past their fortieth birthday, "however they are required to have two facelifts for every single facelift of their male counterparts."[9] Two of the anchors profiled in this book, Judy Woodruff and Paul Zahn, experienced the harshness of youth over experience when the younger Paula Zahn was brought in to CNN to replace the aging and more experienced Judy Woodruff. Though both women are notable in their own right, the youth-obsessed nature of television news impacted both of their careers. Most recently Zahn left CNN, only to be replaced by a younger woman, Campbell Brown, formerly of NBC, who CNN hopes will revive its late-night audience.

In addition to their attractive appearance, newscasters need to exhibit competence, intelligence, strength, and gravitas. This "all things to all people" requirement is reminiscent of the notion of rhetorical multitasking that has been found in the rhetoric of successful female rhetors, such as Elizabeth Dole. Rhetorical multitasking is the ability to establish more than one task when a woman speaks.[10] In addition to trying to meet the needs of many different types of audiences when they speak, from this study several characteristics of the rhetoric of women broadcasters can be found. They are meticulous in their preparation for interviews. For example, the notecards for which Barbara Walters is famous helped her to establish herself as competent when very few women were appearing on news broadcasts. Christiane Amanpour created a niche for herself by becoming an expert on global issues and traveling the world to report her stories. Young Dana Bash described the grunt work that she did for years at CNN, "taking the tapes, logging them in, writing on them what happened." She noted, "sometimes you didn't even get paid for it."[11] Katie Couric worked her way up to anchor, after several jobs that were anything but glamorous. Her first job at ABC News included getting sandwiches for the anchor.[12] Along the way she was told that she didn't have the talent to be on air, let alone anchor, in one instance being told by the news director that she might have a chance to anchor only if she would try it at a "really, really small market."[13]

All the women profiled in this book, as well as other women in broadcasting and journalism, have some similar traits. These traits include intelligence and drive. To become successful in broadcasting requires a work ethic uncommon in other professions. The advice that Katie Couric gives young women interested in broadcasting has been the path of most of the women in this book: "get a good, solid liberal arts education, and focus on areas such as economics, government, foreign policy, and Russian history. Learn as much as you can, and make sure that learning continues through your first, lowly jobs. Be patient and tenacious, because smart, dedicated people will eventually make themselves known."[14] All of the women in this book are accomplished academically, many musically, and all have traveled extensively. These women exhibit an insatiable curiosity and many of them have extraordinary patriotism and the desire to be seen and heard in a field that began in a male tradition and is continuing on more equal footing. The passion for their profession and their excellence that has been demonstrated through their interviews with leaders of every magnitude on a global stage has ensured that despite obstacles, women in broadcasting are now seen and heard—stay tuned.

NOTES

1. Maurine H. Beasley, *First Ladies and the Press: The Unfinished Partnership of the Media Age* (Evanston, Illinois: Northwestern University Press, 2005), xix.

2. James Poniewozik, "Here's the News: Old Is In. The Hottest Anchor Is the Most Traditional. But for TV News to Survive, Change Would Do It Good," *Time*, April 2, 2007, 68.

3. Mark Halperin and John F. Harris, *The Way to Win: Taking the White House in 2008* (New York: Random House, 2007), 34.

4. Bob Schieffer, *Face the Nation: My Favorite Stories from the First 50 Years of the Award-winning News Broadcast* (New York: Simon and Schuster, 2004), 97.

5. Lesley Stahl, *Reporting Live* (New York: Simon and Schuster, 1999), 404.

6. Alessandra Stanley, "In Iraq, Couric Hones Her Hard-News Image," *The New York Times*, September 5, 2007, Arts, 1.

7. Geert Hofstede, *Cultures and Organizations: Software of the Mind* (London: McGraw-Hill, 1991), 14.

8. Ibid., 262.

9. Christine Craft e-mail correspondence with Nichola D. Gutgold, July 5, 2006.

10. Molly Meijer Wertheimer and Nichola D. Gutgold, *Elizabeth Hanford Dole: Speaking from the Heart* (Westport, Connecticut: Praeger Press, 2004), 127.

11. Dana Bash, interview with Nichola D. Gutgold, March 15, 2007.

12. Jacci Duncan, *Making Waves: 50 Greatest Women in Radio and Television* (Kansas City: McMeel Publishing, 2001), 84.

13. Ibid., 85.

14. Ibid., 87.

BIBLIOGRAPHY

ABC News transcripts, *20/20*, April 12, 2000. "Who Killed JonBenét? Former Lead Detective of the JonBenet Ramsey Murder Investigation Believes Patsy Ramsey is the Murderer."

ABC News, *Good Morning America*, November 12, 2003. "Britney Spears, Exclusive Interview with Pop Star."

ABC News, *Primetime Live* (ABC 10:00 p.m. EST) June 14, 1995, transcript #406 accessed from http://web.lexis-nexis.com.

ABC News transcripts. "Elian Gonzalez successfully reunited with his father; President Clinton Comments; Live Coverage Continues of Protestors and Rioters in Miami." ABC News Special Report: Elian Gonzalez, April 22, 2000.

ABC News transcripts, *20/20*, January 12, 1996. lexisnexis@prod.lexisnexis.com

———. *20/20* October 14, 1994. lexisnexis@prod.lexisnexis.com

———. *20/20* October 7, 1994. lexisnexis@prod.lexisnexis.com

———. *World News Tonight with Peter Jennings*, June 18, 1987. lexisnexis@prod.lexisnexis.com.

Adler, Ronald B., Lawrence B. Rosenfeld, and Russell F. Proctor. *Interplay: The Process of Interpersonal Communication*. 8th ed. Fort Worth: Harcourt-Brace, 2001.

Alan, Jeff, with James M. Lane. *Anchoring America: The Changing Face of Television News.* Chicago and Los Angeles: Bonus Books, 2003.

Alder, Jonathan. "Looksism in TV News." *Newsweek*, November 6, 1989, 72.

Allen, Craig M. "Gender Breakthrough Fit for a Focus Group." *Journalism History* 28:4, Winter, 2003, 154–62.

———. *News is People: The Rise of Local TV News and the Fall of News from New York*. Ames: Iowa State University Press, 2001.

Amanpour, Christiane. "Commentary." *The Quill*, Chicago, 2005, 40.

———. Speech before the Los Angeles World Affairs Council, "While America Slept: Bombs, but Then What?" December 6, 2002, http://www.lawac.org/speech/amanpour (accessed September 22, 2007).

Anderson, Bonnie M. *News Flash Journalism, Infotainment and the Bottom Line Business of Broadcast News*. San Francisco, Jossey-Bass, 2004.

Anderson, Karrin Vasby. "From Spouses to Candidates: Hillary Rodham Clinton, Elizabeth Dole, and the Gendered Office of U.S. President. " *Rhetoric & Public Affairs* 5, no. 1 (Spring 2002): 105–32.

Armstrong, Rob. *Covering Politics: A Handbook for Journalists*. Ames, Iowa, Blackwell Publishing, 2004.

Auletta, Ken. *Backstory: Inside the Business of News*. New York: The Penguin Press, 2003.

———. "Promise Her the Moon." *The New Yorker* (New York), 14 February 1994.

———. "The Dawn Patrol: The Curious Rise of Morning Television, and the Future of Network News." *The New Yorker*, August 8, 2005. http://www.newyorker.com/printables/fact/050808fa_fact1 (accessed August 22, 2006).

———. *Three Blind Mice: How the TV Networks Lost Their Way*. New York: Vintage Books: 1991.

———. *Whom Do Journalists Work For?* The Red Smith Lecture in Journalism John W. Gallivan Program in Journalism, Ethics an Democracy, University of Notre Dame (Kansas City: Universal Press Syndicate, 2005).

Balducci, Leslie. "Anchor Juggles Life, Career Like Rest of Us." *Chicago Sun-Times*, May 26, 1996, F53.

Baldwin, Louis. *Women of Strength: Biographies of 196 Who Have Excelled in Traditionally Male Fields, A.D. to the Present*. Jefferson, North Carolina: McFarland Press, 1996.

Barker, Olivia. "Couric's Style Goes from 'Today' to 'Evening': New Job May Bring Subtler Clothes, Hair." *USA Today*, August 10, 2006, 1D.

Bauder, David. "CBS Is Taking 'Evening News' in a New Direction." *The Morning Call* (Allentown, PA) September 19, 2006, E5.

———. "Chung-Condit Interview Lures Viewers to ABC." *The Milwaukee Journal-Sentinel*, August 30, 2001.

———. "CNN Yanks Zahn 'Sexy' Promotion." Associated Press Online, January 8, 2002.

Beasley, Maurine H. *First Ladies and the Press: The Unfinished Partnership of the Media Age*. Evanston, Illinois: Northwestern University Press, 2005.

Becker, Anne. "An Age-Old Problem: TV Newswomen Say Discrimination Persists. It's Just Harder to Prove." *Broadcasting and Cable*, October 31, 2005, 12–13.

Becker, Anne and P. J. Bednarski. "*CBS Evening News* to Be Shown Live on Internet." *Broadcasting & Cable* (accessed 17 August 2006). http://www.broadcastingcable.com/article/CA6363379.html (accessed 9/5/2006).

Bergen, Peter. *The Osama Bin Laden I Know.* Free Press, 2006.

Biagi, Shirley. *Newstalk II State of the Art Conversation with Today's Broadcast Journalists.* Belmont: Wadsworth Publishing Company, 1987.

Birkner, Gabrielle. "Today Is Couric's Last; Tomorrow, Her New Look." *New York Sun Times*, May 31, 2006. www.nysun.com/article/33587 (accessed 11 July 2006).

Bliss, Edward Jr. *Now the News: The Story of Broadcast Journalism.* New York: Columbia University Press, 1991.

Blue, Rose and Joanne E. Bernstein. *Diane Sawyer: Superwoman.* Hillside, New Jersey: Enslow Publishing, 1990.

Blumberg, Skip. "Interviews with Interviewers . . . About Interviewing" videotape produced with grants from National Endowment of the Arts, 1985.

Boedecker, Hal. "PBS Celebrates Anchor's Career." *Daily Press* (Norfolk, VA), July 26, 2006, D5.

Bradley, P. *Women and the Press: The Struggle for Equality.* Evanston, Illinois: Northwestern University Press, 2005).

Brecher, Elinor J. "Elizabeth Vargas: Tuning in at the Top." *Puerto Rico Herald*, June, 2002, www.puertorico-herald.org/issues/2002.vol6n24 (accessed November 15, 2006).

Brown, Les. "ABC with Barbara Waters." *The New York Times*, April 21, 1976, 1.

Buchman, Patti. "Title VII Limits on Discrimination Against Television Anchorwoman on the Basis of Age-Related Appearance." *Columbia Law Review*, vol. 85, no. 1, January, 1985, 190–215.

"CBS Alters Photo to Slim Couric Down." http://msnbc.msn.com/id/14584870/from/ET/ (accessed August 30, 2006). *CBS News Evening News* cbsnews_evening_news_newsletter-dgn2=psu.edu@cbsig.com (e-mail received September 5, 2006).

CBS This Morning, September 5, 2006 (transcribed from broadcast).

CNN Breaking News. "Sen. John Kerry Arrives at Boston's Faneuil Hall to Deliver His Concession Speech," November 3, 2004 http://edition.cnn.com/TRANSCRIPTS/0411/03/bn.03.html (accessed January 2, 2006).

CNN Breaking News, September 11, 2001, 19:05. CNN.com transcripts.

CNN Special Presentation. "In the Footsteps of Bin Laden." August, 2006 (recorded from television August 23, 2006).

———. "An In-Depth Look at Islam." October 13, 2001 (obtained from Pennsylvania State University Library).

CNN transcript, "A Global Forum with President Clinton," transcript #320-6, (accessed October 19, 2006).

CNN, *Larry King Live*, November 1, 2006, recorded from television.

CNN March 31, 2001, "Milosevic's Legacy Still Scares Balkans." http://transcripts .cnn.com/TRANSCRIPTS/0103/31/smn.14.html (accessed October 20, 2006).

CNN Special Presents, 8:00 p.m. EST, September 24, 2006. "Where Have All the Parents Gone?" http://web.lexisexis.com.ezaccess.libraries.psu.edu/universe/document (accessed October 14, 2006).

CNN Presents Christiane Amanpour Interviews President of Syria. http://www.cnn .com/2005/WORLD/meast/10/12/alassad.transcript/index.html (accessed August 22, 2007).

CNN, *Paula Zahn Now*, January 26, 2004.

CNN Tribute, "America Remembers: The Events of September and America's Response." DVD, 2003, CNN.

Campbell, Karlyn Kohrs. "The Discursive Performance of Femininity: Hating Hillary." *Rhetoric & Public Affairs* (1998).

"Candy Crowley's Spectacular View of the Inauguration," January 20, 2001, http:// cnnstudentnews.cnn.com/2001/ALLPOLITICS/stories/01/20/crowley.debrief/ (accessed January 2, 2006).

Carmody, John. "Boston TV Job for Times' Lydon." *The Washington Post*, January 7, 1977, B8.

Carmody, John and Lee Lescaze. "Anchors Away: The Crew's Changing at ABC News." *The Washington Post*, April 20, 1978, B1.

Carter, Bill. "Tender Trap." *New York Times*, August 23, 1992, 23.

———. "Bush's Iran-Contra Response." *The New York Times*, October 14, 1992, A–22.

———. "Chung to Join Rather as CBS News Anchor." *The New York Times*, May 18, 1993, C18.

———. "Sawyer Makes New Deal with ABC." *The New York Times*, February 17, 1994, A-4.

———. *Desperate Networks*. New York: Doubleday, 2006.

Castro, Janice. "Women in Television: An Uphill Battle." *Channels*, January, 1988.

Chung, Connie. "The Business of Getting 'The Get': Nailing an Exclusive Interview in Prime Time." *The Joan Shorenstein Center Press Politics Public Policy, Discussion Paper D-28*, April 1998.

"Chung and Povich, On Screen and Off." *St. Louis Post-Dispatch* (Missouri), November 9, 2005, E6.

Clark, Amy Sara. *"Connie Chung's Serenade Gag a Web Hit."* June 20, 2006, http:/ /www.cbsnews.com/stories/2006/06/20/entertainment/main1736320.shtml (accessed November 12, 2006).

Clayman, Steven and John Heritage. *The News Interview: Journalists and Public Figures on the Air.* Cambridge: Cambridge University Press, 2002.

Cohen, Patricia. "Stop the Press, Boys! Women Claim Space on the Op-Ed Pages." *The New York Times*, March 15, 2007. www.thewhitehouseproject.org (accessed March 21, 2007).

Collins, Scott. "Chung Quits after Show Cancelled." *The San Diego Union Tribune*, March 27, 2003, E-7.

"Connie Chung Joins CNN." *People's Daily* (Beijing), January 24, 2002. http://english.peopledaily.com.cnn (accessed November 8, 2006).

"Couric's Audience Shrinks." LATimes.com, September 11, 2006. http://www.latimes.com/entertainment/news/la-et-qtcbs12sep12,1,632636.story?coll=la-headlines-entnews&track=crosspromo (accessed September 11, 2006).

Cooper, Anderson. "Judgment Day Arrives for Senator Joe Lieberman." *360 Degrees* 10:00 p.m. EST August 8, 2006.

Cozby, Paul C. "Self Disclosure a Literature Review." *Psychological Bulletin* 79:2. 1973, 73–91.

———. "Self-Disclosure, Reciprocity, and Liking." *Sociometry* 35, no. 1 (March 1972): 151–60.

Craft, Christine. *Too Old, Too Ugly, and Not Deferential to Men*. Rocklin, CA: Prima Publishing, 1986.

Cram, Peter. MD, MBA; A. Mark Fendrick, MD; John Inadomi, MD; Mark E. Cowen, MD, SM; Daniel Carpenter, PhD; Sandeep Vijan, MD, MS. "The Impact of a Celebrity Promotional Campaign on the Use of Colon Cancer Screening: The Katie Couric Effect," *Journal of Internal Medicine* 163, no. 13 (July 14, 2003): 1601–5.

Cronkite, Walter. *A Reporter's Life*. New York: Knopf, 1996.

Crouse, Timothy. *The Boys on the Bus: Riding with the Campaign Press Corps*. New York: Random House, 1972.

Dickerson, Nancy. *Among Those Present*. New York: Random House, 1976.

Dobbs, Michael. "The Amanpour Factor: How Television Fills the Leadership Vacuum on Bosnia." *The Washington Post*, July 23, 1995, C2.

Dow, Bonnie J. *Prime-Time Feminism: Television, Media Culture and the Women's Movement Since 1970*. Philadelphia: University of Pennsylvania Press, 1996.

Duncan, Jacci, ed. *Making Waves: The 50 Greatest Women in Radio and Television*. Kansas City: McMeel Publishing, 2001.

Easton, Nina J. "Unsung Heroes II." *American Journalism Review*, July/August, 2002.

Ekstrom, Mats. "Information, Storytelling and Attractions: TV Journalism in Three Modes of Communication." *Media, Culture and Society* 22 (2000): 465–92.

"Election Reflections: Candy Crowley." Monday, December 18, 2000, 1 p.m. EST http://www.cnn.com/chat/transcripts/2000/12/18/crowley.html (accessed January 2, 2007)

Ellerbee, Linda. *And So It Goes: Adventures in Television*. New York: G. P. Putnam, 1986.

———. *Move On: Adventures in the Real World*. New York: G. P. Putnam, 1991.

Engstrom, Erika. "Looking Through a Gendered Lens: Local U.S. Television News Anchors' Perceived Career Barrier." *Journal of Broadcasting and Electronic and Electronic Media* 44, no. 4: 6.

Feran, Tom. "Chung and Rather: A Team on the Go." *Plain Dealer* (Cleveland, Ohio), July 20, 1993, 13C.

Ferretti, Fred. "Barbara Walters at ABC." *The New York Times*, April 22, 1976, 66.

Fillo, Maryellen. "Senate Race 'Like Christmas Morning' for Media; National Press Converges on State to Cover the Political Story of the Summer That Is Seen as a Referendum on War." *Hartford Courant*, August 8, 2006, A2.

Foote, Joe S., ed. *Live from the Trenches*. Carbondale and Edwarsville: Southern Illinois University Press, 1998.

Foote, Joe S. *Television Access and Political Power*. New York: Praeger Publishers, 1990.

Frank, Reuven. *Out of Thin Air The Brief Wonderful Life of Network News*. New York: Simon and Schuster, 1991.

Fraser, Benson P. and William J. Brown. "Media, Celebrities, and Social Influence: Identification With Elvis Presley." *Mass Communication & Society* 5, no. 2 (2002): 183–206.

Gee, Dana. "War Journalist Would Grill bin Laden: CNN Documentary: Christiane Amanpour Traces Footsteps of Most-Wanted Terrorist." *The Vancouver Province*, July 16, 2006, C7.

Glenn Gavin. "She's Not Just the Host—She's Also the Story's Main Reporter." *Miami Herald*, August 23, 2006.

Gold, Matea. "Moving Past 'Today'; Katie Couric Shoots Down Skeptics Who This She's Too Soft for the Evening News." *Los Angeles Times*, May 30, 2006, 1E.

Goodman,Walter. "A Reporter's Debut on '60 Minutes.'" *The New York Times*, November 4, 1996.

Graham, Elizabeth E., Carole A. Barbato, and Elizabeth M. Perse. "The Interpersonal Communication Motives Model." *Communication Quarterly* 41, no. 2 (Spring, 1993): 172–86.

Gunther, Marc. *The House That Roone Built: The Inside Story of ABC News*. New York: Little, Brown and Company, 1994.

Guttenplan, D. D. "Britain: Dumb and Dumber? A Transatlantic Spat Over the Quality of 'Quality Press.'" *Columbia Journalism Review* (July/August 1997), http://archives.cjr.org/year/97 (accessed January 24, 2006).

Hackett, Robert A. "Decline of a Paradigm? Bias and Objectivity in News Media." *Critical Studies in Communication* 1, no. 3 (September, 1984): 229–59.

Hagan, Joe. "ABC New's Vargas Girl Asks: Why So Few Women in Prime Time?" *New York Observer*, December 12, 2004. http://www.observer.com/node/50209 (accessed September 23, 2007).

———. "Charlie the Conquerer," *New York Magazine*, June 19, 2006. http://nymag.com/news/media/17255/index.html (accessed December 17, 2006).

Halperin, Mark and John F. Harris. *The Way to Win: Taking the White House in 2008*. New York: Random House, 2007.

Harris, Rob. "How to Be Christiane Amanpour: TV News Correspondent." *The Guardian* (Manchester, UK), May 30, 2005, 28.

Hart, Roderick P. *Modern Rhetorical Criticism*. Needham Heights: Allyn and Bacon, 1997.

HBO Special. "The Journalist and the Jihadi: The Life of Daniel Pearl." Transcribed from television, October 29, 2006.

Heffernan, Virginia. "Asking Simple Questions of AIDS Victims and Getting Simple, Powerful Answers." *The New York Times*, September 23, 2006, B10.

———. "A Mastermind of Terror and Allure." *The New York Times*, August 23, 2006, E6.

———. "Was Killing of Shepard an Anti-Gay Hate Crime?" *The New York Times*, November 26, 2004, E, 34.

Hess, Stephen and Marvin Kalb. *The Media and the War on Terrorism* (Washington, D.C: Brookings Institute Press, 2003).

Huff, Richard. "Chung Done at CNN as Network Pulls Show." *Daily News* (New York), March 26, 2003, 98.

———. "CNN: Out, Darn Spot." *Daily News* (New York) January 8, 2002, 74.

Huff, Richard, David Bianculli, and Helen Kennedy. "CNN Calmly Brings Attack to the World." *Daily News*, December 17, 1998, 46.

Hume, Ellen. "The New Paradigm of News." *Annals of the American Academy of Political and Social Science* 546, (Jul., 1996): 141–53.

Jacobs, Jerry. *Changing Channels: Issues and realities in Television News*. Mountainview, CA: Mayfield Publishing, 1990.

Jamieson, Kathleen-Hall. *Beyond the Double Bind*. New York: Oxford University Press, 1995.

Johnson, Haynes. "Historic Meeting of Heads of State—and a One-Eyed King; The Visit." *The Washington Post*, November 23, 1977, A3.

Johnson, Peter. "CBS' Big Gamble—News Head Ober Defends Anchor Team." *USA Today*, November 29, 1993, 1D.

Jubera, Drew. "Clinton, Reporter Trade Jabs." *Atlanta Journal and Constitution*, May 4, 1994, B1.

"Katie Couric Weighs Anchor." http://www.cbsnews.com/stories/2006/09/05/eveningnews/main1966506.shtml (accessed September 5, 2006).

"Katie Ready to Hit the Ground Running." www.tmz.com/2006/08/29katie-ready-to-hit-the-ground-running/ (accessed September 5, 2006).

Kelleher, Ellen. "Queen of the Questioners: Barbara Walters Puts Her Success Down to Iron Will and Stamina." *Financial Times* (London, England), November 30, 2004, Media, 9.

Kim, Janet. "Lecture Honors Daniel Pearl." *The Stanford Daily*, October 17, 2006, 1.

Kinzer, Stephen. "Where There's War, There's Amanpour." *The New York Times*, October 9, 1994, 57.

Kiviat, Barbara. "10 Questions for Andrea Mitchell." *Time,* September 14, 2005, http://www.time.com/time/magazine/article/0,9171,1093739-1,00.html (accessed January 3, 2006).

Klein, Edward. *Katie: The Real Story.* New York: Crown Publishers, 2007.

Krebs, Albin. *New York Times*, December 14, 1976, 34.

Kurtz, Howard., "Diane Sawyer, On the Ground and in High Gear." *The Washington Post,* February 19, 2007, C-1.

———. "Katie Couric, Thinking About Tomorrow; After 15 Years at 'Today,' CBS-Bound Host Is Ready to Begin Her Next Chapter." *The Washington Post*, May 30, 2006, C-1.

Kurtz, Howard and Candy Crowley. "Are Journalists Quietly Rejoicing Over Democratic Takeover of Congress?; Did Media Scapegoat Rumsfeld?" *Reliable Sources*, CNN, November 12, 2006, 10:00 a.m. EST.

Last, Jonathan P. "New Anchors Lack Stamina and Gravitas." *Philadelphia Inquirer*, September 24, 2006, C3.

Lauzen, Martha M. and David M. Dozier. "Recognition and Respect Revisited: Portrayal of Age and Gender in Prime-Time Television." *Mass Communication & Society* 8, no. 3 (2005): 241–56.

Liorente, Liz. "Talent, Versatility, Class: ABC New Personality Elizabeth Vargas Finds Balance as a Mother, a Wife and a Super-journalist." *Hispanic Magazine*, December, 2004.

Lipton, Joshua. "Barbara Walters." *Columbia Journalism Review* 40, no. 4 (Nov–Dec 2001): 80.

Lowry, Brian. "The Fluff Factor." *Broadcasting & Cable*. November 13, 2004, 48.

Malone, Mary. *Connie Chung: Broadcast Journalist.* Hillside, New Jersey: Enslow Publishers, 1992, 48.

Manchester, William. *The Death of a President: November 1963*. New York: Harper and Row, 1967.

Marlane, Judith. *Women in Television News Revisited*. Austin: University of Texas Press, 1999.

Matousek, Mark. "Gritty Woman CNN's Judy Woodruff Balances Hard News and Hard Knocks." *AARP Magazine*, September & October 2004. http://www.aarpmagazine.org/people/Articles/a2004-09-13-mag-woodruff.html (accessed January 29, 2007).

Matusow, Barbara. *The Evening Stars: The Making of the Network News Anchor.* Boston: Houghton Mifflin Company, 1983.

McCombs M. E. and D. L. Shaw. "The Agenda Setting Function of Mass Media." *Public Opinion Quarterly* 36, no 2: 176–87.

McDonough, Kevin. "Catch This 'Anchor' Before It Sinks." *The Morning Call* (Allentown, PA), August 22, 2007, E5.

McPherson-Shilling, Liless and Linda K. Fuller. *Dictionary of Quotations in Communications*. Greenwich, CT: Greenwood Press, 1997.

Media Bistro, The DC Fishbowl Interview, September, 14, 2006.

Milbank, Dana. "In the House, Suddenly Righteous Republicans." *The Washington Post*, January 4, 2001, A2.

Mitchard, Jacquelyn. "Katie Unplugged." *Parade*, August 12, 2006, 6.

Mitchell, Andrea. *Talking Back . . . to Presidents, Dictators, and Assorted Scoundrels*. New York: Viking, 2005.

Mitchell, Andrea. "There Is No Freedom of the Press Here." MSNBC.com, July 21, 2005, http://www.msnbc.msn.com/id/8616820/ (accessed January 11, 2007).

Muller, Judy. *Now This: Radio, Television . . . and the Real World*. New York: G. P. Putnam, 2000.

NBC News transcripts, *The Today Show*, "Secretary of State Condoleezza Rice Demands and Gets Apology from Sudanese Government for Rough Handling of Aides and Reporters Traveling with Her." July 21, 2005, Thursday 7 a.m. EST.

NBC News transcripts, NBC News Special Report: Inauguration of George W. Bush. January 20, 2001.

NBC News transcripts, *The Today Show* 7:00 a.m. EST January 2, 2007, " Former President Gerald Ford's Funeral Today," Reporters: Andrea Mitchell.

NBC News, *The Today Show*, September 11, 2001, DVD on loan from the Television News Archives, Vanderbilt University.

NBC News transcripts, *The Today Show*. January 20, 1997.

———. October 23, 1997.

———. April 22, 1999.

———. July 19, 1999.

———. June 11, 2003.

———. June 28, 2005.

———. May 31, 2006.

Neuhaus, Cable. "Whatever Katie Wants." *AARP*, November–December, 2006, http://www.aarpmagazine.org/people/couric.html (accessed September 28, 2006).

"New Kids on the Block." *The New York Times*, September 10, 2006, B2.

Oppenheimer, Jerry. *Barbara Walters: An Unauthorized Biography*. New York: St. Martin Press, 1990.

Ostrow, Joanne. "Stahl Upbeat on News: CBS Pro in Denver for Lecture Series." *Denver Post*, March 28, 1999, J-1.

Page, Clarence. *Nieman Reports* 58, no. 4 (Winter, 2004): 57.

Paisner, Daniel. *The Imperfect Mirror: Inside Stories of Television Newswomen*. New York: William Morrow, 1989.

Pauley, Jane. *Skywriting A Life Out of the Blue*. New York: Ballantine Books, 2005.

Peel, Elizabeth. "Barbara Walters: Star of the Morning." *Newsweek*, May 6, 1974, 57.

Persico, Joseph E. *Edward R. Murrow, An American Original*. New York: Dell Publishing, 1983.

Phil Donahue Show. "Newswomen." 1987, distributed by "Films for the Humanities."

Poniewozik, James. "Katie Couric: The New Anchor Is Shaking Up The News." *Time,* April 30, 2006. http://www.time.com/time/magazine/article/0,9171,1187398,00 .html. (accessed August 30, 2006).

Potter, Deborah. "Breaking the Mold." *American Journalism Review* 28, no. 3 (Jun–Jul 2006).

Price, Cindy J. and Shawn S. Wuff. "Does Sex Make a Difference? Job Satisfaction of Television Network Correspondets." *Women's Studies in Communication* 28, no. 2 (Fall, 2005): 208.

"Promotional Photo of Slimmer Couric Was Altered by CBS." *The Morning Call* (Allentown, PA), August 31, 2006, A11.

Rakow, Lana F. and Kimberlie Kranich. "Women and Sign in Television News." *Journal of Communication* 41, no. 1 (Winter, 1999): 8.

Rakow, Lana F. and Laura A. Wackwitz, eds. *Feminist Communication Theory Selections in Context.* Thousand Oaks: Sage, 2004.

Rather, Dan, with Mickey Herskowitz. *The Camera Never Blinks: Adventures of a TV Journalist.* New York: William Morrow, 1977.

Ready to Begin Her Next Chapter." *Washington Post,* May 30, 2006, C-1.

Reasoner, Harry. *Before The Colors Fade.* New York: Knopf, 1981.

Reed, Julia. "Woman in the News." *Vogue* 182, no. 2 (February, 1992): 218.

Roush, Matt. "Bleary Opening for Chung's 'Eye to Eye.'" *USA Today,* June 17, 1993, 3D.

"Rice Gets Apology for Incident in the Sudan." *USA Today,* July 21, 2005, http:// www.usatoday.com/news/world/2005-07-21-rice-sudan_x.htm (accessed January 4, 2006).

Robertson, Lori. "We Have a Breaking Story." *American Journalism Review,* October, 2001, 1.

Robinson, Mary. Interview with Nichola D. Gutgold, November 1, 2006.

Rush, Ramona R., Carol E. Oukrop and Pamela J. Creedon, eds. *Seeking Equity for Women in Journalism and Mass Communication Education: A 30-Year Update.* Mahweh, New Jersey: Lawrence Erlbaum Associates, 2004.

Ryan, Marie-Laure, ed. *Narrative Across Media: The Languages of Storytelling.* Lincoln and London: University of Nebraska Press, 2004.

Ryan, Suzanne C. "Zahn's Job Starts with 'The Most Challenging Story of Our Careers.'" *The Boston Globe,* October 6, 2001, F3.

Sanders, Marlene and Marcia Rock. *Waiting for Prime Time: The Women of Television News.* Chicago: University of Illinois Press, 1994.

Saunders, Dusty. "CNN Digs Deep on bin Laden." *Rocky Mountain News,* August 22, 2006, 2D.

Schieffer, Bob. *Face the Nation: My Favorite Stories from the First 50 Years of the Award-winning News Broadcast.* New York: Simon and Schuster, 2004.

———. *This Just In: What I Couldn't Tell You on Television.* New York: Putnam, 2003.

Schudson, Michael. *The Power of News*. Cambridge: Harvard University Press, 1995.

Sennett, Richard. *Authority*. New York: Knopf, 1993.

Shales, Tom. "Connie Chung, Stressing the Obvious." *The Washington Post*, April 25, 1988, B1.

———. "Covering the Big Story in Jerusalem: The News People as Newsmakers." *The Washington Post*, November 21, 1977, C1.

Shephard, Richard F. "Barbara Walters Gets the Interview." *The New York Times*, December 21, 1976, 67

Sheridan, Patricia. "Breakfast with Andrea Mitchell." *Pittsburgh Post-Gazette*, October 9, 2006, http://www.post-gazette.com/pg/06282/728480-129.stm (accessed January 19, 2007).

Shister, Gail. "Chung and Rather—A Surprise TV Pairing." *Philadelphia Inquirer*, May 18, 1993, F1.

Silver, James. "She Doesn't Do Froth." *The Independent* (London), July 10, 2006, 10.

60 Minutes, "Nancy Pelosi: Two Heartbeats Away: Lesley Stahl Profiles the Woman Who Could Become the Next Speaker of the House." October 20, 2006, accessed online: http://www.cbsnews.com/stories/2006/10/20/60minutes/main2111089.shtml.

60 Minutes 7:00 p.m. EST CBS, September 24, 2006, lexisnexis@prod.lexisnexis.com accessed October 1, 2006.

Sklarewitz, Norman. "Political Journalism." September 1, 2006, http://airtranmagazine.com/contents/2006/09/candy-crowley/ (accessed January 2, 2007).

Stahl, Lesley. *Reporting Live*. New York: Simon and Schuster, 1999.

Stanley, Alessandra. "For the New Face of CBS News, a Subdued Beginning." *The New York Times*, September 6, 2006, A15.

Steinberg, Jacques. "ABC Rejects Dual Anchors in 2nd Shuffle." *The New York Times*, May 24, 2006, Section A,1.

———. "'60 Minutes' May Be Too Few for All the Stars." *The New York Times*, June 3, 2005, C1.

Stone, Vernon A. "Trends in the Status of Minorities and Women in Broadcast News." *Journalism Quarterly*, 65:288–93.

Strachan, Alex. "The Truth Chaser: "Christiane Amanpour Never Lets up Her Pursuit of the Story." *Ottowa Citizen*, July 29, 2006, K1.

Strachen, Alex. "Christiane Amanpour: Serious, Fearless and Fiercely Intelligent: CNN Stalwart Does News the Old-fashioned Way—Without Apology." *Edmonton Journal* (Alberta), July 18, 2006, c1.

"Syrian President Says He Can Help Broker Peace: ABC News' Diane Sawyer Talks Exclusively to President Bashar al-Assad About Iraq and Mideast Peace." ABC News, February 5, 2007, http://abcnews.go.com.

TV Guide. "Why Are There Still No Female Dan Rathers?" August 1, 1981, 1.

———. April 6, 2006, http://www.newsmax.com/archives/articles/2006/4/6/112752.shtml (accessed August 26, 2006).

The Museum of Broadcast Communications, http://www.museum.tv.com.

The Theodore H. White Lecture with Judy Woodruff. Joan Shorenstein Center Press, Politics, Public Policy. Harvard University John F. Kennedy School of Government, November 1, 2001.

Toomey, Coleen, producer. *The President and the Press*, Films for the Humanities and Sciences, 1998.

Trotta, Liz. *Fighting for Air in the Trenches with Television News*. New York: Simon and Schuster, 1991.

Turnbull, Barbara. "Primetime Diva Has Paid Her Dues." *Toronto Star*, May 15, 2006, E-7.

"U.S. Newsroom Employment Falls; Small Gains for Women and Minorities." *Media Report to Women* 32, no. 2 (Spring 2004).

Vanocur, Sandy. "Will Arledge Preside Over ABC News?" *The Washington Post*. March 9, 1977, B1.

"Vargas, Woodruff to Share Anchor Desk at ABC." MSNBC.com, December 9, 2005, www.msnbc.com/id/10335483 (accessed November 15, 2006).

Vavrus, Mary Douglas. *Postfeminist News: Political Women in the Media Culture*. Albany: State University of New York Press, 2002.

Velshi, Ali. Candy Crowley. "Stories Behind the Stories." CNN, May 28, 2006.

Walsh, Amy. "Life with Tyson Is 'Torture, Pure Hell' Says His Wife." *St. Petersburg Times* (Florida), September 30, 1988, 2C.

Walters, Barbara. *How to Talk with Practically Anybody about Practically Anything*. New York: Doubleday, 1970.

Ward, Monique L. and Kristen Harrison. "The Impact of Media Use on Girls' Beliefs about Gender Roles, Their Bodies and Sexual Relationships: A Research Synthesis." In Ellen Cole and Jessica Henderson Daniel, eds., *Featuring Females* (Washington, D.C., APA, 2005).

Weber, Keith and B. R. Patterson. "Construction and Validation of a Communication-Based Emotional Support Scale." Communication Research Reports 13 (1), 1996, 69–76.

Wenner, Kathryn S. "She's Not Bashful; CNN Producer Dana Bash Moves to the Other Side of the Camera to Become a White House Correspondent." *American Journalism Review*, January, 2003, http://www.ajr.org/Article.asp?id=2738 (accessed February 28, 2007).

"Who's Talking? An Analysis of Sunday Morning Talk Shows." The White House Project, September 5, 2001 (paper distributed at Forum for Leadership, Washington, D.C., 2001).

Wilbert, Caroline. "Connie Chung Show Canceled; Veteran Anchor to Leave CNN." *The Atlanta Journal-Constitution*, March 26, 2003, 1D.

Will, George F. "Dole's Tobacco Debacle." *The Washington Post*, July 7, 1996, C07.

Williams, Patricia J. "Guaranteed Authentic." *Oprah Magazine*, March 2007, 214.

Winfrey, Oprah. "The O Interview." *O: The Oprah Winfrey Magazine,* September, 2005, 209.

Wolf, Naomi. *The Beauty Myth: How Images of Beauty Are Used Against Women.* New York: Perennial, 1991, 2002.

Woodruff, Judy. "Generation Next Changes the Face of the Workforce." PBS, December 14, 2006. http://www.pbs.org/newshour/bb/business/july-dec06/geny_12-14.html.

Woodruff, Judy with Kathleen Maxa. *This is Judy Woodruff at the White House.* Menlo Park, CA and London: Addison-Wesley Publishing, 1982.

Wulf, Steve. "Barb's Wired." *Time* 146, no. 19 (Nov. 6, 1995): 68.

www.abc.go.com/theview/hosts/walters.html

www.cnn.com/ALLPOLITICS/stories/1999/03/02/lewinsky/

www.cnn.com/ALLPOLITICS/stories/1999/03/04/lewinsky.excerpts/

www.shemadeit.org

www.forbes.com/lists/2006/53/AU0O.html (accessed March 30, 2007).

www.monahancenter.org/about/index.html (accessed August 22, 2006)

www.newyorkmetro.com/nymetro/news/people/features/2433/.

Yandell, Steven. "Caring in the Midst of a Crisis." *Dynamic Chiropractic* 13, no. 11 (May 22, 1995).

Yuan, Elizabeth. "Staying on Top of Your Game." CNN, July 28, 2006, 3:48 p.m. EST.

Zoglin, Richard. "Morning Companion." *Time*, April 26, 2004, http://www.time.com/time/magazine/article/0,9171,994011,00.html.

Zoglin, Richard. "Star Power: Diane Sawyer, with a New Prime-time Show and a $1.6 Million Contract, Is Hot. But Are Celebrity Anchors Like Her Upstaging the News?" *Time*, August 7, 1989, 46–51.

INDEX

20/20, 19, 45, 46, 50, 51, 71, 83

48 Hour Investigates, 154

60 Minutes, 42, 152, 154, 157

ABC, xii, 4, 10, 11,18, 32, 37, 39–40, 43, 45, 47, 51, 56, 67, 69, 70–80, 86, 115, 149, 152, 200

ABC News, 1, 11, 14, 23, 38, 40–44, 71, 81, 147, 170, 195, 202

Agnew, Spiro, 2

Allen, Craig M., 8

Amanpour, Christiane, 91–110, 196, 202; career, 94–97; communication style, 101–2, 106–9; confrontation with Bill Clinton, 97–99; early life, 93–94; education, 94

An In Depth Look at Islam, 95

anchor, 1; media portrayals of, 9–10; obstacles facing women anchors, 12–20; sexist treatment of, 12–13

Anderson, Bonnie, 19, 21–22

Arledge, Roone, 23, 42, 44, 147

Associated Press, 169, 171

The Atlantic Journal-Constitution, 170

Auletta, Ken, 16, 22, 169

The Barbara Walters Special, 38, 53

Bash, Dana, 25, 113–18, 202; career, 115; communication style, 116–18; education, 115

Batchelor, Clara Couric, 170

Beasley, Maurine, 2, 195

Beutel, Bill, 35

bin Laden, Osama, 91–92, 104, 109

Blair, Tony, 104

Blitzer, Wolf, 122

bona fide occupational qualification (BFOQ), 24

The Boys on the Bus: Riding with the Campaign Press Corps, 64

The Brand New Kid, 173

Brinkley, David, 69

Broadcasting & Cable, 20

Brokaw, Tom, 6, 68–69, 80, 169

Brookings Institute, 121

Brown, Campbell, 202

Brown, Dan, 85
Buchanan, Pat, 119
Burke, Kenneth, 49–50
Bush, Barbara, 118, 177–78
Bush, George H. W., 49, 119
Bush, George W., 119, 120, 124, 138, 183
Bush, Laura, 115–16

The Cavalier Daily, 170
CBS, 1, 12, 15, 33–34, 41, 45, 54, 55, 64–70, 76, 80, 96, 134, 146, 152–54, 167, 184, 185, 191, 195–96, 199–200
CBS Evening News, 15, 72, 146, 167, 184–87, 195, 197
CNN, 10, 19, 21–24, 43, 71, 92–93, 95–98, 102, 105, 106, 108–109, 114–15, 118, 120–21, 124, 133, 135–37, 146, 159–61, 163, 170–71, 198–99, 202
CNN Presents: God's Warriors, 198
Camp David, xi, 133
Carter, Jimmy, 119–20, 131, 135, 199
Castro, Fidel, 36
Chancellor, John, 11, 40, 43, 169
Chase, Sylvia, 66
Chung, Connie, xi, 63–79, 81; career, 66–73; communication style, 77–79; education, 65
Civil Rights Act, Title VII, 5
Clarke, Richard, 156
Clinton, Bill, 49, 64, 85, 138, 179
Clinton, Hillary, 50, 53–54, 64, 128–30, 180, 182–84
Clinton, Roger, 64
Clinton, Virginia, 64
Condit, Gary, 71, 76–77
Couric, Emily, 170, 173
Couric, John M., Jr., 170
Couric, Katie, xii, 4, 6, 12, 16, 25, 56, 80, 167–91, 196, 201–2; career, 170–72; communication style, 188–91; education, 170; *Couric &*

Co., 186; "The Couric Effect," 172; *Katie Couric's Notebook*, 186
Craft, Christine, 7, 17, 18
Cronkite, Walter, 1, 2, 5–6, 11, 19, 43, 168, 191
Crouse, Timothy, 64
Crowley, Candy, 25, 118–25, 196, 198; career, 120–21; communication style, 122–25; education, 118
Curry, Ann, 173, 176

The Daily News (Philadelphia), 126
The Daily Show with Jon Stewart, 72
Daly, John, 6, 176
Dateline NBC, 172
The Da Vinci Code, 80, 83
Dean, Howard, 137–39
Deaver, Mike, 129
Dickerson, John, 7, 8
Dickerson, Nancy, 4, 7, 8
Dobbs, Lou, 117–18. *See also Lou Dobbs Tonight*
Dole, Bob, 178–79
Dole, Elizabeth, 178, 202
Downs, Hugh, 35
Dozier, David M., 6
The Drudge Report, 11
DuMont, 11

Edwards, Douglas, 6
Edwards, Elizabeth, 161–62
Edwards, John, 162
Edwards, Stephanie, 35
Ellerbee, Linda, 18
Extreme Makeover, 24
Eye to Eye with Connie Chung, 68, 71–72

FCC. *See* Federal Communications Commission
Face the Nation, 153–54
Federal Communications Commission (FCC), 5, 17, 178

Ferri, Anthony J., 8
Foote, Joe, 18
Ford, Gerald R., 131
Frederick, Pauline, 4

Gates, Bill, 75, 78
George magazine, 182
Gibson, Charles, "Charlie," 6, 11, 14, 82, 185, 195
Gingrich, Newt, 64, 70, 74–77
Giuliani, Rudy, 130
Glick, Marian, 11
Gonzalez, Alberto, 118
Good Morning America, 11, 35, 115, 147, 151–52, 160
Goodwin, Doris Kearns, 190
Gore, Al, 155–56, 183
Greenspan, Alan, 127
Gresham's Law, 132
Gumbel, Bryant, 169, 171

Harding, Tonya, 64, 77
Hart, Roderick P., 3, 14, 49, 163, 168–69, 201
Hartford Courant (Connecticut), 124
Hartman, Rome, 185
Hartz, Jim, 35
Harvard University, 8
Hazlewood, Joseph, 64
Hearst Publications, xi, 25
His Girl Friday, 182
Hofstede, Geert, 201
Hollywood Walk of Fame, 31
Huntley, Chet, 69

Imus, Don, 127
iPhone, 195
infotainment, 21–22, 67
In the Footsteps of bin Laden, 94, 109, 198

Jackson, Jesse, 119
Jamieson, Kathleen Hall, 13

Jennings, Peter, 11, 35, 69
Johnson, Lady Bird, 35
Johnson, Lyndon, 35
The Journal of Medicine, 172

Kennedy, John (Jack) F., 11, 34, 126, 168–69
Kennedy, John F. Jr., 181–82
Kerrigan, Nancy, 64, 74
Kerry, John, 122–23
Khatami, Mohammad, 99–100
King, Larry, 55–56, 122
Kurtz, Howard, 121
KYW, 126

Larry King Live, 43, 158
Last, Jonathan, 13, 168
Lauzen, Martha M., 6
Lazio, Rick, 128
Leno, Jay, 177
Levy, Chandra, 76–77
Lewinsky, Monica, 54–55
Lieberman, Joseph, 124, 162
Live from the Headlines, 161
Living History, 182
Lou Dobbs Tonight, 10. *See also* Lou Dobbs
Lunden, Joan, 12

The MacNeil/Lehrer News Hour, 137
MSNBC, 10, 161
MSNBC Live, 126
Maples, Marla, 147
Marlane, Judith, 3
McGee, Frank, 35–37
McGovern, George, 36
McGrady, Phyllis, 80
Metromedia, 18
Miklaszewski, Jim, 176
Milosevic, Slobodon, 101–2
Mitchell, Andrea, xi, 8, 25, 126–31; career, 126–27; communication style, 128–31; education, 126

Monahan, Jay, 172–73
Moonves, Les, 6
Mudd, Roger, 5
Murphy Brown, 9–10, 172
Murrow, Edward R., 43, 94, 100, 103, 104, 106; "Murrow's Boys," 12, 200
Myers, Lisa, 6

NBC, 33–35, 37–42, 46, 55, 67–70, 120, 126, 134, 168, 171–72, 177, 200–201
NBC News, 127, 135
NBC Nightly News with Brian Williams, 126
National Colorectal Cancer Research Alliance, 172
News Flash, 21
Newsweek, 83
New York Daily News, 185
New York Magazine, 81
The New York Times, 38, 45, 51, 92, 152, 200
Nielsen Media Research, 187
Nixon, Pat, 196
Nixon, Richard, 35, 146, 150, 196
Norville, Deborah, 23–24, 171
Not for Women Only, xi, 37

The Oprah Winfrey Show, 24

PBS, 135, 137, 199
Parsons, Estelle, 33
Paula Zahn Now, 161
Pauley, Jane, 12, 170
Pearl, Daniel, 109
Petraus, David, 116
The Philadelphia Inquirer, 168
Povitch, Maury, 65, 67–68, 72–73
Presley, Lisa Marie, 147–49
Prime Time Live, 4, 85, 147, 152, 169
"professional beauty qualification," 23
Putin, Vladimir, 196

Rabin, Yitzhak, 198
Ramsey, John, 84
Ramsey, JonBenét, 84
Ramsey, Patsy, 84–85
Rather, Dan, 5, 6, 11, 16, 19, 68–71, 81, 197
Reader's Digest, 67
Reagan, Ronald, 115, 119, 129, 131, 154
Reasoner, Harry, xii, 39–42, 56
Reporting Live, 8, 153
Reynolds, Frank, 1
rhetorical multitasking, 202
Rice, Condoleezza, 127–28, 133, 187–89
Rizzo, Frank, 129
Robinson, Max, 43
Roker, Al, 173
Rooney, Andy, 2
Rubin, James, 100
Russert, Tim, 14, 171

Saturday Night with Connie Chung, 68
Savitch, Jessica, 11
Sawyer, Diane, 4, 17, 25, 82, 145–52; career, 146–47; communication style, 150–51; education, 146
Schieffer, Bob, 6, 55, 167, 197
Schonfeld, Reese, 92, 170–71
Schulbert, Stuart, 36
Schwartz, Stu, 115
September 11, 2001, 173–77
Sevareid, Eric, 106
SheSource.org, 2
Shepard, Matthew, 83–84
Shriver, Maria, 12
Slate.com, 7
Smee, Thomas, 8
Smith, Harry, 169
Society of Professional Journalists, 20–21
Sorensen, Erik, 70
Spears, Britney, 147
spina bifida, 136, 196

Spiro, Agnew, 2
Stahl, Lesley, 4, 17, 25, 66, 152–58,
    197, 199; career, 153–55;
    communication style, 156–58;
    education, 153
The Swan, 24
Swayze, John Cameron, 6

TV Guide, 6, 169
television beauty qualification, 23–24
Thatcher, Margaret, 196
Thomas, Helen, xi
Three Mile Island, 127, 146
The Today Show, 4, 14–15, 23, 33–37,
    39, 45, 170–74, 177–79, 182, 184,
    189–90, 200
The Tonight Show, 177
Trotta, Liz, 4
Trump, Donald, 149, 169
Tsongas, Paul, 119
Turner Broadcasting, 18
Tyndall, Andrew, 6

USA Today, 70, 73
United Press International, 170

Vargas, Elizabeth, 79–86, 197; career,
    80–81; communication style, 84–86;
    education, 80; Hispanic heritage,
    82; pregnancy, 11, 14, 179
Vasil, Janet, 5
The View, 51–52, 197

Wallace, Mike, 5, 54
Walters, Barbara, xi, xii, 11, 31–56, 71,
    79, 169, 196–97; co-anchor of *ABC*

Evening News, 37–41;
    communication style, 49–56; early
    career, 35–37; education, 33
Walters, Lou, 23, 32–33
Watergate, 65–66, 197
The Washington Post, 42–43, 45, 92,
    98, 151, 179
WASH, 120
WBRU, 94
Weinberger, Caspar, 178
WFMZ-TV, 5
The White House Project, 15
Williams, Brian, 6
Williams, Mary Alice, 12
WJAR, 94
WLKY-TV, 146
Wolf, Naomi, 13, 23
Woodruff, Bob, 14, 25, 197, 201
Woodruff, Judy, 6, 12, 132–40, 202;
    career, 134–35; communication
    style, 137–40; education, 134
WPIX-TV, 33
WTOP, 127
WTVJ, 171
Wulff, Shaun S., 8

XM satellite radio, 125

Yeltsin, Boris, 196
YouTube, 72

Zahn, Paula, 25, 158–64, 199, 202;
    career, 158–61; communication
    style, 162–64; education, 160
Zemin, Jiang, 196
Zucker, Jim, 177

ABOUT THE AUTHOR

Nichola D. Gutgold is associate professor of communication arts and sciences at Penn State Lehigh Valley where she enjoys teaching a variety of communication courses in media and film. She is the author of numerous articles as well as coauthor of the book *Elizabeth Hanford Dole: Speaking from the Heart* (Praeger, 2004), and author of *Paving the Way for Madam President* (Lexington Books, 2006).

Newscaster drawings by **Harry J. Hayes**.